iOS Programming Cookbook

Over 50 exciting and powerful recipes to help you unearth the promise of iOS programming

Hossam Ghareeb

BIRMINGHAM - MUMBAI

iOS Programming Cookbook

First published: March 2017

Production reference: 2310317

Published by Packt Publishing Ltd.
Livery Place
35 Livery Street
Birmingham
B3 2PB, UK.

ISBN 978-1-78646-098-1

www.packtpub.com

Credits

Author
Hossam Ghareeb

Reviewer
Siddharth Shekar

Acquisition Editor
Larissa Pinto

Content Development Editors
Johann Barretto
Samantha Gonsalves

Technical Editor
Pranav Kukreti

Copy Editors
Dhanya Baburaj
Shaila Kusanale

Project Coordinator
Devanshi Doshi

Proofreader
Safis Editing

Indexer
Mariammal Chettiyar

Graphics
Jason Monteiro

Production Coordinator
Deepika Naik

Cover Work
Deepika Naik

About the Author

Hossam Ghareeb is a software engineer who graduated from Alexandria University in 2012. He found his passion in mobile development, especially iOS development. Currently, he is a senior iOS developer at Noon e-commerce in Dubai.

Hossam has built his experience by learning tips and tricks from the managers he works with, open source projects, and online tutorials. He discovered that the best way to pay this back is to share his experience with others and help people get experience in iOS development.

> *First of all, big thanks to my parents whom I owe for everything I have and the good things that they taught me. I would like to thank my wife for her support and encouragement to keep writing the book. I want to thank my son Yusuf for inspiring me despite of all the time this took me away from him. Thanks to all the mentors that I've met over the years. Last but not least, special thanks to Samantha Gonsalves, the content editor of the book, for her cooperation and support in completing the book and to the reviewers for their comments and suggestions.*

About the Reviewer

Siddharth Shekar is a game developer with over 5 years of industry experience in game development, 11 years of experience in C++, C#, and other programming languages, and is adept at graphics libraries and game engines such as Unity and Unreal. He has also published games on the iOS, Android, Amazon, and Windows Phone App Stores.

Siddharth is also the author of *Learning Cocos2d-x Game Development*, *Learning iOS 8 Game Development Using Swift*, and *Cocos2d Cross-Platform Game Development Cookbook*, all published by Packt Publishing.

Currently, he is a lecturer in the Games Department at Media Design School, Auckland, New Zealand. He teaches graphics programming and PlayStation 4/PS Vita native game development and mentors final year production students.

More information about Media Design School and Siddharth Shekar can be found at www.mediadesignschool.com.

I would like to thank my parents for supporting me in everything that I choose to do. I would also like to thank Media Design School for encouraging me to continue working on this book. Finally, I would like to thank Packt Publishing for putting this book together and offering me the opportunity to review the book.

www.PacktPub.com

For support files and downloads related to your book, please visit www.PacktPub.com.

Did you know that Packt offers eBook versions of every book published, with PDF and ePub files available? You can upgrade to the eBook version at www.PacktPub.com and as a print book customer, you are entitled to a discount on the eBook copy. Get in touch with us at service@packtpub.com for more details.

At www.PacktPub.com, you can also read a collection of free technical articles, sign up for a range of free newsletters and receive exclusive discounts and offers on Packt books and eBooks.

https://www.packtpub.com/mapt

Get the most in-demand software skills with Mapt. Mapt gives you full access to all Packt books and video courses, as well as industry-leading tools to help you plan your personal development and advance your career.

Why subscribe?

- Fully searchable across every book published by Packt
- Copy and paste, print, and bookmark content
- On demand and accessible via a web browser

Customer Feedback

Thanks for purchasing this Packt book. At Packt, quality is at the heart of our editorial process. To help us improve, please leave us an honest review on this book's Amazon page at https://www.amazon.com/dp/178646098X.

If you'd like to join our team of regular reviewers, you can e-mail us at customerreviews@packtpub.com. We award our regular reviewers with free eBooks and videos in exchange for their valuable feedback. Help us be relentless in improving our products!

Table of Contents

Preface

iOS is evolving every year to provide a better experience for its users. Not only the system, but also the hardware of iPhone and iPad devices, which require a powerful system like the iOS to utilize the features of hardware is evolving. The latest release of iOS now comes with great features to give iOS developers the chance to develop mobile apps with new ideas or enhance the experience of current apps with new features. The book tries to cover the new features of iOS and let iOS developers get their hands dirty by writing sample demos with the features to understand how they work. The book is not meant to be a theory book, which talks about technical things, such as new APIs, or about any specific topic. The book is a cookbook that takes you within minutes to the point and guides you to build a simple demo to understand what is going on using examples, which is the best way to make things stick in your mind.

What this book covers

Chapter 1, *Swift Programming Language,* is a simple revision of Swift 3 and an explanation of the most important topics in Swift.

Chapter 2, *The Essentials,* covers the most commonly used UI components, such as UIView, gestures, stack views, and so on.

Chapter 3, *Integrating with Messages App,* talks about one of the hottest features in iOS—how to integrate with the iOS Messages app to add your own stickers or develop extensions.

Chapter 4, *Working with Interface Builder,* provides tips and tricks while dealing with interface builders, such as storyboards and XIB files. Get your hands dirty with Autolayout and size classes and know how to work with them.

Chapter 5, *Working with UITableView,* covers one of the most important components in iOS that all iOS developers should be aware of.

Chapter 6, *Animations and Graphics,* gives your apps a better look by teaching you how to animate views and draw simple shapes.

Chapter 7, *Multimedia,* helps you to deal with audio and video in iOS. It provides information about how to use filters thanks to the Core Image framework.

Chapter 8, *Concurrency*, overcomes the fear of using concurrency in iOS by helping you understand how to use dispatch queues and NSOperationQueues with simple examples.

Chapter 9, *Location Services*, covers the most commonly used operations in location services, such as getting a user's location, adding pins, navigation, and geofencing.

Chapter 10, *Security and Encryption*, discusses how to secure your app and protect your user's sensitive information using Touch ID for authentication and saving data in a device's Keychain.

Chapter 11, *Networking*, covers how to establish networking in an iOS app to retrieve data and parse it.

Chapter 12, *Persisting Data with Core Data*, takes you through the workings of Core Data to persist data and perform CRUD (creation, reading, updating, and deletion) operations.

Chapter 13, *Notifications*, helps you overcome the hassle of dealing with push notification and setup and gets you started with configuring your project and server to send and receive notifications.

Chapter 14, *App Search*, looks at making your app content searchable from Spotlight and Safari suggestions.

Chapter 15, *Optimizing Performance*, showcases how to measure the performance of your app and how to enhance it.

What you need for this book

Any Mac hardware-running macOS system, such as MacBook Pro, MacBook Air, Mac Mini, iMac, or Mac Pro.

Some chapters require testing on an iOS device with iOS 10.0 or later version.

The software requirements are Xcode 8.1 or later, which requires a Mac running macOS 10.11.5 or later, and iOS Simulator 10.0 or later.

Who this book is for

If you are an iOS developer on a quest to develop your perfect iOS app, then this book is for you. It would also prove to be a valuable resource for those who want to get up and running with iOS development through a clear, practical approach. In order to unleash the full potential of this book, basic Swift programming knowledge is necessary.

Sections

In this book, you will find several headings that appear frequently (Getting ready, How to do it, How it works, There's more, and See also).

To give clear instructions on how to complete a recipe, we use these sections as follows:

Getting ready

This section tells you what to expect in the recipe, and describes how to set up any software or any preliminary settings required for the recipe.

How to do it...

This section contains the steps required to follow the recipe.

How it works...

This section usually consists of a detailed explanation of what happened in the previous section.

There's more...

This section consists of additional information about the recipe in order to make the reader more knowledgeable about the recipe.

See also

This section provides helpful links to other useful information for the recipe.

Conventions

In this book, you will find a number of text styles that distinguish between different kinds of information. Here are some examples of these styles and an explanation of their meaning.

Code words in text, database table names, folder names, filenames, file extensions, pathnames, dummy URLs, user input, and Twitter handles are shown as follows: " The `sort` function gives us another flexibility by which you can provide a closure that returns the comparison result between any two items in the list to determine which should come first in the list."

A block of code is set as follows:

```
{ (parameters) ->returnType in
  // block of code goes here
}
```

Any command-line input or output is written as follows:

```
cd path_to_directory
```

New terms and **important words** are shown in bold. Words that you see on the screen, for example, in menus or dialog boxes, appear in the text like this: "Under **Relationship Segue**, click on **view controllers** to make this view controller part of the view controllers list on the tab bar controller."

Warnings or important notes appear in a box like this.

Tips and tricks appear like this.

Reader feedback

Feedback from our readers is always welcome. Let us know what you think about this book-what you liked or disliked. Reader feedback is important for us as it helps us develop titles that you will really get the most out of.

To send us general feedback, simply e-mail feedback@packtpub.com, and mention the book's title in the subject of your message.

If there is a topic that you have expertise in and you are interested in either writing or contributing to a book, see our author guide at www.packtpub.com/authors.

Customer support

Now that you are the proud owner of a Packt book, we have a number of things to help you to get the most from your purchase.

Downloading the example code

You can download the example code files for this book from your account at http://www.packtpub.com. If you purchased this book elsewhere, you can visit http://www.packtpub.com/support and register to have the files e-mailed directly to you.

You can download the code files by following these steps:

1. Log in or register to our website using your e-mail address and password.
2. Hover the mouse pointer on the **SUPPORT** tab at the top.
3. Click on **Code Downloads & Errata**.
4. Enter the name of the book in the **Search** box.
5. Select the book for which you're looking to download the code files.
6. Choose from the drop-down menu where you purchased this book from.
7. Click on **Code Download**.

You can also download the code files by clicking on the **Code Files** button on the book's webpage at the Packt Publishing website. This page can be accessed by entering the book's name in the **Search** box. Please note that you need to be logged in to your Packt account.

Once the file is downloaded, please make sure that you unzip or extract the folder using the latest version of:

- WinRAR / 7-Zip for Windows
- Zipeg / iZip / UnRarX for Mac
- 7-Zip / PeaZip for Linux

The code bundle for the book is also hosted on GitHub at `https://github.com/PacktPubl` `ishing/iOS-Programming-Cookbook`. We also have other code bundles from our rich catalog of books and videos available at `https://github.com/PacktPublishing/`. Check them out!

Downloading the color images of this book

We also provide you with a PDF file that has color images of the screenshots/diagrams used in this book. The color images will help you better understand the changes in the output. You can download this file from `https://www.packtpub.com/sites/default/files/down` `loads/iOSProgrammingCookbook_ColorImages.pdf`.

Errata

Although we have taken every care to ensure the accuracy of our content, mistakes do happen. If you find a mistake in one of our books-maybe a mistake in the text or the code-we would be grateful if you could report this to us. By doing so, you can save other readers from frustration and help us improve subsequent versions of this book. If you find any errata, please report them by visiting `http://www.packtpub.com/submit-errata`, selecting your book, clicking on the **Errata Submission Form** link, and entering the details of your errata. Once your errata are verified, your submission will be accepted and the errata will be uploaded to our website or added to any list of existing errata under the Errata section of that title.

To view the previously submitted errata, go to `https://www.packtpub.com/books/conten` `t/support`and enter the name of the book in the search field. The required information will appear under the **Errata** section.

Piracy

Piracy of copyrighted material on the Internet is an ongoing problem across all media. At Packt, we take the protection of our copyright and licenses very seriously. If you come across any illegal copies of our works in any form on the Internet, please provide us with the location address or website name immediately so that we can pursue a remedy.

Please contact us at `copyright@packtpub.com` with a link to the suspected pirated material.

We appreciate your help in protecting our authors and our ability to bring you valuable content.

Questions

If you have a problem with any aspect of this book, you can contact us
at questions@packtpub.com, and we will do our best to address the problem.

Swift Programming Language

1

In this chapter, we will cover the following topics:

- Using closures to create self-contained code
- Creating enumerations to write readable code
- Working with protocols and delegates
- Using extensions to extend classes functionality
- Working with memory management and ARC
- Using error handling
- Using generics to write generic and reusable code

Introduction

Welcome to our first chapter in *iOS Programming Cookbook*. We will start our journey in this book with a revision or emphasize on the most important and commonly used topics in Swift programming language. Before talking about these topics, ensure that you have a basic knowledge about Swift programming language and have used it before.

It has been more than 2 years since Apple released the awesome programming language-Swift. Swift is meant to be easy to code, easy to learn, safe, and intuitive. For each version of Swift, Apple introduces some awesome features and enhancements in the language. As we see in Swift 2.0, Swift came with higher performance, and new APIs such as error handling, and some enhancements. Swift is not meant to be available in iOS development only; you may find it in other platforms later in the future, thanks to the announcement of Apple that Swift will become open source.

Our recipes in this chapter will focus on the most important topics in Swift that will be used frequently in iOS development. When you focus on these topics and learn them properly, you will find using them in development will make your life easier and your code will be more organized. There are many people who can write code, but only few can write awesome code. Thus, mastering these topics is very important to be a good developer and to help you and others working on a project.

 For the latest features of Swift, ensure that you are using the latest version of Xcode.

Using closures to create self-contained code

Closures are self-contained lines of code to be executed and passed like any other data types. You should be familiar with blocks or at least heard about them in Objective-C or C. This recipe will help you to understand closure syntax and get familiar in using them.

Getting ready

Closures syntax in Swift is pretty easy and is easier than the syntax in C or Objective-C. The general form of closure is as follows:

```
{ (parameters) ->returnType in
    // block of code goes here
}
```

As you see, you first put open curly braces, add list of parameters and the return type, then the keyword `in`, followed by lines of code in your closure. Closures are first-class type, which means it can be nested, passed in parameters, returned from function, and so on.

How to do it...

1. Go to Xcode and create a new playground file called `Closures` to test code about closures in it.
2. To see closures in action, copy and paste this piece of code in the playground file (the output of each statement is printed on the right):

```
var names = ["David", "Jones", "Suzan", "Naomi", "Adam"]
```

```
names.sort() // ["Adam", "David", "Jones", "Naomi", "Suzan"]
names.sort{ (str1: String, str2: String) ->Bool in
  return str1 > str2
}

// ["Suzan", "Naomi", "Jones", "David", "Adam"]
```

How it works...

Swift provides us with a built-in system function called `sort`. The function can sort any collection of data. The function, by default, will sort the collection in an ascending order. The `sort` function gives us another flexibility by which you can provide a closure that returns the comparison result between any two items in the list to determine which should come first in the list.

As we saw, the default `sort` function sorts our data in an ascending order; in order to do any other logic, we can sort with closure that gives you two items as parameters to decide how to compare them. The `sort` function sorts the collection in place, and that's why the names variable is created as `var` not `let`. If the names collection is defined as `let`, you will not be able to use the `sort()` function. There is another function called `sorted()`, which returns a totally new sorted collection without changing the original one. It's available in both versions of the collection with `var` or `let`.

There's more...

Even though the closure syntax looks simple, but Swift can make it simpler. Let's see how closure syntax can be optimized.

Inferring type

When closures are passed as argument like what we did in the `sort` function, Swift can infer the types of closure parameters and return type. In that case, we can omit the parameters and return types, as there is no need to write them. In our previous example, when we infer types, the `sort` function would be like this:

```
names.sort{ str1, str2 in
  return str1 > str2
}
```

As you can see, the `String` types and the return type have been omitted.

Omitting the return keyword

Swift can make your life easier than that. When closure body consists of only one expression, the `return` keyword can be omitted. So, the new version of `sort` function will be like this:

```
names.sort({ str1, str2 in str1 > str2})
```

Shorthand arguments

To reach the maximum awesomeness of Swift, you can refer to the argument list with names `$0`, `$1`, and so on. When you decide to use the shorthand arguments, you can omit the list of parameters. You may ask what about the `in` keyword, will it be alone? The answer is no, we won't leave it alone; we can omit it as well completely. Here is the final version of our `sort` function:

```
names.sort({ $0 > $1})
```

Creating enumerations to write readable code

Using enumerations is one of the best practices that you should follow while writing any software project and not only iOS projects. Once you find that you have a group of related values in your project, create `enum` to group these values and to define a safe type for these values. With enumerations, your code becomes more readable and easy to understand, as it makes you define new types in your project that map to other value. In Swift, enumerations have been taken care of and have become more flexible than the ones used in other programming languages.

Getting ready

Now, we will dive into enumerations and get our hands dirty with it. To do so, we will create a new playground file in Xcode called `Enumerations` so that we can practice how to use enumerations and also see how it works.

Writing enumerations is meant to be easy, readable, and straightforward in syntax writing in Swift. Let's see how enum syntax goes:

```
enum EnumName{
}
```

You see how it's easy to create enums; your enumeration definition goes inside the curly braces.

How to do it...

Now, let's imagine that we are working on a game, and you have different types of monsters, and based on the type of monster, you will define power or the difficulty of the game. In that case, you have to use enum to create a monster type with different cases, as follows:

1. Type the following code to create enum with name Monster:

```
enum Monster{
   case Lion
   case Tiger
   case Bear
   case Crocs
}

enum Monster2{
   case Lion, Tiger, Bear, Crocs
}
```

2. Use the '.' operator to create enums variables from the previously created enum:

```
var monster1 = Monster.Lion
let monster2 = Monster.Tiger
monster1 = .Bear
```

3. Use the switch statement to check the value of enum to perform a specific action:

```
func monsterPowerFromType(monster:Monster) ->Int {
   var power = 0
   switch monster1 {
     case .Lion:
        power = 100
     case .Tiger:
        power = 80
```

```
     case .Bear:
        power  = 90
     case .Crocs:
        power = 70
  }
  return power
}

let power = monsterPowerFromType(monster1) // 90

func canMonsterSwim(monster:Monster) ->Bool{
  switch monster {
    case .Crocs:
        return true
    default:
        return false
  }
}

let canSwim = canMonsterSwim(monster1) // false
```

How it works...

Now, you have a new type in your program called `Monster`, which takes one value of given four values. The values are defined with the `case` keyword followed by the value name. You have two options to list your cases; you can list each one of them in a separate line preceded by the `case` keyword, or you can list them in one line with a comma separation. I prefer using the first method, that is, listing them in separate lines, as we will see later that we can add raw values for cases that will be more clear while using this method.

If you come from a C or Objective-C background, you know that the enums values are mapped to integer values. In Swift, it's totally different, and they aren't explicitly equal to integer values.

The first variable `monster1` is created using the enum name followed by '.' and then the type that you want. Once `monster1` is initialized, its type is inferred with `Monster`; so, later you can see that when we changed its value to `Bear`, we have just used the '.' operator as the compiler already knows the type of `monster1`. However, this is not the only way that you will use enums. Since enums is a group of related values, so certainly you will use it with control flow to perform specific logic based on its value. The `switch` statement is your best friend in that case as we saw in the `monsterPowerFromType()` function.

We've created a function that returns the monster power based on its type. The `switch` statement checks all values of monster with '.' followed by an enum value. As you already know, the `switch` statement is exhaustive in Swift and should cover all possible values; of course, you can use default in case it's not possible to cover all, as we saw in the `canMonsterSwim()` function. The `default` statement captures all non-addressed cases.

There's more...

Enumerations in Swift have more features, such as using enums with raw values and associated values.

Enum raw values

We saw how enums are defined and used. Enum cases can come with predefined values, which we call raw values. To create enums with raw values, the following rules should be adhered:

- All raw values should be in the same type.
- Inside the enum declaration, each raw value should be unique.
- Only possible values allowed to use are strings, characters, integer, and floating point numbers.

Assigning raw values

When you assign raw values to enum, you have to define the type in your enum syntax and give value for each case:

```
enum IntEnum: Int{
    case case1 = 50
    case case2 = 60
    case case3 = 100
}
```

```
67
68  enum Emoji: Character{
69      case Happy = "😀"
70      case Neutral = "😐"
71      case Sad = "😞"
72  }
```

Swift gives you flexibility while dealing with raw values. You don't have to explicitly assign a raw value for each case in enums if the type of enum is Int or String. For Int type enums, the default value of enum is equal to the value of previous one + 1. In case of the first case, by default it's equal to 0. Let's take a look at this example:

```
enum Gender: Int{
    case Male
    case Female
    case Other
}
var maleValue = Gender.Male.rawValue   // 0
var femaleValue = Gender.Female.rawValue // 1
```

We didn't set any raw value for any case, so the compiler automatically will set the first one to 0, as it's a no set. For any following case, it's value will be equal to previous case value + 1. Another note is that .rawValue returns the explicit value of the enum case. Let's take a look at another complex example that will make it crystal clear:

```
enum HTTPCode: Int{
    case OK = 200
    case Created  // 201
    case Accepted // 202
    case BadRequest = 400
    case UnAuthorized
    case PaymentRequired
    case Forbidden
}
```

```
let pageNotFound = HTTPCode.NotFound
let errorCode = pageNotFound.rawValue   // 404
```

We have explicitly set the value of first case to `200`; so, the following two cases will be set to `201` and `202`, as we didn't set raw values for them. The same will happen for `BadRequest` case and the following cases. For example, the `NotFound` case is equal to `404` after incrementing cases.

Now, we see how Swift compiler deals with `Int` type when you don't give explicit raw values for some cases. In case of `String`, it's pretty easier. The default value of `String` enum cases will be the case name itself. Let's take a look at an example:

```
enum Season: String{
    case Winter
    case Spring
    case Summer
    case Autumn
}

let winter = Season.Winter

let statement = "My preferred season is " + winter.rawValue // "My
preferred season is Winter"
```

You can see that we could use the string value of `rawValue` of seasons to append it to another string.

Using Enums with raw values

We saw how easy it is to create enums with raw values. Now, let's take a look at how to get the raw value of enums or create enums back using raw values.

We already saw how to get the raw value from enum by just calling `.rawValue` to return the raw value of the enum case.

To initialize an enum with a raw value, the enum should be declared with a type; so in that case, the enum will have a default initializer to initialize it with a raw value. An example of an initializer will be like this:

```
let httpCode = HTTPCode(rawValue: 404)   // NotFound
let httpCode2 = HTTPCode(rawValue: 1000) // nil
```

The `rawValue` initializer always returns an `optional` value because there will not be any matching enum for all possible values given in `rawValue`. For example, in case of `404`, we already have an enum whose value is `404`. However, for `1000`, there is no enum with such value, and the initializer will return `nil` in that case. So, before using any enum initialized by the `rawValue` initializer, you have to check first whether the value is not equal to `nil`; the best way to check for enums after initialization is by this method:

```
if let httpCode = HTTPCode(rawValue: 404){
    print(httpCode)
}
if let httpCode2 = HTTPCode(rawValue: 1000){
    print(httpCode2)
}
```

The condition will be true only if the initializer succeeds to find an enum with the given `rawValue`.

Enums with associated values

Last but not least, we will talk about another feature in Swift enums, which is creating enums with associated values. Associated values let you store extra information with enum case value. Let's take a look at the problem and how we can solve it using associated values in enums.

Suppose we are working with an app that works with products, and each product has a code. Some products codes are represented by QR code format, but others by UPC format. Check out the following image to see the differences between two codes at `http://www.mokemonster.com/websites/erica/wp-content/uploads/2014/05/upc_qr.png`):

The UPC code can be represented by four integers; however, QR code can be represented by a string value. To create an enum to represent these two cases, we would do something like this:

```
enum ProductCode{
    case UPC(Int, Int, Int, Int)
    case QR(String)
}

var productCode = ProductCode.UPC(4, 88581, 1497, 3)
productCode = ProductCode.QR("BlaBlaBla")
```

First, UPC is a case, which has four integer values, and the second is a QR, which has a string value. Then, you can create enums the same way we created before in other enums, but here you just have to pass parameters for the enum. When you need to check the value of enum with its associated value, we will use a `switch` statement as usual, but with some tweaks:

```
switch productCode{
case .UPC(let numberSystem, let manufacturerCode, let productCode, let
checkDigit):
    print("Product UPC code is \(numberSystem) \(manufacturerCode)
\(productCode) \(checkDigit)")
case .QR(let QRCode):
    print("Product QR code is \(QRCode)")
}

// "Product QR code is BlaBlaBla"
```

Working with protocols and delegates

Protocol is a set of methods and properties for a particular task to which classes, structure, or enumeration can be conformed.

Getting ready

The syntax of protocol goes like this:

```
protocol ProtocolName{
    // List of properties and methods goes here....
}
```

The keyword `protocol` followed by the protocol name and curly braces are the building blocks of any protocol you need to write. Classes, structures, or enumeration can then conform to it like this:

```
class SampleClass: ProtocolName{
}
```

After class name, you type `colon` and the super class name that this class extend from if any, followed by a list of protocols that you want to conform to with a comma separation.

How to do it...

1. Create a new playground file in Xcode called `Protocols` as usual.
2. Complete the following example using the following protocol:

```
protocol VehicleProtocol{
  // properties
  var name: String {set get} // settable and gettable
  var canFly: Bool {get} // gettable only (readonly)
  // instance methods
  func numberOfWheels() ->Int
  func move()
  func stop()
  // class method
  staticfuncpopularBrands() -> [String]
}

class Bicycle: VehicleProtocol{
  var name: String
  var canFly: Bool{
    return false
}
init(name: String){
self.name = name
}
func numberOfWheels() -> Int {
  return 2
}
func move() {
 // move logic goes here
}
func stop() {
 // stop logic goes here
}
static func popularBrands() -> [String] {
```

```
      return ["Giant", "GT", "Marin", "Trek", "Merida", "Specialized"]
    }
  }

  class Car: VehicleProtocol{
    var name: String
    var canFly: Bool{
      return false
    }
  init(name: String){
    self.name = name
  }
  funcnumberOfWheels() ->Int {
    return 4
  }
  func move() {
    // move logic goes here
  }
  func stop() {
    // stop logic goes here
  }
  static func popularBrands() -> [String] {
    return ["Audi", "BMW", "Honda", "Dodge", "Lamborghini", "Lexus"]
  }
}

let bicycle1 = Bicycle(name: "Merida 204")
bicycle1.numberOfWheels() // 2

let car1 = Car(name: "Honda Civic")
car1.canFly  // false

Bicycle.popularBrands() // Class function
// ["Giant", "GT", "Marin", "Trek", "Merida", "Specialized"]
  Car.popularBrands() // ["Audi", "BMW", "Honda", "Dodge", "Lamborghini",
"Lexus"]
```

How it works...

We started by defining VehicleProtocol that has a list of properties and functions that every vehicle should have. In properties, we have two types of properties: name, which is marked as {get set}, and canFly, which is marked as {get}. When you mark a property {get set}, it means it's gettable and settable, whereas {get} means it only gettable, in other words, it's a read-only property. Then, we added four methods, out of which three methods-numberOfWheels(), move(), and stop()-are instance methods. The last one-popularBrands()- marked as static is a type method. Types methods can be called directly with type name, and there is no need to have instance to call it.

Then, we created two new classes, Bicycle and Car, which conform to VehicleProtocol, and each one will have different implementations.

There's more...

We have already covered the most important parts of protocols and how to use it, but still they have more features, and there are many things that can be done with it. We will try here to mention them one by one to see when and how we can use them.

Mutating methods

Swift allows you mark protocol methods as mutating when it's necessary for these methods to mutate (modify) the instance value itself. This is applicable only in structures and enumerations; we call them value types. Consider this example of using mutating:

```
protocol Togglable{
    mutating func toggle()
}

enum Switch: Togglable{
    case ON
    case OFF
    mutating func toggle() {
        switch self {
        case .ON:
            self = OFF
        default:
            self = ON
        }
    }
}
```

The `Switch` enum implements the method `toggle`, as it's defined in the protocol `Togglable`. Inside `toggle()`, we could update self-value as function marked as `mutating`.

Delegation

Delegation is the most commonly used design pattern in iOS. In delegation, you enable types to delegate some of its responsibilities or functions to another instance of another type. To create this design pattern, we use protocols that will contain the list of responsibilities or functions to be delegated. We usually use delegation when you want to respond to actions or retrieve or get information from other sources without needing to know the type of that sources, except that they conform to that protocol. Let's take a look at an example of how to create use delegate:

```
@objc protocol DownloadManagerDelegate {
    func didDownloadFile(fileURL: String, fileData: NSData)
    func didFailToDownloadFile(fileURL: String, error: NSError)
}
class DownloadManager{
    weak var delegate: DownloadManagerDelegate!
    func downloadFileAtURL(url: String){
        // send request to download file
        // check response and success or failure
        if let delegate = self.delegate {
            delegate.didDownloadFile(url, fileData: NSData())
        }
    }
}

class ViewController: UIViewController, DownloadManagerDelegate{
    func startDownload(){
        letdownloadManager = DownloadManager()
        downloadManager.delegate = self
    }
    func didDownloadFile(fileURL: String, fileData: NSData) {
        // present file here
    }
    func didFailToDownloadFile(fileURL: String, error: NSError) {
        // Show error message
    }
}
```

The protocol `DownloadManagerDelegate` contains methods that would be called once the specific actions happen to inform the class that conforms to that protocol. The `DownloadManager` class performs the download tasks asynchronously and informs the delegate with success or failure after it's completed. `DownloadManager` doesn't need to know which object will use it or any information about it. The only thing it cares about is that the class should conform to the delegate protocol, and that's it.

Class-only protocols

We mentioned before that classes, structures, and enumerations could adopt protocols. The difference among them is that classes are reference types, whereas structures and enumerations are value types. If you find yourself having some specific actions that will be done only via reference types, mark it as `class` only. To do so, just mark it as follows:

```
protocol ClassOnlyProtocol: class{
    // class only properties and methods go here
}
```

Add a colon : and the `class` keyword to mark your protocol as class only.

Checking protocol conformance

It would be very useful to check whether an object conforms to a specific protocol or not. It's very useful when you have a list of objects, and only some of them conform to specific protocol. To check for protocol conformance, do the following:

```
class Rocket{
}

var movingObjects = [Bicycle(name: "B1"), Car(name:"C1"), Rocket()]

for item in movingObjects{
    if let vehicle =  item as? VehicleProtocol{
        print("Found vehcile with name \(vehicle.name)")
        vehicle.move()
    }
    else{
        print("Not a vehcile")
    }
}
```

We created a list of objects, and some of them conform to `VehicleProtocol` that we created earlier. Inside the `for-loop` we casted each item to `VehicleProtocol` inside `if` statement; the cast will succeed only if this item already conforms to that protocol.

Optional requirements

You see that when you list your properties and methods in a protocol, the type that conforms to that protocol should adopt to all properties and methods. Skipping one of them will lead to a compiler error. Some protocols may contain methods or properties that are not necessary to implement, especially with delegates. Some delegate methods are meant to notify you something that you don't care about. In that case, you can mark these methods as optional. The keyword `optional` can be added before properties and methods to mark them as optional. Another thing, the protocol that has optional stuff should be marked with `@Objc`. Take a look at the following example:

```
@objc protocol DownloadManagerDelegate {
    func didDownloadFile(fileURL: String, fileData: NSData)
    optional func didFailToDownloadFile(fileURL: String, error: NSError)
}
```

It's the new version of `DownloadManagerDelegate`, which marks `didFailToDownloadFile` method as optional.

Using extensions to extend classes functionality

For its name, extensions are used to extend an existing functionality. In Swift, you can extend classes, structures, protocols, and enumerations. Extensions are similar to categories in Objective-C except that extensions don't have names. It's very useful to add functionality to any type that you don't have access to its source code, such as native classes `String`, `NSArray`, and so on.

Getting ready

In Swift, syntax is pretty easy, and that's why it is awesome. To extend any type, just type the following:

```
extension TypeToBeExtended{
}
```

Inside the curly braces, you can add your extensions to the type to be extended. In extension, you can do the following:

- Adding instance- or class-computed properties
- Adding instance or class methods
- Adding new initializers
- Defining subscripts
- Adding nested types
- Conforming to protocols

Once you create an extension to any type, the new functionality will be available for all instances in the whole project.

How to do it...

1. Create a new playground file in Xcode called Extensions.
2. Create extension for double value by adding computing properties, as follows:

```
extension Double{
  var absoluteValue: Double{
    return abs(self)
  }
  var intValue: Int{
    return Int(self)
  }
}

extension String{
  var length: Int{
    return self.characters.count
  }
}

let doubleValue: Double = -19.5
doubleValue.absoluteValue // 19.5
doubleValue.intValue // 19

extension Int{
  func isEven() ->Bool{
    return self % 2 == 0
  }
  func isOdd() ->Bool{
    return !isEven()
```

```
    }
    func digits() -> [Int]{
      var digits = [Int]()
      var num = self
      repeat {
        let digit = num % 10
        digits.append(digit)
        num /= 10
      } while num != 0
      return digits
    }
}

let num = 12345
num.digits()  // [5, 4, 3, 2, 1]
```

How it works...

In Double type, we have added two computed properties. The computed properties are properties that will be calculated every time when it's called. We've added a property called absoluteValue, which returns the absolute value; same for intValue, which returns the integer value of double. Then, for any double value in the whole project, these two properties are accessible and can be used.

In the Int type, we have defined three new instance methods. The isEven() method should return true if this number is even, false otherwise, and the same logic applies for isOdd(). The third method that has some more logic is digits(), which returns array of digits in the number. The algorithm is simple; we get the last digit by getting the remainder of dividing the number by 10, and then skip the last digit by dividing by 10.

There's more...

Extensions are not meant to add new properties and methods only. You extend types by adding new initializers, mutating methods, and by defining subscripts.

Mutating instance methods

When you add instance methods, you can let them mutate (modify) the instance itself. In methods we've added before, we just do some logic and return a new value, and the instance value remains the same. With mutating, the value of instance itself will be changed. To do so, you have to mark your instance method with the `mutating` keyword. Let's take a look at an example:

```
extension Int{
    mutating func square(){
        self = self * self
    }
    mutating func double(){
        self = self * 2
    }
}

var value = 8
value.double() // 16
value.square() // 256
```

When you mark your method as `mutating`, it lets you to change self and assign new value to it.

Adding new initializer

Extensions allow you to add new initializer to the currently available initializer for any particular type. For example, let's take a look at the CGRect class. CGRect has three initializers: empty `init`; `init` with origin and size; and `init` with x, y, width, and height. We will add new initializer with a center point and a rectangular size. Let's take a look at how to do it:

```
extension CGRect{
    init(center:CGPoint, size:CGSize){
        let x = center.x - size.width / 2
        let y = center.y - size.height / 2
        self.init(x: x, y: y, width: size.width, height: size.height)
    }
}

let rect = CGRect(center: CGPoint(x: 50, y: 50), size: CGSizeMake(100, 80))
// {x 0 y 10 w 100 h 80}
```

Define subscripts

One of features that extensions provide to us is the ability to define subscripts to a particular type. Subscripting allows you to get value by calling `[n]` to get information at index *n*. Like array, when you access item at that index, you can do the same with any type you want. In the following example, we will add subscripting support to the `String` type:

```
extension String{
    subscript(charIndex: Int) -> Character{
        let index = startIndex.advancedBy(charIndex)
        return self[index]
    }
}
let str = "Hello"
str[0] // "H"
```

To add subscript to type, just add the keyword `subscript` followed by `index` and the return type. In our preceding example, the subscript will return the character at a given index. We advanced the `startIndex`, which is a property in the `String` type and points to the first character by the input `charIndex`. Then, we return the character at that `Index`.

Working with memory management and ARC

If you are coming from the old school where **MRC (Manual Reference Counting)** was being used for memory management, you definitely know how much headache developers suffer to manage memory in iOS. With iOS 5, Apple introduced **ARC (Automatic Reference Counting)**, and life became easier in terms of memory management. Though ARC manages your memory automatically, some mistakes may ruin your memory with no mercy if you didn't understand the concept of memory management.

Getting ready

Before checking how to manage memory and avoid some common mistakes, I would like to highlight some notes:

- Assigning a class instance to variable, constant, or properties will create a strong reference to this instance. The instance will be kept in memory as long as you use it.
- Setting the reference to `nil` will reduce its reference counting by one (once it reaches zero, it will be deallocated from memory). When your class deallocated from memory, all class instance properties will be set to `nil` as well.

How to do it...

1. Create two classes, `Person` and `Dog`, with a relation between them, as shown in the following code snippet (this code snippet has a memory issue called reference cycle):

```
class Dog{
   var name: String
   var owner: Person!
   init(name: String){
      self.name = name
   }
}
class Person{
   var name: String
   var id: Int
   var dogs = [Dog]()
   init(name: String, id: Int){
      self.name = name
      self.id = id
   }
}
let john = Person(name: "John", id: 1)
let rex = Dog(name: "Rex")
let rocky = Dog(name: "Rocky")
john.dogs += [rex, rocky] // append dogs
rex.owner = john
rocky.owner = john
```

2. Update the reference type of owner property in the `Dog` class to break this cycle:

```
class Dog{
  var name: String
  weak var owner: Person!
  init(name: String){
    self.name = name
  }
}
```

How it works...

We have started our example by creating two classes, `Person` and `Dog`. The `Person` class has one-to-many relation to the `Dog` class via the property array `dogs`. The `Dog` class has one-to-one relation to class `Person` via the property `owner`. Everything looks good, and it works fine if you tested, but unfortunately we did a terrible mistake. We have a retain cycle problem here, which means we have two objects in memory; each one has a strong reference to the other. This leads to a cycle that prevents both of them from being deallocated from memory.

This problem is a common problem in iOS, and not all developers note it while coding. We call it as parent-child relation. Parent (in our case, it's the `Person` class) should always have a `strong` reference to child (the `Dog` class); child should always have a `weak` reference to the parent. Child doesn't need to have `strong` reference to parent, as child should never exit when parent is deallocated from memory.

To solve such a problem, you have to break the cycle by marking one of these references as `weak`. In step 2, we see how we solved the problem by marking the property owner as `weak`.

There's more...

The reference cycle problem can happen in situations other than relations between classes. When you use closure, there is a case where you may face a retain cycle. It happens when you assign a closure to a property in class instance and then this closure captures the instance. Let's consider the following example:

```
class HTMLElement {

let name: String
let text: String?

lazy var asHTML: () -> String = {
```

```
if let text = self.text {
return "<\(self.name)>\(text)</\(self.name)>"
        } else {
return "<\(self.name) />"
        }
    }

init(name: String, text: String? = nil) {
        self.name = name
self.text = text
    }
}

let heading = HTMLElement(name: "h1", text: "h1 title")
print(heading.asHTML()) // <h1>h1 title</h1>
```

We have the `HTMLElement` class, which has closure property `asHTML`. Then, we created an instance of that class which is `heading`, and then we called the closure to return HTML text. The code works fine, but as we said, it has a reference cycle. The instance set closure to one of its property, and the closure captures the instance (happens when we call `self.name` and `self.text` inside the closure). The closure in that case will retain `self` (have a strong reference to the `heading` instance), and at the same time, `heading` already has a strong reference to its property `asHTML`. To solve reference cycle made with closure, add the following line of code as first line in closure:

```
[unownedself] in
```

So, the class will look like this:

```
class HTMLElement {

let name: String
let text: String?

lazy var asHTML: () -> String = {

        [unownedself] in

if let text = self.text {
return "<\(self.name)>\(text)</\(self.name)>"
        } else {
return "<\(self.name) />"
        }
    }

init(name: String, text: String? = nil) {
        self.name = name
```

```
self.text = text
    }
}
```

The `unowned` keyword informs the closure to use a weak reference to self instead of the strong default reference. In that case, we break the cycle and everything goes fine.

Using error handling

In any iOS project, a lot of operations may fail and you have to respond to these errors in your project. Since Swift 2, a new mechanism has been added to the language for responding and dealing with errors in your project. You can now throw and catch errors when you do any operation that may fail for some reason. Suppose, you do some logic to request some data in a JSON format from a remote server and then you save this data in a local database. Can you imagine how many errors may happen for these operations? Connection may fail between your app and the remote server, failing to parse the JSON response, database connection is closed, database file doesn't exist, or another process is writing in database and you have to wait. Recovering from these errors allows you take the appropriate action based on the error type.

Getting ready

Before starting to learn how to handle errors in Swift, you first have to be familiar with how to represent in errors that are going to happen in your program. Swift provides you with a protocol called `ErrorType` that your errors types should adopt. Then, to represent errors, here comes the role of enumerations to help you. You create a new enum, which lists all error cases, and this enum should conform to the `ErrorType` protocol. The syntax of using enum with `ErrorType` will be something like this:

```
enum DBConnectionError: ErrorType{
    case ConnectionClosed
    case DBNotExist
    case DBNotWritable
}
```

As we see it's pretty straightforward. You create enum representing the error that conforms to `ErrorType` protocol, and then list all errors as cases in the enum.

How to do it...

1. As usual, let's create a new playground named `ErrorHandling`.
2. Let's create now a new error type for a function that will sign up a new user in a system:

```
enum SignUpUserError: ErrorType{

    case InvalidFirstOrLastName
    case InvalidEmail
    case WeakPassword
    case PasswordsDontMatch
}
```

3. Now, create the sign up function that throws errors we made in the previous step, if any:

```
func signUpNewUserWithFirstName(firstName: String, lastName: String,
email: String, password: String, confirmPassword: String) throws{

    guard firstName.characters.count> 0 &&lastName.characters.count> 0
else{

        throw SignUpUserError.InvalidFirstOrLastName
    }

    guard isValidEmail(email) else{
        throw SignUpUserError.InvalidEmail
    }

    guard password.characters.count> 8 else{
        throw SignUpUserError.WeakPassword
    }

    guard password == confirmPassword else{
        throw SignUpUserError.PasswordsDontMatch
    }

    // Saving logic goes here

    print("Successfully signup user")

}

func isValidEmail(email:String) ->Bool {
```

```
            let emailRegex = "[A-Z0-9a-z._%+-]+@[A-Za-z0-9.-]+\\.[A-Za-
z]{2,}"
            let predicate = NSPredicate(format:"SELF MATCHES %@", emailRegex)
            return predicate.evaluateWithObject(email)
        }
```

4. Now, let's see how to use the function and catch errors:

```
        do{
            trysignUpNewUserWithFirstName("John", lastName: "Smith", email:
"john@gmail.com", password: "123456789", confirmPassword: "123456789")
        }
        catch{
          switch error{
            case SignUpUserError.InvalidFirstOrLastName:
              print("Invalid First name or last name")
            case SignUpUserError.InvalidEmail:
              print("Email is not correct")
            case SignUpUserError.WeakPassword:
              print("Password should be more than 8 characters long")
            case SignUpUserError.PasswordsDontMatch:
              print("Passwords don't match")
            default:
              print(error)
          }
        }
```

How it works...

We started our code example by creating a new error type called `SignUpUserError`, which conforms to `ErrorType` protocol. As we see, we listed four errors that may happen while signing up any user in our system, such as invalid first name or last name, invalid e-mail, weak password, and passwords that don't match. So far, so good!

Then, we create a function `signUpNewUserWithFirstName`, which takes user input values, and as we can see, we have marked it with the `throws` keyword. The keyword `throws` says that this function may throw an error anytime during execution, so you be prepared to catch errors thrown by this method.

Inside the implementation of the function, you will see a list of `guard` statements that checks for user input; if any of these `guard` statements returned `false`, the code of `else` statement will be called. The statement `throw` is used to stop execution of this method and throw the appropriate error based on the checking made.

Catching errors is pretty easy; to call a function that throws error, you have to call it inside the `do-catch` block. After the `do` statement, use the `try` keyword and call your function. If any error happens while executing your method, the block of code inside the `catch` statement will be called with a given parameter called `error` that represents the error. We've created a `switch` statement that checks the type of `error` and prints a user-friendly statement based on the error type.

There's more...

The information that we previously presented is enough for you to deal with error handling, but still there are a couple of things considered important to be known.

Multiple catch statements

In the preceding example, you will notice that we've created a `catch` statement, and inside, we used a `switch` statement to cover all cases of error. This is a correct way, but for your reference, we have another way to do this. Consider the following:

```
catch SignUpUserError.InvalidFirstOrLastName{

}
catch SignUpUserError.InvalidEmail{

}
catch SignUpUserError.WeakPassword{

}
catch SignUpUserError.PasswordsDontMatch{

}
```

After the `do` statement, you can list `catch` statement with the type of error that this statement will catch. Using this method has a condition that the `catch` statements should be exhaustive, which means it should cover all types of errors.

Disable error propagation

Functions that usually throw an error, in some cases, don't throw an error. In some cases, you may know that calling a function like these with some kind of parameters will never throw an error. In that case, Swift gives you an option to disable error propagation via calling this method with `try!` instead of `try`. Calling throwing functions via `try!` will disable error propagation, and if an error is thrown in that case, you will get a runtime error. So, it's better to take care while using `try!`.

Using generics to write generic and reusable code

Generic code is used to write reusable and flexible functionalities that can deal with any type of variables. This helps in writing reusable and clean code regardless of the type of objects your generic code deals with. An example of using generics is when you use `Array` and `Dictionary`. You can create an array of `Int` or `String` or any type you want. That's because `Array` is natively created and can deal with any type. Swift gives you the ability to write generic code very easily as you will see in this section.

Getting ready

Before learning how to write generic code, let's see an example of a problem that generics solve. I bet you are familiar with stack data structures and have been using it in one of the computer science courses before. Anyway, it's a kind of collection data structure that follows **LIFO (Last in first out)**. It has very commonly used APIs for these operations, which are pop and push. Push inserts new item to the stack; pop returns the last inserted one. It's just a simple overview, as we will not explain data structures in this book as it's out of topic.

How to do it...

Here, we will create the stack data structure with/without generics:

1. Create a new playground named `Generics`.
2. Let's create the data structure stack with type `Int`:

```
class StackInt{
```

```
      var elements = [Int]()

  func push(element:Int)
  {
    self.elements.append(element)
  }
  func pop() ->Int
  {
    return self.elements.removeLast()
  }
  func isEmpty()->Bool
  {
    returnself.elements.isEmpty
  }
}

var stack1 = StackInt()
stack1.push(5)      // [5]
stack1.push(10)   //[5,10]
stack1.push(20) // [5,10,20]
stack1.pop()    // 20
```

3. Let's see the same created stack but with a generics fashion:

```
class Stack <T>{
  var elements = [T]()
  func push(element:T)
  {
    self.elements.append(element)
  }
  func pop()->T{
    return self.elements.removeLast()
  }
}

var stackOfStrings = Stack<String>()
stackOfStrings.push("str1")
stackOfStrings.push("str2")
stackOfStrings.pop()

var stackOfInt = Stack<Int>()
stackOfInt.push(4)
stackOfInt.push(7)
stackOfInt.pop()
```

How it works...

The first class we created, StackInt, is a stack that can work only with the Int type. It's good if you are going to use it with Int type only. However, a famous data structure like it can be used with different types, such as String or Double. It's not possible to create different stack class for each type, and here comes the magic of generics; instead we created another class called Stack marked with <T> to say it's going to deal with the generic type T, which can be Int, String, Double, and so on. Then, we create two stack instances, stackOfStrings and stackOfInt, and both share the same code as their class is built with generics.

2
The Essentials

In this chapter, we will cover the following topics:

- Using UIView via code or interface builder to build your own custom views
- Working with navigation controller and navigation bar
- Working with stack views
- Working with UICollectionView
- Working with gestures like swipe, pan, rotation, and tap
- Using 3D touch

Introduction

Game on, your swift weapons are ready for iOS development. This chapter will be considered your first station in our journey through this book. We will cover some of the most commonly used UI components for building your app screens in this chapter. We will start with the godfather of all UI components--the UIView. Then, we will introduce navigation controller, stack views, collection views, and the gesture recognizers. These components are important because you will use them frequently in iOS development and should be known by any iOS developer. This is not applicable to the last recipe (3D Touch), since it's a new feature in iOS devices; but, it's still important, as all new upcoming devices will have this feature, so you should be ready and be aware of how to utilize it in your app.

Using UIView via code or interface builder to build your own custom views

UIViews are the base building blocks of any iOS app. Think of LEGO; kids build their own buildings and blocks using tiny base blocks. The same logic is used in iOS; all UI screens you see are just a building of UIViews. All native/custom UI components extend from UIView; in other words, UIView is the base class of all UI components. To master iOS development and building the layout of any app, you have to be familiar with UIView.

Getting ready

We will see in this recipe how to create/use UIViews programmatically (hardcoded) or via interface builder. The fast and recommended way is to create your UIViews via interface builder (XIB files or Storyboards); but of course, in some cases, you will need to build custom UIViews, and in that case you will build your own custom UIViews programmatically.

How to do it...

1. Go to Xcode and create a new iOS project with template **Single View Application**. Set the name of the project to `UIViews`.
2. Now, select the storyboard file and open the single page view controller:

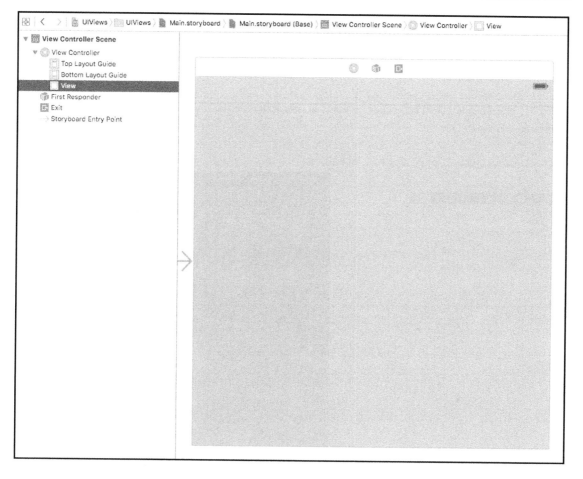

3. In the Attribute Inspector in the right-hand side bar, set the size of the **View Controller** to iPhone 4.7-inch size.

4. Open the **View Controller** view, and from **Object Library** in the right-hand side bar, drag two UIViews. In the first UIView and from the **Size Inspector** tab in the right side bar, set the frame of the first one to *(x = 0, y = 0, width = 375, height = 300)*, and from the **Attribute Inspector** tab, set red as the background color. In the second UIView, set the frame to *(x = 0, y = 300, width = 375, height = 300)*.

5. Rename the two views by selecting each one and hit the *Enter* key. The title will be converted to a text field where you can rename your views. Change the first view to RedView and the second one to BlueView. You should see something like this:

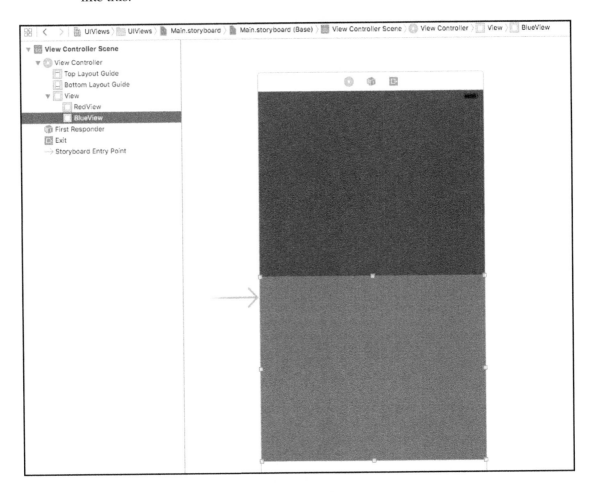

6. Take an outlet for your views. Click on **Assistant Editor** at the top bar to open the `ViewController.swift` file, and drag the view to the source code file to add outlets by selecting each view and holding the *Ctrl* key:

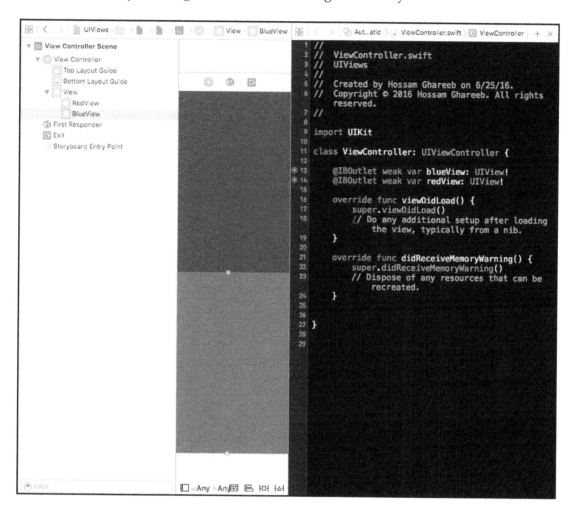

7. Now, open the `ViewController.swift` file in the `viewDidLoad` function and add the following code:

```
let yellowView = UIView(frame: CGRectMake(0, 0, 200, 100))
yellowView.backgroundColor = UIColor.yellowColor()
self.redView.addSubview(yellowView)
let brownView = UIView(frame: CGRectMake(100, 50, 200, 100))
brownView.backgroundColor = UIColor.brownColor()
self.redView.insertSubview(brownView, belowSubview: yellowView)
```

8. Now, build and run the project; you should see something like this:

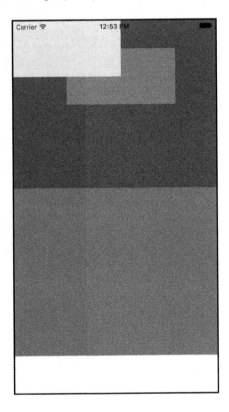

How it works...

First, we created the project with the **Single View** template; there are multiple templates that you can use or start with for your empty project. Then, we set the layout size of the view controller to a 4-inch size iPhone, as the project is intended to be for iPhone only, not iPad. This doesn't mean that your app will work on a 4-inch (iPhone 6 and iPhone 6s) iPhone only; it indicates what the layout will look like. We will see in later chapters how to design your app's UI, regardless of the screen size via size classes and auto layout.

Then, we saw how simple it is to add UIViews via interface builder. We added the red and blue views without wiring any line of code, and you can see how to change the view's properties in Attribute Inspector.

We add outlets to your views in the `ViewController.swift` file, which act as a reference to your components created in interface builder. So, you can access them any time in your code and do any specific action on them, such as hiding, resizing, translation, or adding subviews.

We then moved to source code to add two views, but programmatically. You first need to initialize the UIView and we used one of its initializers, which takes a frame to initialize with. The frame specifies the size and location (on superview) of the view. Then, we change the background color using one of its properties: `.backgroundColor`. I recommend opening the documentation of UIView, where you will see a list of properties and functions to be used.

Creating UIViews is nothing without presenting them onscreen, and to present it, you have to add a subview to any other view. The most common method used is `addSubview()`, which adds the view as a subview to the superview and on top of the view hierarchy. In some cases, adding on the top is not what you want, and you need some flexibility to choose where to add your view in the view hierarchy; that's why, `UIView` provides you with another three methods to insert a subview:

- Function `insertSubview(brownView, belowSubview: yellowView)`: This adds a subview below any other subview that you have in your view hierarchy. This method requires having a reference to the view you want to add below a subview.
- Function `insertSubview(view, atIndex: 2)`: This is a very flexible function to add any subview to your view hierarchy at any index. The index is 0 indexed, and 0 means the first subview.
- Function `insertSubview(view, aboveSubview: superview)`: This adds a subview above any other subview you have in your view hierarchy. This method requires having a reference to the view you want to add above a subview.

Using these methods, you have a full customization, where you can place your UIViews programmatically.

There's more...

We saw how to add UIViews using interface builder or programmatically. These are the most commonly used ways in UIViews while working on an iOS app. In some cases, native components don't fit your needs, and you have to build your own custom UIView. Let's see in action how to build a custom UIView. In the following example, we will see how to build a circular progress bar programmatically and how to use or customize it using interface builder.

Go to Xcode and create a new Swift class CircularProgressBar, which extends UIView. Then, add the following code:

```
@IBDesignable
class CircularProgressBar: UIView {

    /// The background fixed color of progress bar
    @IBInspectable var progressFixedColor : UIColor = UIColor.whiteColor()
    /// The progressive color
    @IBInspectable var progressColor : UIColor = UIColor.redColor()
    /// The line width of the progress circle
    @IBInspectable var lineWidth:CGFloat = 5.0
    /// The layer where we draw the progressive animation.
    private var progressiveLayer : CAShapeLayer?

    func updateProgess(progress:CGFloat, animated:Bool,
     duration:CFTimeInterval){
        if self.progressiveLayer == nil{
            self.setNeedsDisplay()
        }
        if progress <= 1.0{
            self.progressiveLayer?.strokeEnd = progress
            if  animated {
                CATransaction.begin()
                let animation = CABasicAnimation(keyPath: "strokeEnd");
                animation.duration = duration
                animation.fromValue = NSNumber(float: 0.0)
                animation.toValue = NSNumber(float: Float(progress));
                animation.timingFunction = CAMediaTimingFunction(name:
                 kCAMediaTimingFunctionEaseInEaseOut)
                self.progressiveLayer?.addAnimation(animation, forKey:
                 "animateStrokeEnd")
                CATransaction.commit()
```

```
            }
        }
    }
    override func drawRect(rect: CGRect) {
        // Drawing code
        let fixedLayer = getShapeLayerForRect(rect, strokeColor:
         progressFixedColor)
        fixedLayer.strokeEnd = 1.0
        self.layer.addSublayer(fixedLayer)
        let progressiveLayer = getShapeLayerForRect(rect, strokeColor:
         progressColor)
        progressiveLayer.strokeEnd = 0.0
        self.progressiveLayer = progressiveLayer
        self.layer.addSublayer(progressiveLayer)
    }
    private func getShapeLayerForRect(rect:CGRect, strokeColor
     sColor:UIColor) -> CAShapeLayer{
        let radius = CGRectGetWidth(rect) / 2 - lineWidth / 2
        let newRect = CGRectMake(lineWidth / 2, lineWidth / 2, radius * 2,
         radius * 2)
        let path = UIBezierPath(roundedRect: newRect, cornerRadius:
         radius).CGPath
        let shape = CAShapeLayer()
        shape.path = path
        shape.strokeColor = sColor.CGColor
        shape.lineWidth = self.lineWidth
        shape.fillColor = nil
        return shape
    }

}
```

Let's explain the code step by step:

1. We marked our class with @IBDesignable, which tells the compiler that this class is a custom UIView that can be rendered in interface builder. This helps you to see what the view looks like without running the on simulator or device.

2. We listed three parameters to set the colors and line width of the progress view. Each parameter is marked as @IBInspectable, which tells the compiler to display these parameters in Attribute Inspector, so you customize these values as well from interface builder.

3. Go to interface builder and add a `UIView` as a subview to the view that is blue. Change its class from `UIView` to `CircularProgressBar` from the Identity Inspector tab. Change its background color to clear color and see how the view will be rendered:

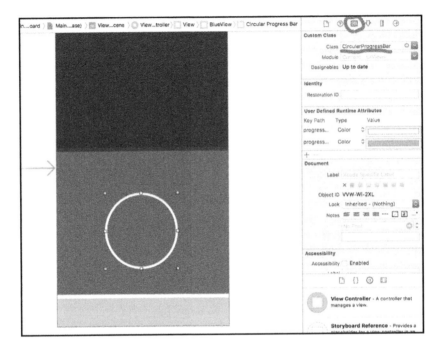

4. Also, if you open the Attribute Inspector, you will see that three additional attributes have been added:

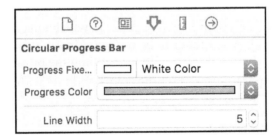

5. Then, we override the drawRect method. This function should be overridden to make a custom drawing in your view. In drawRect, we created two circular shapes. One shape is the fixed circle shape, which acts as a background. It's strokeEnd value is 1, as it's fixed and a complete circle. The second shape is the progressive circle, which will be animated via strokeEnd to show its progress. We used the getShapeLayerForRect function to create a circle via the CAShapeLayer class in the CoreAnimation framework.

More information about drawing with Bezier Path and Core Animation can be found in Chapter 5, *Animations and Graphics*.

6. Then, we add the updateProgess function that updates the progress by animating the progressive layer strokeEnd property.

7. Now, take a look at an outlet of the progressive view in ViewController.swift:

```
@IBOutlet weak var circularProgressView: CircularProgressBar!
```

8. Then override viewDidAppear method to update the progress value to 75% like this:

```
override func viewDidAppear(animated: Bool) {
    super.viewDidAppear(animated)
    self.circularProgressView.updateProgess(0.75, animated: true,
     duration: 2)
}
```

9. Now, build and run; you should see the progress updates with animation:

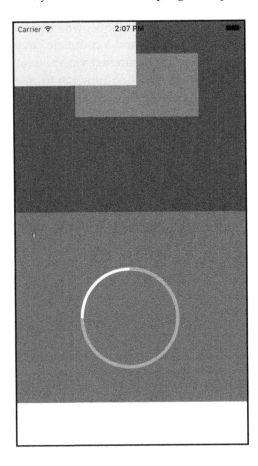

Working with navigation controller and navigation bar

In iOS, we have multiple native view controllers that manage list of other view controllers, such as UINavigationController, UITabBarViewController, or UIPageViewController. Navigation controller is one of the most common controllers used to manage list of view controllers, and all iOS developers or users are familiar with this component. This component is one of the essential components that every iOS developer should know how to master and use.

Getting ready

In this recipe, we will see how to build an iOS app which uses a navigation controller. We will see how to push and pop between the view controllers of the navigation controller. We will discuss the navigation bar, which you can see at the top of the navigation controller, and how to customize it.

There is some information that you should know about `UINavigationController`:

- The view controllers that it manages are put in a stack; when you push a view controller, you put it at the top of the stack. Also, when you pop a view controller, you remove the top one from the stack and display the preceding one.
- `UINavigationController` has three main items--the left item, middle item, and right item.
  - **Left Item:** By default, you will see a back button (except for the root), and its title is set to the `title` property of the preceding view controller. You can add a custom button in the by setting `leftBarButtonItem` or `leftBarButtonItems` properties in the navigation item of the displayed view controller.
  - **Middle Item:** By default, a label with the current view controller `title` property is displayed. You can add custom middle view by setting the `titleView` property in the navigation item of the displayed view controller.
  - **Right Item:** This is the same as left item; but by default, there is nothing to display. You can use the `rightBarButtonItem` or `rightBarButtonItems` properties in the navigation item.

How to do it...

1. Create a new Xcode project with a **Single View** template named `NavigationController`.
2. From Object library, drag a navigation controller to the storyboard, and set the entry point of the storyboard to the navigation controller.

3. By default, the navigation controller in interface builder comes with a root view controller, which is a `UITableViewController`. We will use this table to display a list of dates, and when you click on one of them, it will push another view controller.

4. Create a new view controller called `MasterViewController` to be the root view controller and make it extend from `UITableViewController`. The source code of `MasterViewController` should look like this:

```
class MasterViewController: UITableViewController {
  var objects = [AnyObject]()
  override func viewDidLoad() {
    super.viewDidLoad()
    let addButton = UIBarButtonItem(barButtonSystemItem: .Add,
     target: self, action: "insertNewObject:")
    self.navigationItem.rightBarButtonItem = addButton
  }
  func insertNewObject(sender: AnyObject) {
    objects.insert(NSDate(), atIndex: 0)
    let indexPath = NSIndexPath(forRow: 0, inSection: 0)
    self.tableView.insertRowsAtIndexPaths([indexPath],
     withRowAnimation: .Automatic)
  }
  // MARK: - Segues
  override func prepareForSegue(segue: UIStoryboardSegue, sender:
   AnyObject?) {
  if segue.identifier == "showDetail" {
    if let indexPath = self.tableView.indexPathForSelectedRow {
      let object = objects[indexPath.row] as! NSDate
      let controller = segue.destinationViewController as!
       DetailViewController
      controller.detailItem = object
    }
   }
  }
}
// MARK: - Table View
override func tableView(tableView: UITableView, numberOfRowsInSection
 section: Int) -> Int {
   return objects.count
}
override func tableView(tableView: UITableView, cellForRowAtIndexPath
 indexPath: NSIndexPath) -> UITableViewCell {
  let cell = tableView.dequeueReusableCellWithIdentifier("Cell",
   forIndexPath: indexPath)
  let object = objects[indexPath.row] as! NSDate
  cell.textLabel!.text = object.description
  return cell
```

```
    }
}
```

5. Then, set the class of the root view controller in the storyboard to be
   MasterViewController from Identity Inspector.

6. Add a new view controller in Xcode called DetailViewController to display
   the details when you select an item from MasterViewController:

```
class DetailViewController: UIViewController {

    @IBOutlet weak var detailDescriptionLabel: UILabel!

    var detailItem: AnyObject? {
        didSet {
            // Update the view.
            self.configureView()
        }
    }

    func configureView() {
        // Update the user interface for the detail item.
        if let detail = self.detailItem {
            if let label = self.detailDescriptionLabel {
                label.text = detail.description
            }
        }
    }

    override func viewDidLoad() {
        super.viewDidLoad()
        // Do any additional setup after loading the view, typically
from
        a nib.
        self.configureView()
    }
}
```

7. Add a new view controller in the storyboard, and set its class to
   DetailViewController.

8. From the prototype cell of the table view in MasterViewController, hold the
   Ctrl key, create a segue to the DetailViewController, and select show as a
   type of the segue.

9. Click on the segue, and set the identifier in the Attribute Inspector to **showDetail**:

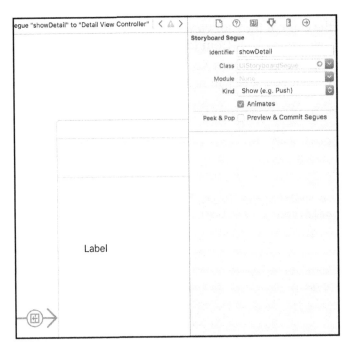

10. Add a `UILabel` as a subview to display the details of the selected item and connect the outlet to source code of `DetailViewController.swift`:

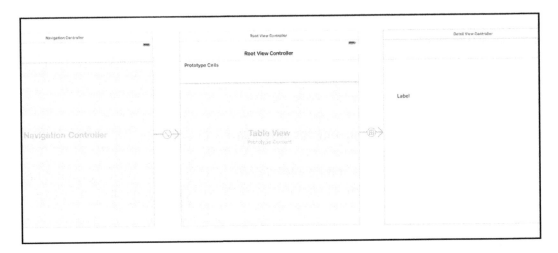

11. Lastly, in the `MasterViewController` in the storyboard, you will see a table view that has a prototype cell. Update the identifier of the cell to `Cell` to match the identifier in the source code.

   If you are not familiar with table views, don't worry, we will explain them in detail in later chapters.

12. Now, build and run. You will see an empty list in `MasterViewController`; click on the add button multiple times; you will see something like this:

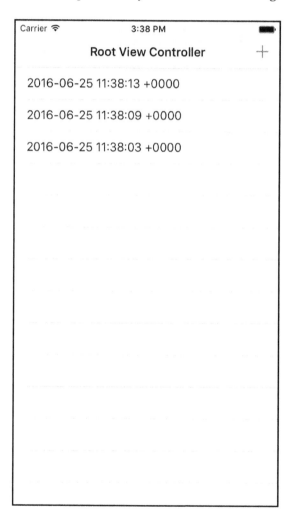

13. Also, when you click on any item, it should navigate you to
    `DetailViewController`:

How it works...

First, we created the `MasterViewController`, which is the root view controller. We made it a subclass of `UITableViewController` to display a table view with list of cells, and when you select any cell, navigation controller will push a new `DetailViewController` as a details view.

In `MasterViewController`, we added a right bar button in the right item that we have explained earlier. First, we create a new `UIBarButtonItem` and set in the `navigationItem.rightBarButtonItem`. This adds a right button at the right and will be visible only to `MasterViewController` and not to all controllers in the navigation stack. The action of the right button will insert a new cell in the table view.

Since we added a segue from the cell to `DetailViewController`, once you select any cell from the table, a new `DetailViewController` will be pushed. In most cases, you will need to pass some information for the newly opened view controller, and in our case, we need to pass the selected item to `DetailViewController`. The `prepareForSegue` method is the best place to do so, and you can differentiate between segues (if you have multiple segues) using their identifiers. When you open `DetailViewController`, you will see a back button automatically added in the navigation bar to go back to the preceding view controller.

There's more...

We saw how to use navigation controller in interface builder and how to set bar button items in the navigation item of view controllers. We will see some other useful APIs to be used in the navigation controller in this section.

Push and pop

We saw in the preceding example how to navigate to another view controller using segues. Additionally, we can do this programmatically by calling the following:

```
self.navigationController?.pushViewController(viewController, animated:
true)
```

This pushes a new view controller with or without animation.

Also, to pop view controllers, we have three functions that we can use:

- The `popViewControllerAnimated` function: This will pop the top view controller and update the UI to the preceding one
- The `popToRootViewControllerAnimated` function: This will pop all view controllers in the stack, but the root view controller
- The `popToViewController:animated` function: This will pop all view controllers in the stack not upto the root but upto a given reference to the view controller to pop to it

Hiding navigation bar

- You can at any time hide or show the navigation bar based on any logic you have in your app by calling:

```
self.navigationController?.setNavigationBarHidden(true, animated: true)
```

> Passing `true` to the preceding function hides the bar, and passing `false` will show the bar. Also, you can specify whether you want to do it with animation or not.

- `UINavigationController` has another awesome property called `hidesBarsOnSwipe` when you set it to `true`. The navigation bar will be hidden automatically when you swipe up a table view or a scroll view. Also, when you swipe down, it will be shown again. This feature is very nice, as it saves a lot of space for the user while scrolling a list of data to see as much data as possible on screen. Let's give it a shot; from our preceding example, open `MasterViewController` and add this line of code in the `viewDidLoad` function:

```
self.navigationController?.hidesBarsOnSwipe = true
```

- Then, build and run; you will note the bar hides or shows while scrolling:

Navigation bar color

Last but not least is changing the color of the navigation bar. It's very rare to find an app that has a different color for the navigation bar in different screens. Most of the apps have one navigation color that is unique for all screens. We will now see how to set the navigation bar coloring globally in your app. Open the `AppDelegate.swift` file, and add these lines of code:

```
UINavigationBar.appearance().tintColor = UIColor.blackColor()
UINavigationBar.appearance().barTintColor = UIColor.cyanColor()
```

We changed the default blue tint color to black color and bar tint color (background color) to cyan color. When you build and run, you should see something like this:

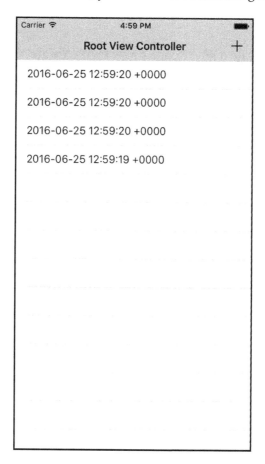

Working with stack views

UIStackView is one of the coolest features introduced in iOS 9.0 for developers. It was a hassle to arrange groups of views horizontally or vertically. You had to get your hands dirty with a lot of Auto Layout constraints to arrange these views properly. UIStackView makes arranging subviews horizontally or vertically easier without you worrying about Auto Layout. Although you don't need to use Auto Layout to arrange your views, as its UIStackview's job, you still need to use Auto Layout to define position and size of the stack view itself. If you're still not convinced about the magic that UIStackView does, you have to give it a shot.

How to do it

1. As usual, let's create a new Xcode project with **Single View** template and name it StackViews.
2. Open the storyboard file and select the view controller and change its size to iPhone 4-inch.
3. From **Object Library**, drag a Vertical stack view and add it as a subview.
4. Change its frame to (X = 20, Y = 20, Width = 280).

5. We need to add constraints to make the stack view's left, right, and top margins to be equal to 20 and to make its `height = 75%` of the device screen. To do so, first select the stack view, and click on the Pin button and set the top, left, and right constraint values to 20:

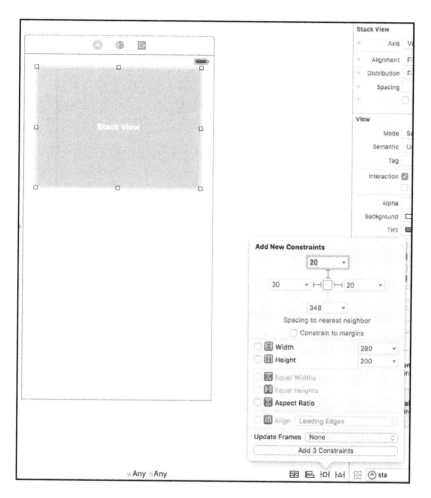

6. For the height constraint, drag the stack view (while holding the *Ctrl* key) to the superview and click on **Equal Heights**:

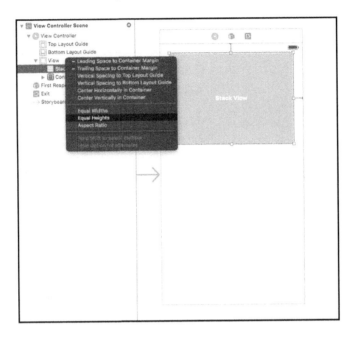

7. Now, the stack view height will be equal to the superview height, but we need it to be 75%. So, open, selecting the stack view. Open the **Size Inspector** tab and double-click on the height constraint. In the multiplier value, change it to 0.75:

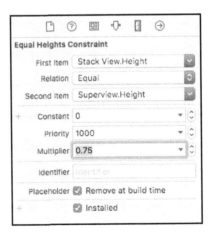

8. You will note that there is a warning in Xcode because your stack view's frame doesn't match the constraints. To solve it, just click on the warning indicator arrow, and then click on the warning indicator triangle that will show a popup asking how you want to fix the warning. Select **Update frames** from the options, and click on **Fix Misplacement**:

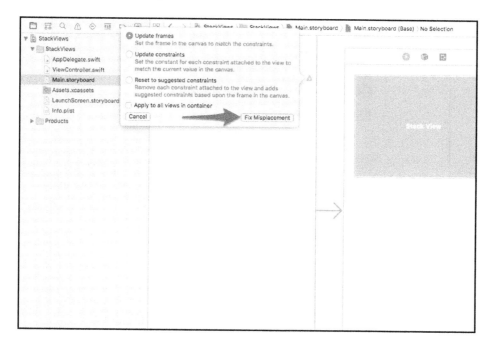

9. Now, your stack view is ready. Let's add some content to it. From the **Object Library**, drag an image view and place it inside the stack view. You will note that the image view size automatically matches the stack view size.

10. Repeat the previous process for two more image views. You will note that stack view automatically lays out the three image views to match the content.

11. Now, select the stack view, click on **Attribute Inspector**, and change its setting to match the following screenshot:

12. Now, set the images for image views to any images you have or use the ones we have in the resources folder for this chapter. You should have something like this:

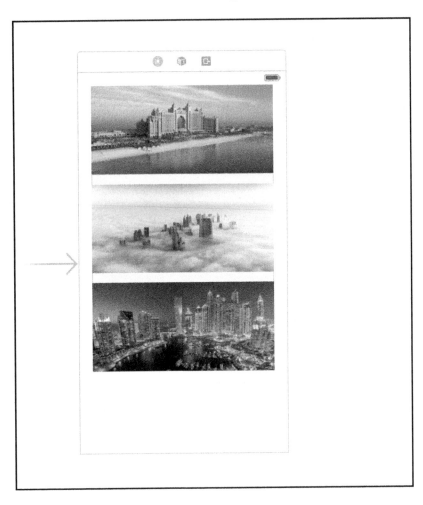

13. Now, build and run in simulator.

How it works...

As we saw in the preceding section, it's easy to manage and work with stack views. Let's take a look at how the preceding example works:

1. We started by placing a vertical `UIStackView` from Object library in our view hierarchy and set its Auto Layout to define its position and size. As we said, you don't have to set any Auto Layout for the subviews of the stack view, but you have to set Auto Layout for the stack view itself.

2. We selected three image views from the **Object Library**, and noted how awesome the stack view is while it automatically lay out the image views to fill the content.

3. From Attribute Inspector, we set some settings to the stack view, which will highlight the most important ones, such as the following:

   - **Axis**: You choose whether you want the stack to layout your subview vertically or horizontally. For example, in horizontal layout, you will note that the first item leading edge will be pinned to the stack's leading edge, and the last item trailing edge will be pinned to the stack's trailing edge. In vertical layout, the layout will be arranged based on top and bottom edges.

   - **Alignment**: This option indicates how the stack view will align your subview relative to the stack view. For example, when you set it to `Center` when the Axis is vertical, stack view will calculate the size of each item and center it horizontally. However, when you set it to `Leading`, all items will be aligned along with the stack view's leading. In our example, we set it to `Fill`, which means the stack view will stretch the arranged views to match the stack view.

   - **Distribution**: The option defines the size of the arranged views. For example, when you set it to `Fill Equally`, the stack view will lay them out, so all arranged views share the same size.

   - **Spacing**: This defines the spacing between the arranged views.

4. When you run the app in different screen size, you will see the magic in how stack views lays out your images equally so that it fits the screen size of the simulator or device.

Working with UICollectionView

`UICollectionView` is a very handy and awesome view when it comes to dealing with grid layout. Collection view helps you create a grid layout (2D cells) easily without hassle.

Collection view is just a scrollable view that lays out multiple cells in a grid layout. So, to create a collection view, you have to specify a data source and delegate exactly like UITableView. Besides that, you need to specify how the layout of your cells will appear. iOS provides you with an abstract class-UICollectionViewLayout-which should be subclassed to customize how the content will be managed. You can create your own custom layouts and describe how you want to lay out your cells. However, thanks to Apple, it provides us with a premade layout called UICollectionViewFlowLayout, which flow the layout by placing the cells one after the other based on their sizes and the spacing between them.

How to do it...

1. Create a new Xcode project with our lovely template **Single View** template and name it Collection View.
2. Open the storyboard file and select our lonely view controller and change its size to iPhone 4-inch.
3. Select the View Controller, go to **Editor** | **Embed In** | **UINavigationController** to automatically make your view controller a root view controller of a navigation controller:

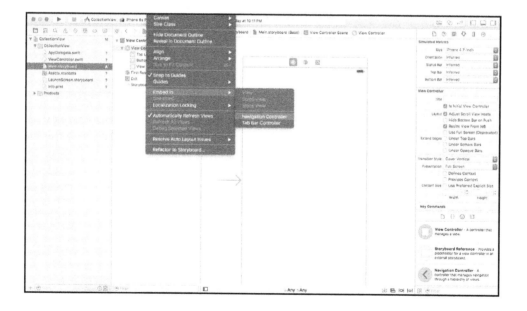

4. From **Object Library**, drag the `UICollectionView` and add it as a subview. Change its frame to (X = 0, Y = 0, Width = 375, Height = 603).

5. Add constraints to make your collection view always at the location *(0, 0)* and with the size same as that of the screen. Open the pin icon, as shown in the following diagram, and set the leading and top constraints to 0. Then, click on the add button:

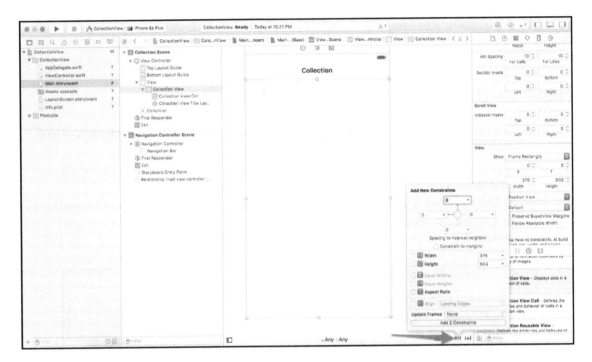

6. Now, we need the constraints for width and height. Holding the *Ctrl* key, drag the collection view, and an arrow will be displayed for you to choose the view you need to select to add constraints with. Drag it to the superview view, and once the list of constraints appears, hold the shift key to allow you to select multiple constraints, select equal width, and equal height, and then press *Enter*.

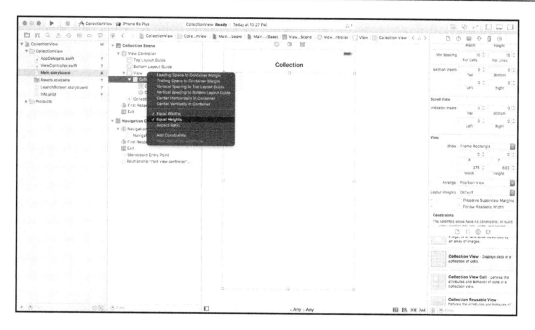

7. Now, regardless of the size of your device's screen, the size of the collection view will be equal to it. Now, open size inspector tab, and in `Min Spacing` section (which identifies the spacing between cells and lines), set them to zeros because we will customize the spacing programmatically:

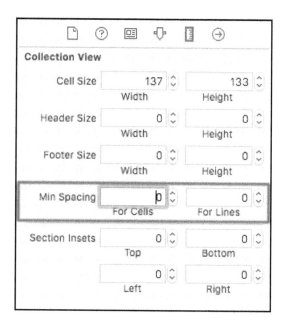

8. From Attribute Inspector, change the background color to white. The default one is black color, which, in my opinion, looks quite unimpressive.

9. To let collection view work properly, it needs to know the delegate and data source. Our `ViewController.swift` will be the delegate and data source. So, to set them in interface builder, hold the *Ctrl* key and drag the collection view to **View Controller**; a list of options for data source and delegate will open. Then, click on each one to set it:

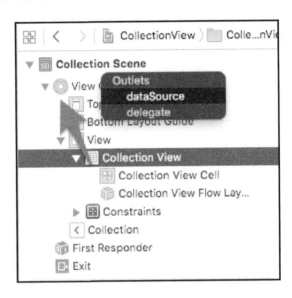

10. Select the prototype cell in the collection view and increase its size a little bit (we will control its size dynamically later via code). Drag a `UIImageView` from Object library, and add it as a subview to the cell. Let its size be identical to the cell size and be at the location *(0, 0)*.

11. Since the cell size will be changed dynamically, we want its image view to be resized automatically as well. For that reason, let's add constraints to the image view by setting its `leading`, `top`, `trailing`, and `bottom` be the same as those of the cell:

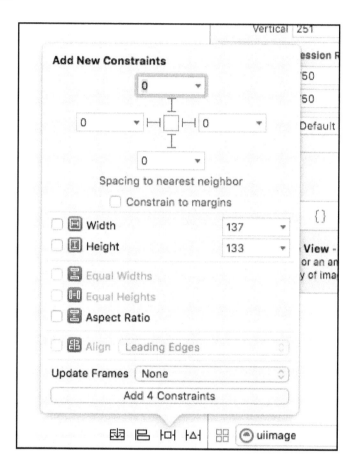

12. Since the collection view cell is customized, it's highly recommended to create a custom `UICollectionViewCell` class to encapsulate the logic/outlets/managing of the custom cell. Create a new file in Xcode, select Cocoa touch class, and set the name to `CustomCollectionViewCell` and the subclass to `UICollectionViewCell`:

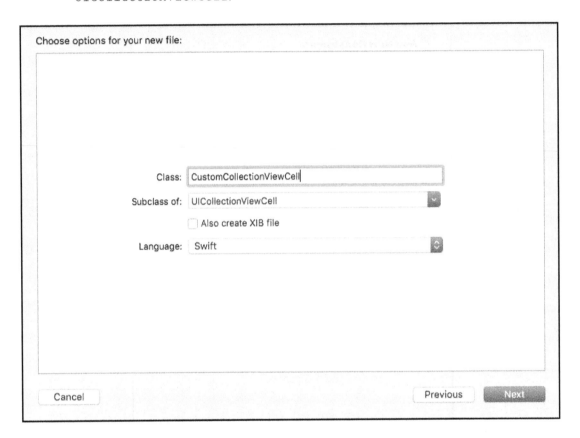

13. Return to storyboard. Let's now select our prototype cell. Also, from Attribute Inspector, change its identifier to cell, and from Identity Inspector, change its class to the newly created `CustomCollectionViewCell` class.

14. Since we changed the class to a custom one, you can now open Assistant Editor to link `IBOutlet` to the image view in `CustomCollectionViewCell`, as follows:

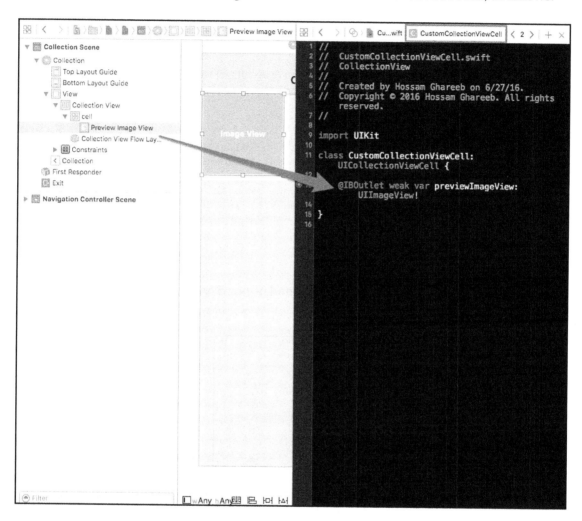

15. Now, everything should be ready in terms of layout. Let's now jump to `ViewController.swift` to write some code. Change the code in `ViewController.swift` to look like this:

```
class ViewController: UIViewController, UICollectionViewDelegate,
UICollectionViewDataSource, UICollectionViewDelegateFlowLayout{

    // MARK: - UICollectionViewDelegateFlowLayout -
    func collectionView(collectionView: UICollectionView, layout
```

```
            collectionViewLayout: UICollectionViewLayout,
sizeForItemAtIndexPath indexPath: NSIndexPath) -> CGSize {
        let width = CGRectGetWidth(collectionView.frame)
        let cellWidth = width / 3
        return CGSizeMake(cellWidth, cellWidth)
    }
    // MARK: - UICollectionViewDatasource -
    func collectionView(collectionView: UICollectionView,
     numberOfItemsInSection section: Int) -> Int {
      return 20
    }

    func collectionView(collectionView: UICollectionView,
     cellForItemAtIndexPath indexPath: NSIndexPath) ->
UICollectionViewCell {
        let cell = collectionView.dequeueReusableCellWithReuseIdentifier
          ("cell", forIndexPath: indexPath) as! CustomCollectionViewCell
        cell.previewImageView.image = UIImage(named: "Dubai.png")
        return cell
    }
  }
```

16. Build and run our app now in the simulator or device; you will see something like this:

How it works...

Although we performed many steps in order to have this result of grid view of images, they are pretty straightforward. The steps are self-explanatory, but we will mention the important points in detail for your reference:

1. We started by setting constraints to the collection view to place it always at the location (0, 0) and with size relative to the super view. For more practice on constraints, check our later chapters. These constraints will automatically resize your collection view to be always equal to the superview, so when you run the app in any device--even iPads--you will see that the collection view size is equal to the screen size.

2. From Size Inspector, we changed the `Min Spacing` for cells and lines to zero. Cells spacing indicates the spacing between any successive items in a row or column. Line spacing indicates the spacing between any successive rows or columns.

3. Then, we added a custom collection view cell, which encapsulates all logic/layout for the prototype cell. You can customize the cell by placing subviews and constraints between them and the superview of the cell. Then, we created a new custom cell class in source files to line your outlets and actions.

4. In source code, where magic happens, we implemented the data source and delegate methods to set the number of cells you need in your layout and which cell to be placed.

5. To customize the flow layout, you can conform to `UICollectionViewDelegateFlowLayout` and implement any optional functions from the flow layout delegate. In the preceding example, we implemented the following:

```
collectionView(collectionView: UICollectionView, layout
  collectionViewLayout: UICollectionViewLayout,
    sizeForItemAtIndexPath indexPath: NSIndexPath) -> CGSize
```

This tells the layout the size of the cell at a given index. In our example, we set the width to be one-third of the screen width (we always display three cells per row), and to make our cells squares, we set the height to be equal to width.

There's more...

Of course, there is much more in `UICollectionView`, especially when it comes to customization. In our example, we saw how we implemented one function from `UICollectionViewDelegateFlowLayout` to set the item size. Other methods that can be implemented are as follows:

```
func collectionView(collectionView: UICollectionView, layout
  collectionViewLayout: UICollectionViewLayout,
   minimumLineSpacingForSectionAtIndex section: Int) -> CGFloat {
   }
   func collectionView(collectionView: UICollectionView, layout
    collectionViewLayout: UICollectionViewLayout,
     minimumInteritemSpacingForSectionAtIndex section: Int) -> CGFloat {
   }
```

The first function lets you specify the spacing between any successive rows and columns. The function gives you the section index if you want to specify a different value for each section in case you have multiple sections.

The second function lets you specify the spacing between any successive cells in a row or column.

Customizable layouts

We explained how to use the `UICollectionViewFlowLayout` subclass that Apple provides us to support flow-based layouts easily. In most cases, this layout gets the job done by customizing the spacing, as we mentioned earlier. However, if you want a fancy customization, such as circular layouts, you have to get your hands dirty and subclass `UICollectionViewLayout` and write your custom code to describe how to manage your content. It's a little bit challenging, but it is worth trying.

Working with gestures like swipe, pan, rotation, and tap

When users use your app, clicking is not only the possible way that user can interact with the app. iOS provides you with gesture recognizers such as the most commonly used gestures by users, such as swipe or tap gestures. Although it is very nice to support gestures in you app, misusing them may lead to a very bad user experience and cause conflicts to your users. Another problem is that most users don't know that you have to swipe in a specific area to get an action done, so it's recommended that you show a tutorial or notes on screen, telling users about what gestures you support so that they become aware of them.

Getting ready

In this recipe, we will show you a simple `UIView` that can interact with multiple gesture recognizers; but before getting started, let's explain briefly the difference between the various gesture recognizers:

- `UITapGestureRecognizer`: This is a gesture recognizer that detects taps on UIViews with any number of taps, for example, detecting double taps on UIView
- `UIPinchGestureRecognizer`: This is a gesture recognizer that detects pinching (zooming) a view with two fingers, similar to zooming pictures in Photos app
- `UIPanGestureRecognizer`: This is a gesture recognizer that detects dragging UIViews
- `UISwipeGestureRecognizer`: This is a gesture recognizer that detects swiping up, down, left, or right
- `UIRotationGestureRecognizer`: This is a gesture recognizer that detects rotating a view with two fingers
- `UILongPressGestureRecognizer`: This is a gesture recognizer that detects long press on UIView to do a specific action

All these gestures are attached to UIViews. A gesture can be attached only to one view but a view can recognize multiple gestures at the same time.

How to do it...

1. Create a new Xcode project called `Gestures` with **Single View** template.
2. Open the storyboard, and in the single view controller, change its size to iPhone 4-inch size.
3. Drag a `UIView` to the center of the screen and set its frame to ($X = 127$, $Y = 259$, *Width = 120, Height = 80*).
4. Change its color to any color you want instead of white.
5. Link it to `ViewController.swift` via `IBOutlet` and call it `sampleView`:

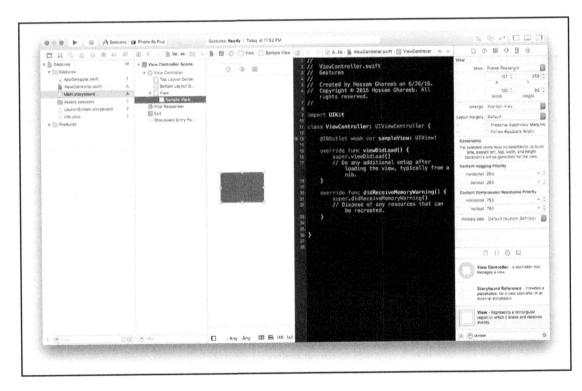

6. Now, open the `ViewController.swift` file, and let's add the following code to set up the `UITapGestureRecognizer`:

```
// MARK: - Tap Gesture -
func setupTapGesture(){
    let tapGesture = UITapGestureRecognizer(target: self, action:
    #selector(handleTapGesture(_:)))
    tapGesture.numberOfTapsRequired = 2
```

```
    self.sampleView.addGestureRecognizer(tapGesture)
}
func handleTapGesture(gesture: UITapGestureRecognizer){
  var newHeight : CGFloat = 80.0
  if CGRectGetHeight(self.sampleView.frame) == 80 {
    newHeight = 200.0
  }
  var frame = self.sampleView.frame
  frame.size.height = newHeight
  self.sampleView.frame = frame
}
```

7. Change the code in `viewDidLoad` to call the setup of `UITapGestureRecognizer`:

```
override func viewDidLoad() {
  super.viewDidLoad()
  setupTapGesture()
}
```

8. Now, when you build and run, you will see that when you double-tap on the view, its height will be updated.

9. Let's now add the pan gesture; add the following two methods to set up the pan gesture:

```
// MARK: - Pan Gesture -
func setupPanGesture(){
  let panGesture = UIPanGestureRecognizer(target: self, action:
    #selector(handlePanGesture(_:)))
  self.sampleView.addGestureRecognizer(panGesture)
}
func handlePanGesture(gesture: UIPanGestureRecognizer){
  let point = gesture.locationInView(self.view)
  self.sampleView.center = point
}
```

10. Update the `viewDidLoad` method to call the setup of
    `UIPanGestureRecognizer`:

```
override func viewDidLoad() {
  super.viewDidLoad()
  setupTapGesture()
  setupPanGesture()
}
```

11. Let's now set up the rotation gesture; add the following two methods to set up
    `UIRotationGestureRecognizer`:

```
// MARK: - Rotation Gesture -
func setupRotationGesture(){
  let rotationGesture = UIRotationGestureRecognizer(target: self,
    action: #selector(handleRotationGesture(_:)))
  self.sampleView.addGestureRecognizer(rotationGesture)
}
func handleRotationGesture(gesture: UIRotationGestureRecognizer){
  self.sampleView.transform = CGAffineTransformRotate
    (self.sampleView.transform, gesture.rotation)
  gesture.rotation = 0
}
```

12. Update the `viewDidLoad` method to call the rotation gesture:

```
override func viewDidLoad() {
  super.viewDidLoad()
  setupTapGesture()
  setupPanGesture()
  setupRotationGesture()
}
```

13. Now, build and run; try to rotate the view with two fingers, and you will see that the view is rotating with it:

14. The last gesture to add is the swipe gesture. Let's first add a subview to our `sampleView` with a different color, for example, red. When you swipe right, we will move it to the right with animation; when you swipe left, we will move it to the left with animation.
15. Go to storyboard, drag a `UIView` with the same size, and add it as a subview to the sample view; set its background color to red.

16. Connect an outlet to the `redView`, like this:

```
@IBOutlet weak var redView: UIView!
```

17. Add the following two functions to set up the swipe gestures:

```
func setupSwipeGestures(){
  let rightSwipeGesture = UISwipeGestureRecognizer(target: self,
    action: #selector(handleSwipeGesture(_:)))
  rightSwipeGesture.direction = .Right
  let leftSwipeGesture = UISwipeGestureRecognizer(target: self,
    action: #selector(handleSwipeGesture(_:)))
  leftSwipeGesture.direction = .Left
  self.sampleView.addGestureRecognizer(rightSwipeGesture)
  self.sampleView.addGestureRecognizer(leftSwipeGesture)
}
func handleSwipeGesture(swipeGesture: UISwipeGestureRecognizer){
  var newXPosition : CGFloat = 0.0
  if swipeGesture.direction == .Right {
    newXPosition = CGRectGetWidth(self.sampleView.frame)
  }
  var frame = self.redView.frame
  frame.origin.x = newXPosition
  UIView.animateWithDuration(0.5) {
    self.redView.frame = frame
  }
}
```

18. Now, update the `viewDidLoad` function to be like this:

```
override func viewDidLoad() {
  super.viewDidLoad()
  setupTapGesture()
//    setupPanGesture()
  setupRotationGesture()
  setupSwipeGestures()
}
```

19. Now, build and run. When you swipe right on the `sampleView`, you will note that the `redView` will be translated to the right with animation. Swiping left will move it back to the original location.

How it works...

As we saw in our previous examples, setting up a gesture recognizer is very easy and simple. The setup can be summarized in three steps:

1. Initialize the gesture with target and action. Target is the object that should be notified when a gesture recognized. The action is the function to be called, and a reference to the gesture will be passed.
2. Configure the gesture. We saw that in the tap gesture when we set the taps required to 2 and in swipe gesture to configure the direction.
3. Adding the gesture to the desired view.

In the action function, it's the best place to handle the gesture and do specific action to your view like moving, rotating, and so on.

The most helpful function in the gesture recognizer is `locationInView()`, which returns a `CGPoint` of the gesture location relative to a given view. We used it in the pan gesture to move the view while dragging. You can use it with the tap gesture also to do specific action at the tapped location.

There's more...

Now, you should be familiar with using gestures, and that is the most commonly used logic in working with gestures. In some cases, while dealing with multiple gestures, you want to control conflicts between them or you have a specific scenario that requires the gesture to not start recognizing, you need to set up a delegate to the gesture recognizer. In these cases, set the `UIGestureRecognizerDelegate` delegate to be notified with a function to solve these problems.

Using 3D touch

Since the launch of iPhone 6s and 6s plus, Apple has introduced a new way of user interaction with mobile apps. A new dimension of touch event has been added by introducing 3D touch. By detecting how hard or deeply the user presses on the screen, you can do a specific action in your app. In the example below, we will see how to get the force of touch and log display on screen.

How to do it...

1. As usual, open Xcode and create a new project with **Single View** template named 3D Touch.
2. Open storyboard, and add a `UILabel` and place it at the center of the screen.
3. Link the label with an `IBOutlet` to `ViewController.swift`.
4. Go to `ViewController.swift` and override the following method:

```
override func touchesMoved(touches: Set<UITouch>, withEvent event:
UIEvent?) {
      if let touch = touches.first {
          if #available(iOS 9.0, *) {
              if traitCollection.forceTouchCapability ==.Available {
                  // 3D Touch is avaialble in this device
                  let force = touch.force / touch.maximumPossibleForce
                  self.forceTouchLabel.text = "\(force)%"
              }
          }
      }
}
```

How it works...

We started our example by overriding the `touchesMoved` function. In iOS, once you interact with the screen, `touchesBegan`, `touchesMoved`, and `touchesCancelled` methods will be called based on the situation. `touchesMoved` is the method that we need, which detects your finger moving on screen.

This method gives you a parameter a touch set. We will only care about the first touch in this set, and we use the if condition to make sure that we have at least one touch object in the set before using it. The `#available(iOS 9.0, *)` checks whether this app works in a device that has iOS 9.0 or later versions, as the API to get force value is available only in iOS 9.0 or later. You will only need that confirmation if you're supporting iOS version before iOS 9.0. If your minimum iOS version is 9, there is no need for that check.

The `traitCollection.forceTouchCapability ==.Available` checks whether your device has a force touch capability. As we know, only specific devices have this hardware feature, such as iPhone 6s and iPhone 6s plus. So, it is the best practice to check the availability of any hardware feature before using it.

There's more...

You may seem disappointed when you think this is the only thing you can do with 3D touch. Actually, there are two other things that you can do with 3D touch, which may seem very interesting to you.

Home screen quick actions

When we see an app icon in iOS, we used to have only two options:

1. Tap the app icon to launch the app.
2. Long press the app icon to drag it somewhere else to organize the app's appearance or click on the delete button to uninstall the app.

You can now force touch the app icon via 3D touch, and you will get a popup with quick actions to select from. In your app, you can define set of static or dynamic actions. Static actions are actions that will appear regardless of your app state. For example, in a chatting app, you may find static actions, such as Create new chat or Go offline. Dynamic actions are actions that will be updated based on the app state. For example, in the same chat app, you may find Reply to John in the quick actions. So, the app may get the last contacted people and display actions to you. It's something like expectation from the app to make your life easier.

To learn more about this feature and other stuff you can do with it, it's highly recommended to visit `Apple developer center`.

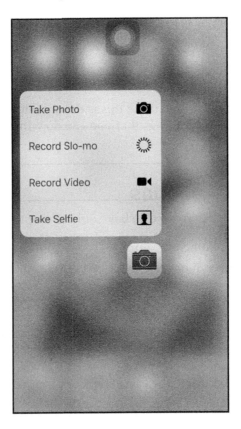

3
Integrating with Messages App

In this chapter, we will cover the following topics:

- Integrating the iMessage app with sticker pack
- Integrating the iMessage app with iMessage app extension

Introduction

In this chapter, we will talk about one of the hot new features of iOS 10, which is integrating the Messages app with stickers and extensions. Competing with the current messaging apps is almost an impossible mission and that's why Apple has opened the door for developers to put their touches to Messages app to make it more interesting and fancy. In iOS 10, you can create app extensions that interact with Messages app to send text, stickers, media files, and much more. We have the following two types of extensions:

- **Stickers**: You can add fancy stickers that users can get/buy from the App Store to integrate with their iMessage app and send them to their friends.
- **iMessages apps**: This is where users can integrate with your app without having to lease the iMessage app. Users can use your app to send content such as documents, payment, and photos.

Integrating iMessage app with sticker pack

Here comes the easy part--the iMessage app with sticker pack. I call it the easy part because, believe it or not, you can create a sticker pack app extension without even writing a single line of code. Just prepare your fancy stickers, create the app extension in Xcode, drag and drop your stickers in Xcode, and there you go. I hear you saying wow, and I bet you are eager to give it a shot.

Getting ready

To create an iMessage app extension, you need to have the Xcode 8.0 or later version. Right now, while I'm writing this chapter, it's available in the beta version. Maybe, while you are reading this chapter, it's available as an official release.

Apple engineers have provided the ability to test these extensions in iOS simulator; so, you don't have to worry about that. In case you want to test these extensions on your device, you need the iOS 10 or later version to be installed on your device. If you are like me now and the official release is not yet available, you can download the iOS 10 Beta version from the Apple developer center and follow the steps to install it on your device.

Stickers

Prepare the stickers that you want to use in the app extension. Your images should follow these rules:

- The images must be in the PNG, APNG, GIF or JPEG format.
- The file must be smaller than 500 KB in size.
- The image cannot be smaller than 100 x 100 points, and cannot be larger than 206 x 206 points.
- Always provide @3x images (300 x 300 pixels to 618 x 618 pixels). The system generates the @2x and @1x versions by downscaling the @3x images at runtime.

 In our recipe, we will use some sample stickers that Facebook uses in its messages app. Copyright is reserved for Facebook, it's used here just for illustration.

How to do it...

1. Ensure that you have the Xcode 8.0 beta version (or the official version, if it's already released).

2. Create a new project and choose the **Sticker Pack Application** template, as shown:

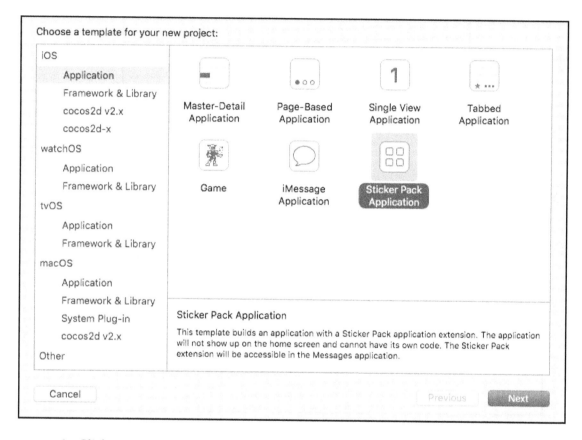

3. Click on **Next** and, in product name, type **FancyEmoji** or any other name you like.

4. The Xcode project will be created, and as you see, without any source code files. I'm not sure whether you feel happy or sad for that, but for me, I felt happy to see a working Xcode project for the first time with no source code file.

5. Open **Stickers.xcstickers**, as shown:

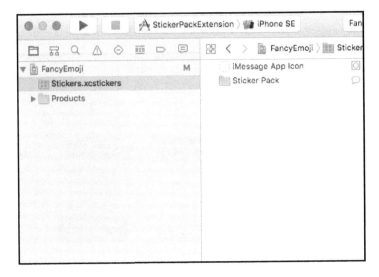

6. Select the `Sticker Pack` folder, where you can drag and drop your stickers.

7. Drag and drop your stickers; now, it should be like this:

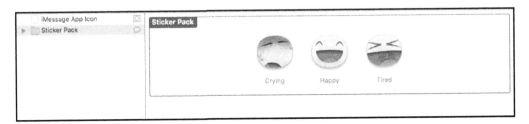

8. Believe it or not, we are done. Choose iPhone 6s Simulator, for example, and run the app.
9. Xcode will ask you to select an app to run your extension. Select **Messages** and click on **Run**, as illustrated in the following screenshot:

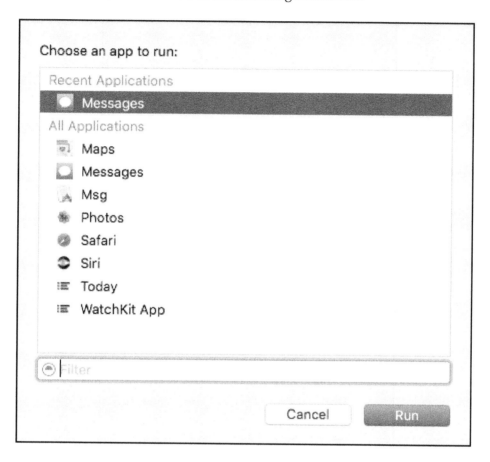

10. You will see something like this, where you can chat with someone called Kate:

11. Click on the App Store icon beside the text area, as follows, and then click on apps like this:

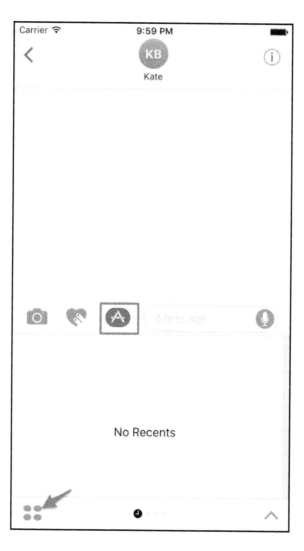

12. Now, choose the sticker pack that we recently created. Wait for a few seconds and you will find that your stickers appear, as shown:

13. Now, choose any sticker to send in your chat and here you go:

How it works...

We first created a new sticker pack template app which, as we see, was very straightforward. Now, prepare your stickers with the criteria illustrated in the *Getting ready* section. Import these stickers by dragging and dropping them in the `Sticker Pack` folder, where all sticker assets should appear. By following these steps, your app extension should be ready to be integrated in the iMessage app.

Running the extension is very easy because it's available to be used in Simulator. Just run the app extension and Xcode will open Messages app with a ready-to-use conversion to test your stickers.

There's more...

To create stickers, Apple provides an amazing tool, which is the Motion app. The Motion app can help you create stunning and animated stickers for iMessages. To get started with the Motion app, you can refer to know how to get it and how to use it. They also provide free project templates to get started in Motion:
`https://developer.apple.com/support/stickers/motion`

Integrating iMessage app with iMessage app

Using iMessage apps will let users use your apps seamlessly from iMessage without having to leave the iMessage. Your app can share content in the conversation, make payment, or do any specific job that seems important or is appropriate to do within a Messages app.

Getting ready

Similar to the Stickers app we created earlier, you need Xcode 8.0 or later version to create an iMessage app extension and you can test it easily in the iOS simulator. The app that we are going to build is a Google Drive picker app. It will be used from an iMessage extension to send a file to your friends just from Google Drive.

Before starting, ensure that you follow the instructions in Google Drive API for iOS from `https://developers.google.com/drive/ios/quickstart` to get a client key to be used in our app.

Installing the SDK in Xcode will be done via CocoaPods. To get more information about CocoaPods and how to use it to manage dependencies, visit `https://cocoapods.org/`.

How to do it...

1. We Open Xcode and create a new iMessage app as shown, and name it `Files Picker`:

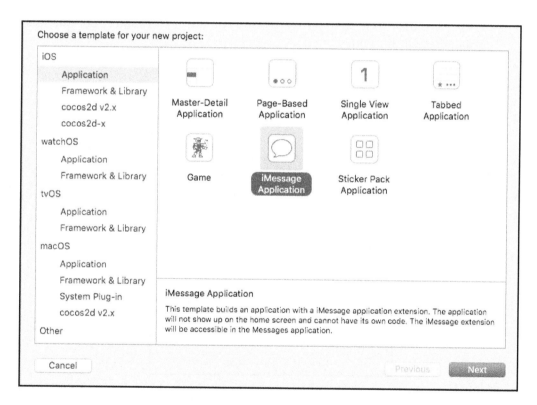

2. Now, let's install Google Drive SDK in iOS using CocoaPods. Open terminal and navigate to the directory that contains your Xcode project by running this command:

```
cd path_to_directory
```

3. Run the following command to create a Pod file to write your dependencies:

```
Pod init
```

4. It will create a Pod file for you. Open it via **TextEdit** and edit it to be like this:

```
use_frameworks!
target 'PDFPicker' do
end

target 'MessagesExtension' do
pod 'GoogleAPIClient/Drive', '~> 1.0.2'
pod 'GTMOAuth2', '~> 1.1.0'
end
```

5. Then, close the Xcode app completely and run the `pod install` command to install the SDK for you.

6. A new workspace will be created. Open it instead of the Xcode project itself:

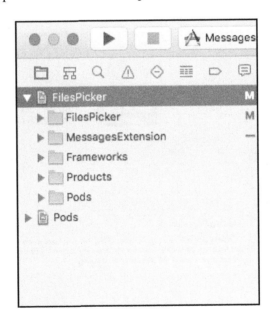

7. Prepare the client key from the Google Drive app you created as we mentioned in the *Getting ready* section, because we are going to use it in the Xcode project.

8. Open `MessagesViewController.swift` and add the following import statements:

```
import GoogleAPIClient
import GTMOAuth2
```

9. Add the following private variables just below the class declaration and embed your client key in the `kClientID` constant, as shown:

```
private let kKeychainItemName = "Drive API"
private let kClientID = "Client_Key_Goes_HERE"
private let scopes = [kGTLAuthScopeDrive]
private let service = GTLServiceDrive()
```

10. Add the following code in your class to request authentication to Google Drive if it's not authenticated and load file info:

```
override func viewDidLoad() {
  super.viewDidLoad()
  // Do any additional setup after loading the view.
  if let auth = GTMOAuth2ViewControllerTouch.
   authForGoogleFromKeychain(forName: kKeychainItemName,
     clientID: kClientID,
     clientSecret: nil)
    {
       service.authorizer = auth
    }
}
// When the view appears, ensure that the Drive API service is
 authorized
// and perform API calls
override func viewDidAppear(_ animated: Bool) {
  if let authorizer = service.authorizer,
    canAuth = authorizer.canAuthorize where canAuth {
    fetchFiles()
  } else {
      present(createAuthController(), animated: true, completion:
        nil)
    }
}
// Construct a query to get names and IDs of 10 files using the
 Google Drive API
func fetchFiles() {
  print("Getting files...")
```

```
      if let query = GTLQueryDrive.queryForFilesList(){
        query.fields = "nextPageToken, files(id, name, webViewLink,
         webContentLink, fileExtension)"
        service.executeQuery(query, delegate: self, didFinish:
         #selector(MessagesViewController.displayResultWithTicket
          (ticket:finishedWithObject:error:)))
      }
    }
    // Parse results and display
    func displayResultWithTicket(ticket : GTLServiceTicket,
                               finishedWithObject response :
GTLDriveFileList,
                                 error : NSError?) {
      if let error = error {
        showAlert(title: "Error", message: error.localizedDescription)
          return
      }
      var filesString = ""
      let files = response.files as! [GTLDriveFile]
      if !files.isEmpty{
        filesString += "Files:n"
        for file in files{
          filesString += "(file.name) ((file.identifier)
           ((file.webViewLink) ((file.webContentLink))n"
        }
      } else {
        filesString = "No files found."
      }
    print(filesString)
    }
    // Creates the auth controller for authorizing access to Drive API
    private func createAuthController() -> GTMOAuth2ViewControllerTouch {
      let scopeString = scopes.joined(separator: " ")
      return GTMOAuth2ViewControllerTouch(
          scope: scopeString,
          clientID: kClientID,
          clientSecret: nil,
          keychainItemName: kKeychainItemName,
          delegate: self,
          finishedSelector:
           #selector(MessagesViewController.viewController
            (vc:finishedWithAuth:error:))
      )
    }
    // Handle completion of the authorization process, and update the
     Drive API
    // with the new credentials.
    func viewController(vc : UIViewController,
```

```
                    finishedWithAuth authResult :
GTMOAuth2Authentication, error : NSError?) {
    if let error = error {
        service.authorizer = nil
        showAlert(title: "Authentication Error", message:
         error.localizedDescription)
        return
    }
    service.authorizer = authResult
    dismiss(animated: true, completion: nil)
    fetchFiles()
}
// Helper for showing an alert
func showAlert(title : String, message: String) {
  let alert = UIAlertController(
      title: title,
      message: message,
      preferredStyle: UIAlertControllerStyle.alert
  )
  let ok = UIAlertAction(
      title: "OK",
      style: UIAlertActionStyle.default,
      handler: nil
  )
  alert.addAction(ok)
  self.present(alert, animated: true, completion: nil)
}
```

11. The code now requests authentication, loads files, and then prints them in the debug area. Now, try to build and run, you will see the following:

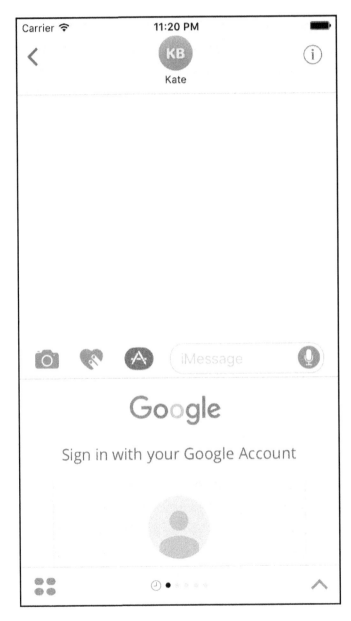

12. Click on the arrow button in the bottom right corner to maximize the screen and try to log in with any Google account you have.

13. Once the authentication is done, you will see the files' information printed in the debug area.

14. Now, let's add a table view that will display the files' information and once a user selects a file, we will download this file to send it as an attachment to the conversation. Now, open the `MainInterface.storyboard`, drag a table view from Object Library, and add the following constraints:

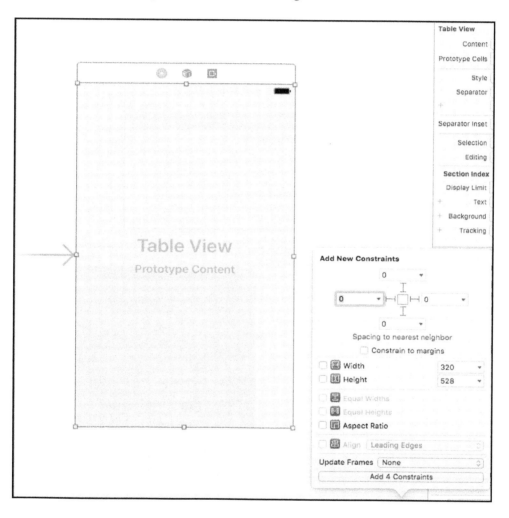

15. Set the delegate and data source of the table view from interface builder by dragging while holding down the *Ctrl* key to the `MessagesViewController`. Then, add an outlet to the table view, as follows, to be used to refresh the table with the files:

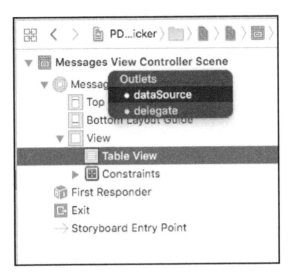

16. Drag a `UITabeView` cell from Object Library and drop it in the table view. For Attribute Inspector, set the cell style to **Basic** and the identifier to `cell`.

17. Now, return to `MessagesViewController.swift`. Add the following property to hold the current display files:

```
private var currentFiles = [GTLDriveFile]()
```

18. Edit the `displayResultWithTicket` function to be like this:

```
// Parse results and display
func displayResultWithTicket(ticket : GTLServiceTicket,
                             finishedWithObject response :
GTLDriveFileList,
                             error : NSError?) {
    if let error = error {
        showAlert(title: "Error", message: error.localizedDescription)
        return
    }
    var filesString = ""
    let files = response.files as! [GTLDriveFile]
    self.currentFiles = files
    if !files.isEmpty{
        filesString += "Files:n"
        for file in files{
            filesString += "(file.name) ((file.identifier)
              ((file.webViewLink) ((file.webContentLink))n"
        }
    } else {
        filesString = "No files found."
    }
    print(filesString)
    self.filesTableView.reloadData()
}
```

19. Now, add the following method for the table view delegate and data source:

```
// MARK: - Table View methods -
func tableView(_ tableView: UITableView, numberOfRowsInSection section:
  Int) -> Int {
    return self.currentFiles.count
}
func tableView(_ tableView: UITableView, cellForRowAt indexPath:
  IndexPath) -> UITableViewCell {
    let cell = tableView.dequeueReusableCell(withIdentifier: "cell")
    let file = self.currentFiles[indexPath.row]
    cell?.textLabel?.text = file.name
    return cell!
```

```
    }

func tableView(_ tableView: UITableView, didSelectRowAt
  indexPath: IndexPath) {
    let file = self.currentFiles[indexPath.row]
    // Download File here to send as attachment.
    if let downloadURLString = file.webContentLink{
        let url = NSURL(string: downloadURLString)
        if let name = file.name{
            let downloadedPath = (documentsPath() as
            NSString).appendingPathComponent("(name)")
            let fetcher = service.fetcherService.fetcher(with: url as!
            URL)
            let destinationURL = NSURL(fileURLWithPath: downloadedPath)
            as URL
            fetcher.destinationFileURL = destinationURL
            fetcher.beginFetch(completionHandler: { (data, error) in
                if error == nil{
    self.activeConversation?.insertAttachment(destinationURL,
                    withAlternateFilename: name, completionHandler: nil)
                }
            })
        }
    }
}
private func documentsPath() -> String{
    let paths = NSSearchPathForDirectoriesInDomains(.documentDirectory,
    .userDomainMask, true)
    return paths.first ?? ""
}
```

20. Now, build and run the app, and you will see the magic: select any file and the app will download and save it to the local disk and send it as an attachment to the conversation, as illustrated:

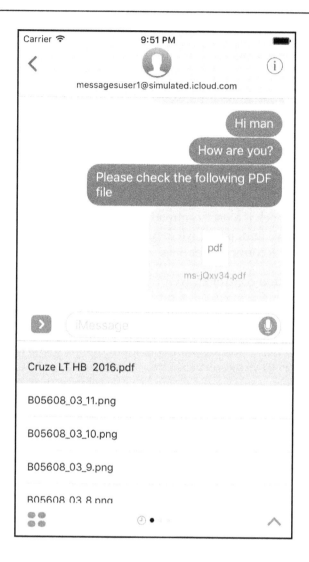

How it works...

We started by installing the Google Drive SDK to the Xcode project. This SDK has all the APIs that we need to manage drive files and user authentication. When you visit the Google developers' website, you will see two options to install the SDK: manually or using CocoaPods. I totally recommend using CocoaPods to manage your dependencies as it is simple and efficient.

Once the SDK had been installed via CocoaPods, we added some variables to be used for the Google Drive API and the most important one is the client key. You can access this value from the project you have created in the Google Developers Console.

In the `viewDidLoad` function, first we check if we have an authentication saved in `KeyChain`, and then, we use it. We can do that by calling `GTMOAuth2ViewControllerTouch.authForGoogleFromKeychain`, which takes the `Keychain` name and client key as parameters to search for authentication. It's useful as it helps you remember the last authentication and there is no need to ask for user authentication again if a user has already been authenticated before.

In `viewDidAppear`, we check if a user is already authenticated; so in that case, we start fetching files from the drive and, if not, we display the authentication controller, which asks a user to enter his Google account credentials.

To display the authentication controller, we present the authentication view controller created in the `createAuthController()` function. In this function, the Google Drive API provides us with the `GTMOAuth2ViewControllerTouch` class, which encapsulates all the logic for Google account authentication for your app. You need to pass the client key for your project keychain name to save the authentication details there, and the finished `viewController(vc : UIViewController, finishedWithAuth authResult : GTMOAuth2Authentication, error : NSError?)` selector that will be called after the authentication is complete. In that function, we check for errors and if something wrong happens, we display an alert message to the user. If no error occurs, we start fetching files using the `fetchFiles()` function.

In the `fetchFiles()` function, we first create a query by calling `GTLQueryDrive.queryForFilesList()`. The `GTLQueryDrive` class has all the information you need about your query, such as which fields to read, for example, `name`, `fileExtension`, and a lot of other fields that you can fetch from the Google drive. You can specify the page size if you are going to call with pagination, for example, 10 by 10 files. Once you are happy with your query, execute it by calling `service.executeQuery`, which takes the query and the finished selector to be called when finished. In our example, it will call the `displayResultWithTicket` function, which prepares the files to be displayed in the table view. Then, we call `self.filesTableView.reloadData()` to refresh the table view to display the list of files.

In the delegate function of table view `didSelectRowAt indexPath:`, we first read the `webContentLink` property from the `GTLDriveFile` instance, which is a download link for the selected file. To fetch a file from the Google drive, the API provides us with `GTMSessionFetcher` that can fetch a file and write it directly to a device's disk locally when you pass a local path to it. To create `GTMSessionFetcher`, use the `service.fetcherService` factory class, which gives you an instance to a fetcher via the file URL. Then, we create a local path to the downloaded file by appending the filename to the documents path of your app and then, pass it to a fetcher via the following command:

```
fetcher.destinationFileURL = destinationURL
```

Once you have set up everything, call `fetcher.beginFetch` and pass a completion handler to be executed after finishing the fetching. Once the fetching is completed successfully, you can get a reference to the current conversation so that you can insert the file to it as an attachment. To do this, just call the following function:

```
self.activeConversation?.insertAttachment(destinationURL,
withAlternateFilename: name, completionHandler: nil)
```

There's more...

Yes, there's more that you can do in the preceding example to make it fancier and more appealing to users. Check the following options to make it better:

1. Show a loading indicator or progress bar while a file is downloading.
2. Check if the file is already downloaded, and if so, there is no need to download it again.
3. Add pagination to request only 10 files at a time.
4. Include options to filter documents by type, such as PDF, images, or even by date.
5. Search for a file in your drive.

Showing progress indicator

As we said, one of the features that we can add in the preceding example is the ability to show a progress bar indicating the downloading progress of a file. Before starting with how to show a progress bar, let's install a library that is very helpful in managing/showing HUD indicators, which is MBProgressHUD. This library is available in GitHub at https://github.com/jdg/MBProgressHUD.

As we agreed before, all packages are managed via CocoaPods, so now, let's install the library via CocoaPods, as shown:

1. Open the Podfile and update it to be as follows:

   ```
   use_frameworks!

   target 'PDFPicker' do

   end

   target 'MessagesExtension' do
       pod 'GoogleAPIClient/Drive', '~> 1.0.2'
       pod 'GTMOAuth2', '~> 1.1.0'
       pod 'MBProgressHUD', '~> 1.0.0'
   end
   ```

2. Run the following command to install the dependencies:

   pod install

3. Now, at the top of the MessagesViewController.swift file, add the following import statement to import the library:

   import MBProgressHUD

4. Now, let's edit the didSelectRowAtIndexPath function to be like this:

   ```
   func tableView(_ tableView: UITableView, didSelectRowAt indexPath:
     IndexPath) {
     let file = self.currentFiles[indexPath.row]
     // Download File here to send as attachment.
     if let downloadURLString = file.webContentLink{
         let url = NSURL(string: downloadURLString)
         if let name = file.name{
             let downloadedPath = (documentsPath() as
              NSString).appendingPathComponent("(name)")
             let fetcher = service.fetcherService.fetcher(with: url as!
   ```

```
        URL)
        let destinationURL = NSURL(fileURLWithPath: downloadedPath)
        as URL
        fetcher.destinationFileURL = destinationURL
        var progress = Progress()
        let hud = MBProgressHUD.showAdded(to: self.view, animated:
        true)
        hud.mode = .annularDeterminate;
        hud.progressObject = progress
        fetcher.beginFetch(completionHandler: { (data, error) in
            if error == nil{
                hud.hide(animated: true)
                self.activeConversation?.insertAttachment
                (destinationURL, withAlternateFilename: name,
                completionHandler: nil)
            }
        })
        fetcher.downloadProgressBlock = { (bytes, written,
        expected) in
            let p = Double(written) * 100.0 / Double(expected)
            print(p)
            progress.totalUnitCount = expected
            progress.completedUnitCount = written
        }
    }
  }
}
```

5. First, we create an instance of MBProgressHUD and set its type to
   annularDeterminate, which means to display a circular progress bar. HUD will
   update its progress by taking a reference to the NSProgress object. Progress
   has two important variables to determine the progress value, which are
   totalUnitCount and completedUnitCount. These two values will be set
   inside the progress completion block, downloadProgressBlock, in the fetcher
   instance. HUD will be hidden in the completion block that will be called once the
   download is complete.

6. Now build and run; after authentication, when you click on a file, you will see something like this:

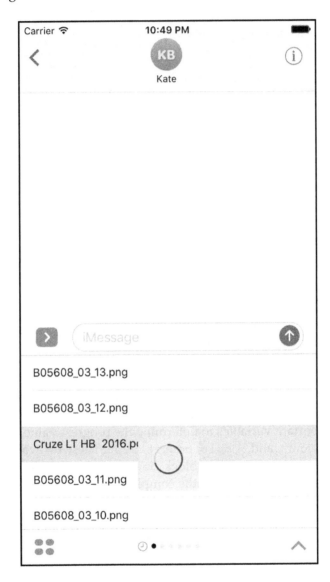

As you can see, the progressive view is updated with the percentage of download to give the user an overview of what is going on.

Request files with pagination

Loading all files at once is easy from the development side, but it's incorrect from the user experience side. It will take too much time at the beginning when you get the list of all the files and it would be great if we could request only 10 files at a time with pagination. In this section, we will see how to add the pagination concept to our example and request only 10 files at a time. When a user scrolls to the end of the list, we will display a loading indicator, call the next page, and append the results to our current results. Implementation of pagination is pretty easy and requires only a few changes in our code. Let's see how to do it:

1. We will start by adding the progress cell design in `MainInterface.storyboard`. Open the design of `MessagesViewController` and drag a new cell along with our default cell.
2. Drag a `UIActivityIndicatorView` from Object Library and place it as a subview to the new cell.
3. Add center constraints to center it horizontally and vertically, as shown:

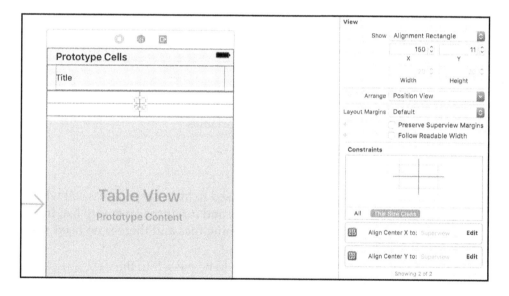

4. Now, select the new cell and go to attribute inspector to add an identifier to the cell and disable the selection, as illustrated:

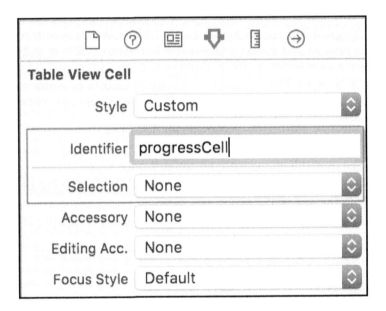

5. Now, from the design side, we are ready. Open `MessagesViewController.swift` to add some tweaks to it. Add the following two variables to the list of our current variables:

```
private var doneFetchingFiles = false
private var nextPageToken: String!
```

6. The `doneFetchingFiles` flag will be used to hide the progress cell when we try to load the next page from Google Drive and it returns an empty list. In that case, we know that we are done with the fetching files and there is no need to display the progress cell any more.

7. The `nextPageToken` contains the token to be passed to the `GTLQueryDrive` query to ask it to load the next page.

8. Now, go to the `fetchFiles()` function and update it to be as shown:

```
func fetchFiles() {
    print("Getting files...")
    if let query = GTLQueryDrive.queryForFilesList(){
        query.fields = "nextPageToken, files(id, name, webViewLink,
         webContentLink, fileExtension)"
        query.mimeType = "application/pdf"
```

```
query.pageSize = 10
query.pageToken = nextPageToken
service.executeQuery(query, delegate: self, didFinish:
  #selector(MessagesViewController.displayResultWithTicket
    (ticket:finishedWithObject:error:)))
    }
  }
```

9. The only difference you can note between the preceding code and the one before that is setting the `pageSize` and `pageToken`. For `pageSize`, we set how many files we require for each call and for `pageToken`, we pass the token to get the next page. We receive this token as a response from the previous page call. This means that, at the first call, we don't have a token and it will be passed as `nil`.

10. Now, open the `displayResultWithTicket` function and update it like this:

```
// Parse results and display
func displayResultWithTicket(ticket : GTLServiceTicket,
                             finishedWithObject response :
GTLDriveFileList,
                                 error : NSError?) {
    if let error = error {
        showAlert(title: "Error", message: error.localizedDescription)
        return
    }
    var filesString = ""
    nextPageToken = response.nextPageToken
    let files = response.files as! [GTLDriveFile]
    doneFetchingFiles = files.isEmpty
    self.currentFiles += files
    if !files.isEmpty{
        filesString += "Files:n"
        for file in files{
            filesString += "(file.name) ((file.identifier)
                ((file.webViewLink) ((file.webContentLink))n"
        }
    } else {
        filesString = "No files found."
    }
    print(filesString)
    self.filesTableView.reloadData()
}
```

11. As you can see, we first get the token that is to be used to load the next page. We get it by calling `response.nextPageToken` and setting it to our new `nextPageToken` property so that we can use it while loading the next page. The `doneFetchingFiles` will be true only if the current page we are loading has no files, which means that we are done. Then, we append the new files we get to the current files we have.

12. We don't know when to fire the calling of the next page. We will do this once the user scrolls down to the refresh cell that we have. To do so, we will implement one of the `UITableViewDelegate` methods, which is `willDisplayCell`, as illustrated:

```
func tableView(_ tableView: UITableView, willDisplay cell:
  UITableViewCell, forRowAt indexPath: IndexPath) {
    if !doneFetchingFiles && indexPath.row == self.currentFiles.count {
        // Refresh cell
        fetchFiles()
        return
    }
}
```

13. For any cell that is going to be displayed, this function will be triggered with the `indexPath` of the cell. First, we check if we are not done with fetching files and the row is equal to the last row, then, we fire `fetchFiles()` again to load the next page.

14. As we added a new refresh cell at the bottom, we should update our `UITableViewDataSource` functions, such as `numbersOfRowsInSection` and `cellForRow`. Check our updated functions, shown as follows:

```
func tableView(_ tableView: UITableView, numberOfRowsInSection
  section: Int) -> Int {
   return doneFetchingFiles ? self.currentFiles.count :
    self.currentFiles.count + 1
}
func tableView(_ tableView: UITableView, cellForRowAt indexPath:
  IndexPath) -> UITableViewCell {
    if !doneFetchingFiles && indexPath.row == self.currentFiles.count{
       return tableView.dequeueReusableCell(withIdentifier:
"progressCell")!
    }
    let cell = tableView.dequeueReusableCell(withIdentifier: "cell")
    let file = self.currentFiles[indexPath.row]
    cell?.textLabel?.text = file.name
    return cell!
}
```

15. As you can see, the number of rows will be equal to the current files' count plus one for the refresh cell. If we are done with fetching files, we will return only the number of files.

Now, everything seems perfect. When you build and run, you will see only 10 files listed, as shown:

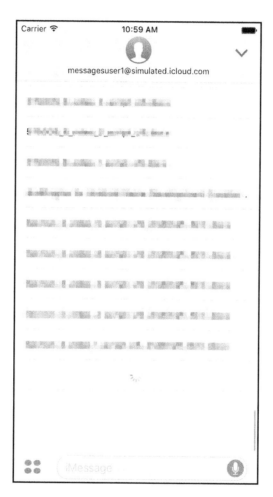

And when you scroll down, you would see the progress cell and that 10 more files will be called.

4

Working with Interface Builder

In this chapter, we will cover the following topics:

- Using storyboards
- Working with Autolayout and constraints
- Designing your interface builder for any size classes in one storyboard
- Embedding view controllers using container view

Introduction

In this chapter, we will talk about a very interesting topic in iOS development, which is working with interface builder. Being an iOS developer requires being professional in dealing with interface builder to build your UI and application flow. Even today, I meet iOS developers who don't know anything about interface builder and still build all screens and components programmatically. Using this method wastes your time and makes your Xcode project huge with hundreds of lines of code just to draw the screens. Within time, Apple introduces new devices every year and sometimes with totally new screen sizes. Without using interface builder and Autolayout, your app will not work properly with these screen sizes, and you will have to write new code to handle these new screens. If you're still not convinced about interface builder magic, stay tuned with us in this chapter to see the magic that we can do in UI without writing a single line of code.

Using storyboards

Storyboards were first introduced in iOS 5, and I still remember my first impression when I started using storyboards. I was impressed and didn't believe it myself. We were struggling with tens of XIB interface files for each screen and for custom table view cells or custom components. In addition to that, when you work on a project that someone else developed, you waste a lot of time trying to figure out which screen is the root screen and how the interactions are between the screens. Storyboards solve all these kinds of problems; when you open it, you will see the whole app flow and see what is going on between screens.

Getting ready

Before getting our example started, make sure that you have the latest version of Xcode 8.0, which is in the beta version now at the time of writing this book. You can still use Xcode 7.x if you want, but you may find little differences between them, especially in the size classes section that we will talk about later.

How to do it...

1. Create a new project and choose the **Tabbed Application** template:

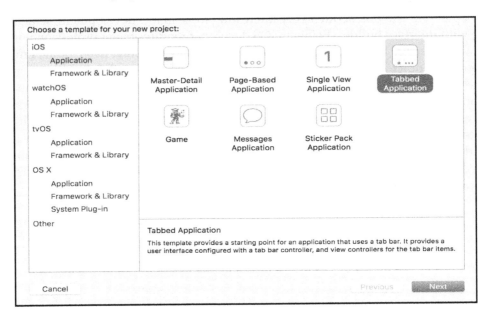

2. Click on **Next**, and in product name, type `PlayWithStoryboard` or any other name you like.

3. Open `Main.storyboard`:

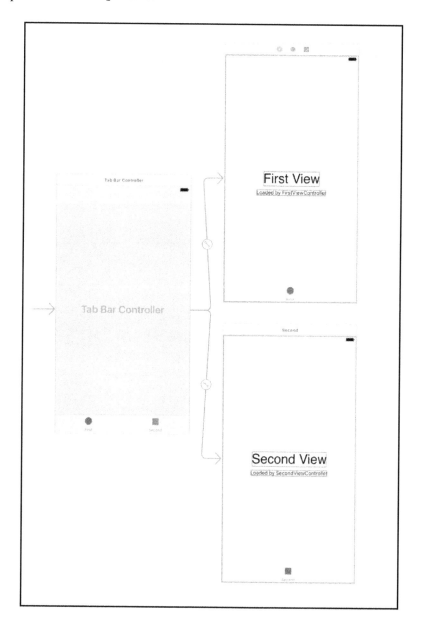

4. You will see a tab bar controller with two view controllers, referenced by segues.

5. Let's now add a third view controller to the tab bar controller. Drag View Controller from **Object Library,** and add a `UILabel` in the center of the screen with the text `Third View`.

6. To add the view controller to the tab bar controller, click on the **Tab Bar Controller** in the storyboard and, while clicking on the *Ctrl* key, drag the pointer to the third view controller till you see this popup:

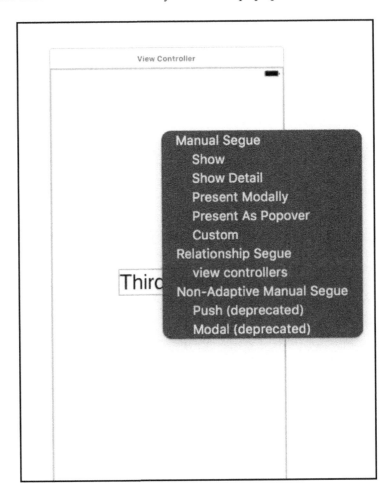

7. Under **Relationship Segue**, click on **view controllers** to make this view controller part of the view controllers list on the tab bar controller.

8. A `TabBarItem` will be added to the third view controller where you can set the title or image the tab bar item represents the view controller. Click on the new item and change its name from item to `Third View`:

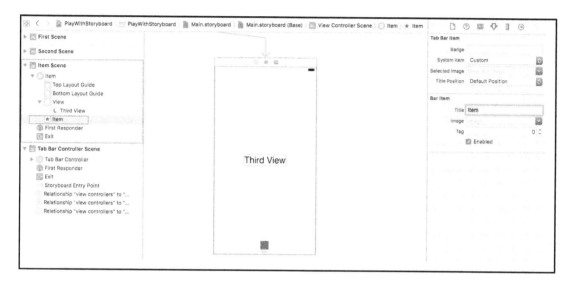

9. Now, build and run; you will see three tabs with three different view controllers.

10. What if we want to embed our first view controller in a navigation controller? In a storyboard, it's pretty easy. Just select the first controller, and in Xcode, go to **Editor** | **Embed In** | **UINavigationController**:

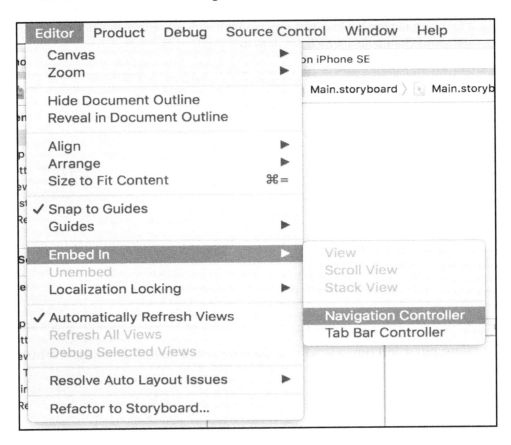

11. Now, storyboard will automatically create a navigation controller with a root view controller, which is the first view controller.

12. Let's now create two new view controllers by dragging two view controllers from **Object Library**.

13. Change the background color of the first one to red and the second one to blue.

14. In the first view controller, add a new UIButton with the title **Go to Red**. Then, pressing the *Ctrl* key, drag the button to add a segue to the red view controller; a list of types of segues will be shown. Click on **Show**:

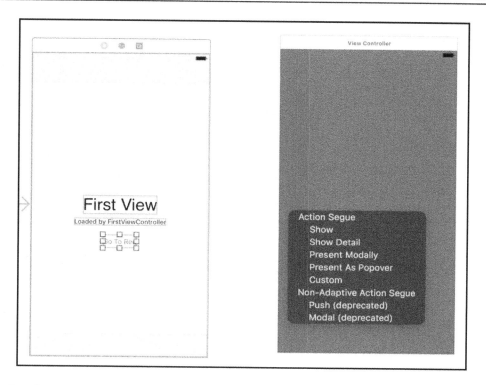

15. Then, select the red view controller and click on **Attribute Inspector** in the right side menu and change its title to **Red View Controller**. Do the same for the blue view controller and change its title to **Blue View Controller**.

16. Go to the red view controller, and add a `UIButton` with title **Go To Blue**. In the same way we added the previous segue, add a **Show** segue to the **Blue View Controller**.

17. The final view for your view controller should look like this:

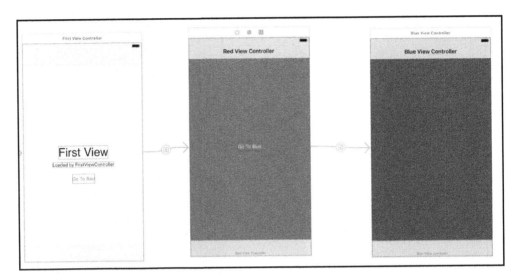

18. Now, build and run, and you will see how to navigate from the first view controller to the red and blue view controllers.

How it works...

We started this demo by giving an introduction in storyboard and by showing how to build your screens and add the connections between them. Connections between screens in storyboard are called segues. Segues have types, as we saw in the menu, and we will learn more about them in the *There's more...* section.

We saw how easy it is to embed any view controller inside the UINavigationController without writing any code to do this. The whole flow of your app will be easy to understand.

There's more...

There are a lot of things that you still can do in segues and UIStoryboard; we will talk about them in the following sections.

Segues attributes

Segues are very useful, and you will not feel that before knowing everything about them. Go to open our storyboard; click on any segue we have, and check its attributes in Attribute Inspector:

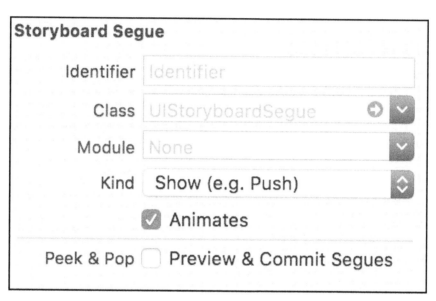

We will focus on **Identifier**, **Kind**, and **Animates** attributes. The Identifier attribute is very useful to identify your segue if you have multiple segues coming out from your view controller. You will need to use this identifier when you want to perform a specific segue programmatically based on any logic in your app. Suppose that the red view controller wants to navigate to the blue view controller without clicking on the Go To Blue button. In that case, you will give the segue an identifier-for example, "goToBlue"-and in the code, you can do the following:

```
self.performSegue(withIdentifier: "goToBlue", sender: self)
```

This will perform the segue that matches the given identifier.

The second attribute that you will see in storyboard is the segue kind, which has multiple kinds, such as `Show`, `Present Modally`, or `Present` as popover. All these kinds affect the animation type presenting in the view controller.

Last but not least is the `Animates` flag. This flag determines whether you want to perform the segue with animation or not. Unfortunately, this property can't be changed in runtime, and it should be configured only from storyboard. What about if you want to perform a segue with/without animation based on some logic in your code? In that case, there is a trick that you can do, that is, duplicate the segue and switch off its `Animates` toggle and give it a different identifier. In the code, you can perform the segue that matches your logic with/without animation.

Preparing for a segue

Now, we know how to perform a segue, but we don't know how to get prepared for a segue. Preparing for a segue means that you can get references to the source and destination view controllers and do some logic to them before performing the segue. You would need this when you want to pass some information from the source view controller to the destination view controller. You can pass objects, change parameters, or do any logic you want to get everything prepared for the segue. To do that, in your view controller that will perform segues, you can override the following method:

```
override func prepare(for segue: UIStoryboardSegue, sender: AnyObject?) {
    if segue.identifier == "goToBlue"{
        let destinationViewController = segue.destinationViewController
        // do whatever if you want with the destination view controller
        here.
    }
}
```

It's very important to check the identifier first before preparing for any segue. It's common to have multiple segues to be prepared, and comparing the identifiers is very important in that case, as each segue will have a different behavior. The `segue.sourceViewController` and `segue.destinationViewController` will get you references to the source and destination view controllers and update or prepare them so that they will be ready for performing the segue.

Unwind segues (exit segues)

A segue will not only help you to go to other screens via push or show (present modally or popover), it can help you to return to your source view controller. The unwind segue will be used to go back to your source view controller not only from the pushed view controller or presented view controller, you can also go back multiple steps in the navigation hierarchy. For example, in the previous demo we built, we have the first view controller, which can be pushed to RedViewController. The RedViewController can be pushed to BlueViewController. We can create the unwind segue, which will help RVC, BVC to go back directly to FVC. I know it's still not clear, and so now, we will do it together to stick this in your mind:

1. In Xcode, create two new Swift classes with a subclass UIViewController-the first one as RedViewController and the second one as BlueViewController.
2. Go to storyboard, and select the red view controller; from Identify Inspector, change the class to RedViewController, which you have already created; do the same for the BlueViewController.
3. Let's now create the unwind segue function in the source view controller, which is the FirstViewController. Open the source file, and add the following function:

```
@IBAction func unwindToFirstViewController(segue: UIStoryboardSegue)
{
}
```

   You will link to this function when you want to go back from red or blue view controllers.

   Any unwind function should be prefixed with "unwind" so that the compiler will understand that this function is the unwind segue function.

4. Go to RedViewController and add a new UIButton with the title **Go To Root**, and do the same in the BlueViewController.

5. We now want to link these buttons to the unwind function that we have created recently in `FirstViewController`. To do this, select the button, and pressing the *Ctrl* key button, drag the **Exit** icon that you will see in the left-hand side of your storyboard in the `FirstViewController` section:

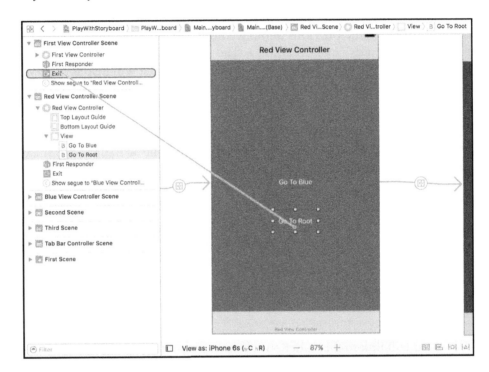

6. When you release the drag on the **Exit** icon, a popup will be shown to select which unwind function you want it to be linked with. In our demo, we have only one unwind function, that is, `unwindToFirstViewControllerWithSegue`, so select it:

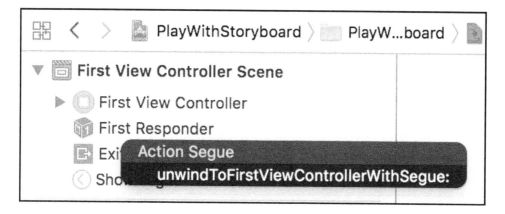

7. Follow the same steps to link the **Go To Root** button in BlueViewController to the same unwind segue in the FirstViewController.

8. Now, everything is fine, except one thing. The unwind function in FirstViewController will be called when you go back from Red or Blue Controllers. But, how can you differentiate between them? We can do this by three methods:

> **Method #1**: Check the type of source view controllers from the passed segue reference in the unwindToFirstViewControllerWithSegue function. Check the following code to know how to do it:

```
@IBAction func unwindToFirstViewController(segue:
UIStoryboardSegue) {
   if let redViewController = segue.sourceViewController as?
   RedViewController{
      print("Coming From Red!")
   }
   if let blueViewController = segue.sourceViewController as?
   BlueViewController{
      print("Coming From Blue!")
   }
}
```

The `segue.sourceViewController` will tell you which view controller you're coming back from and that's what we have used in our comparison. The `segue.destinationViewController` will be always a `FristViewController` instance.

Method #2: Provide each unwind segue you created a different identifier and, inside the `unwindToFirstViewControllerWithSegue` function, you can compare this to know from where you are coming. Let's try this. Select the unwind segue in `RedViewController` and give it an identifier `comingFromRed`:

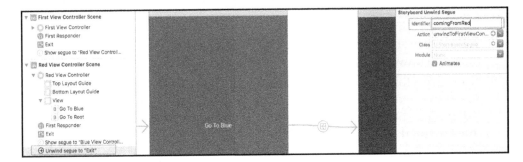

Do the same for the unwind segue in `BlueViewController`, and give it an identifier `comingFromBlue`. Now, let's go to the unwind function `unwindToFirstViewControllerWithSegue` and update it like this:

```
@IBAction func unwindToFirstViewController(segue:
UIStoryboardSegue) {
    if segue.identifier == "comingFromRed"{
        print("Coming From Red!")
    }
    if segue.identifier == "comingFromBlue" {
        print("Coming From Blue!")
    }
}
```

Now, try to build and run; open the red controller and click on the button to go to root folder, then open the blue controller and click on the button to go to root. Now, check the log; you will see the printed messages, as follows:

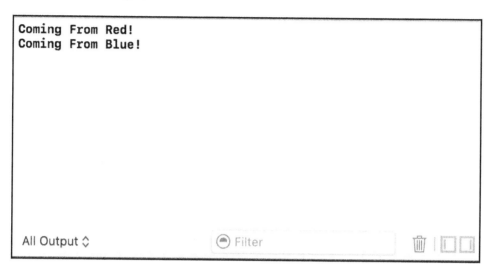

```
Coming From Red!
Coming From Blue!
```

All Output ⬍   ⬤ Filter   🗑 | ▢ ▢

Method #3: The other thing you can do is to create different unwind functions in the `FirstViewController` and link each unwind segue to a different function. For example, you may create two functions like this:

```
@IBAction func unwindToFirstViewControllerFromRed(segue:
 UIStoryboardSegue) {
}
@IBAction func unwindToFirstViewControllerFromBlue(segue:
 UIStoryboardSegue) {
}
```

Also, in storyboard, you can link each button to its own unwind function.

Custom segues

Custom segues help you to create your own custom transitions between the source and destination view controllers. Suppose that you have a view controller, and you're going to present another view controller with custom animation, such as the scale animation. Custom segue can help you in this by creating a new segue, which extends UI, and you can add your own customization. Creating custom segues is very straightforward; check out the following steps to see how to create and use a custom segue:

1. Create a new Swift class, which extends `UIStoryboardSegue`.
2. Inside the class, override the `perform()` function to add your custom code to perform the segue like this:

```swift
class ScaleSegue: UIStoryboardSegue {

    override func perform() {
        if let fromView = self.sourceViewController.view, let toView =
        self.destinationViewController.view{
            var frame = toView.frame
            let screenHeight = UIScreen.main().bounds.size.height
            let screenWidth = UIScreen.main().bounds.size.width
            frame.size = CGSize(width: 2 * screenWidth / 3, height:
             screenHeight / 2)
            toView.frame = frame
            if let window = UIApplication.shared().keyWindow{
                toView.center = window.center
                window.insertSubview(toView, aboveSubview: fromView)
                toView.transform = CGAffineTransform(scaleX: 0, y: 0)
                UIView.animate(withDuration: 0.5, animations: {
                    toView.transform = CGAffineTransform(scaleX: 1, y: 1)
                })
            }
        }
    }
}
```

3. We first got the `fromView`, which is the view of the `sourceViewController`, and then `toView`, which is the view of the `destinationViewController`. We updated the frame of the `toView` to be centered on the screen and takes half the height and two-thirds of the width of the screen size. To animate the view with a scale animation, we first set the scale to `0` by setting view transform to `CGAffineTransform(scaleX: 0, y: 0)`, and then we set it back to `1` with an animation duration equal to 0.5 second.

4. Now, go to storyboard and add a new view controller with yellow background. In any view controller you want to display the yellow view controller with the custom segue that we have recently created, add a `UIButton` and create a segue to the yellow view controller. Select the segue to change its attributes, and type `ScaleSegue` in the `Class` attribute:

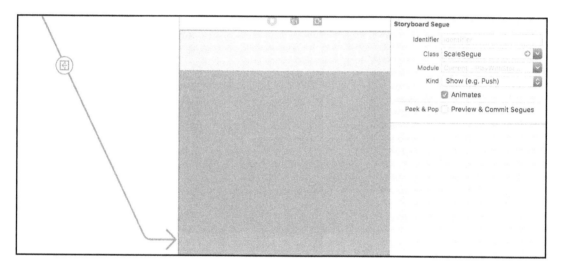

5. Now, when you build and run, you will see something like this:

Working with Autolayout and constraints

Autolayout is one of the best things that happened in iOS. I still remember the old days when I had to write too much code just for positioning views on screen and change their their sizes to be relative to the screen size. With Autolayout now, you can do a lot of things and add constraints to your views without writing a single line of code. Mastering Autolayout will help you to avoid the hassle of different screen sizes and even orientation changes.

Getting ready

In the demo project that we are going to do in this section, we will use the same project used in the preceding section to add some Autolayout constraints to see what they can do. You can use Xcode 8.0 as recommended, but you still can use earlier versions; however, you will notice some differences in screenshots.

How to do it...

1. If you run the demo app we created in the previous section, you will see that views are not aligned properly, as we didn't add any constraints. For example, check how the label appears when you open the third view controller when you click on the third tab:

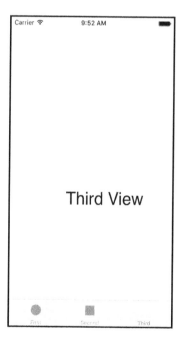

2. As you see, the label is not centered in the iPhone SE simulator.

3. Using constraints, you can center any view horizontally or/and vertically in its container view. To do this, click on the label that you want to be in the center, press the *Ctrl* key and drag the label to the super view. A pop-up list of constraints will appear, as follows:

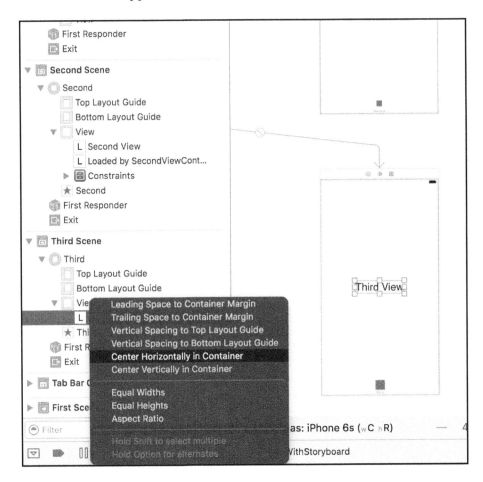

4. To select multiple constraints at the same time, press the *Shift* key and select **Center Horizontally** and **Center Vertically** and then click on *Enter*. Now, the label will be centered, regardless of the size of screen or the frame size of the view controller view.

5. Now, try to open one of the constraints that you have created to see its properties:

6. Keep the constant value at zero, but set Multiplier to 1.5 and see what happens:

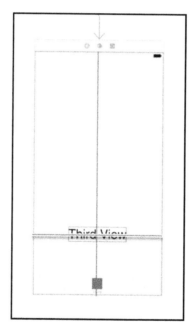

7. The title Y center will be 1.5 times the center of its super view.

8. Let's now go to the yellow view controller that was showing with the custom segue in the preceding section. Let's add two buttons whose sizes are relative to the view controller's frame size.

9. Select the view controller, and from **Object Library**, drag two `UIButton`. Place both of them at the bottom and besides each other like this:

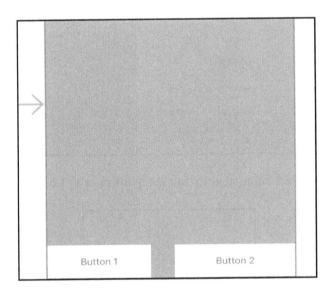

10. What we want to do is add margins of 6 px at the left, right, and bottom of each edge for both buttons. The height will be relative to the view size, which is 1/10. The width of each button will be 0.5 * view width - 9 px. The 9 is the sum of 6 px at edges and 3 px in between the buttons. To do this, select the first button, and then click on the **Pin** button:

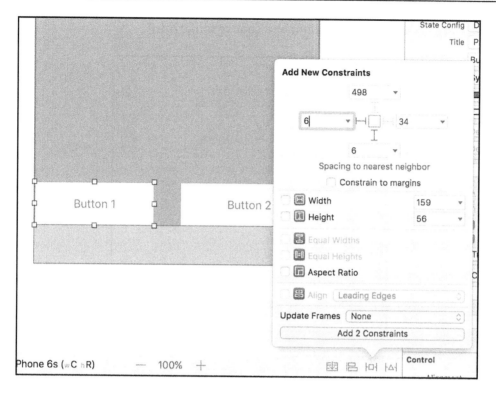

11. The Pin view helps you to add constraints around the button. We selected only the left and bottom constraints and added 6 px margins to it.

12. As we did before, drag the button while pressing the *Ctrl* key to add constraints relative to the super view. As shown in the preceding popup, select equal width and equal height to add the width and height constraints.

13. Click on the width constraint and change it like this:

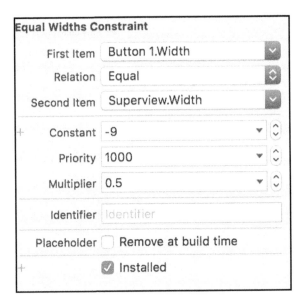

14. Do the same for the height constraint and change the multiplier to 0.1.
15. Apply the same constraints for the second button.
16. Now, you will notice a yellow icon at the top of your view controller, which indicates that the constraints don't match the view's frames. To fix this, click on the icon and a list of mismatched constraints will be listed. Click on one of them, and a popup will appear, check **Apply to all views in container** and click on **Fix Misplacement**:

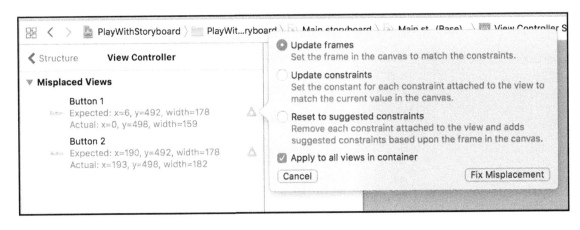

17. Automatically, the frames will be updated like this:

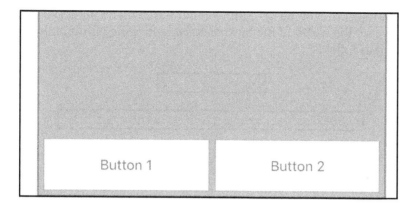

18. Let's build and run the app now. Open the yellow view controller with the custom segue we made in the previous section. You will see something like this:

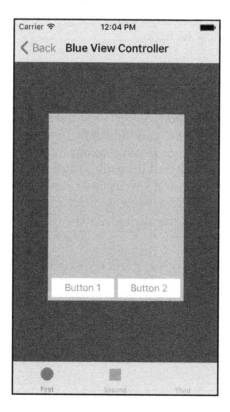

How it works...

To understand Autolayout, you have to think about it as a mathematical equation. For example, when we set the width of the buttons to be half of the width of the super view - 9px, just think of it as follows:

$$w1 = w2 * m + C$$

where C is the constant and m is the multiplier.

Each view needs to have sufficient constraints that identify its frame. For example, you can't set the left, width, and height constraints without setting a constraint specifying the y position. The y position can be set using Top, Bottom, or centering vertically; you have many options, but most important is that all constraints need to specify the x and y positions and the width and height should be there.

You will not master Autolayout just by building a demo app; you have to start using it right now for all the projects you will build. The more you use it the more you will become professional in using it and know its tricks.

There's more...

Don't think that Autolayout can be built only via interface builder. I know there are still some people who build everything programmatically (hardcoded) without using any interface builder files. I haven't been able to figure out why they prefer to do this even today. No offence if you're one them; but it's really weird for me. Anyway, you can still build Autolayout programmatically and specify your constraints so easily. To add a constraint, you need to have an instance of `NSLayoutConstraint`, which encapsulates the relation between the two views and the attributes to be used. The equation that `NSLayoutConstraint` looks like this:

```
firstItem.firstAttribute {==,<=,>=} secondItem.secondAttribute * multiplier
+ constant
```

`firstItem` and `secondItem` are the two views, for which you will add a constraint. `firstAttribute` is the attribute of the `firstItem`, which is a value of enum values for `NSLayoutAttribute`. The enum has values, such as `bottom`, `edge`, `width`, and so many attributes worth checking.

Updating constraints

Once constraints are created via interface builder or programmatically, you can update them in runtime if you have a reference to them. Constraints created via interface builder can be referenced via IBOutlets. To update a constraint, you can change only the constant value, unlike multiplier that can't be changed once it's created. So, if you have a view that its *y* position is changed in runtime, you can have a reference to the constraint that specifies its *y* position and can update the constant value in runtime.

You can animate the changing in constraint constant like how you did with animating the changing in frame. To animate the updated value, perform the following:

```
self.view.layoutIfNeeded()
constraint.constant = newValue
UIView.animate(withDuration: 0.5) {
    self.view.layoutIfNeeded()
}
```

Designing your interface builder for any size classes in one storyboard

Autolayout doesn't solve all your problems in building the UI screen. The big change nowadays in all screen sizes in iOS leads to different behaviors based on screen size. To build a universal app (iPhone and iPad) at the same time, most probably you need to build to two storyboards, which means you have to put in double efforts. However, what if you have a different UI in a landscape mode, 99% percent you would write code to handle this stuff, which is painful. More painful is the iPhone 6 plus screen size, which is huge enough to hold more details than the other iPhones, where some apps have a different UI only specific for iPhone 6 plus. Check out the following two screenshots for the Calendar app in landscape mode.

Here is the screenshot in any normal iPhone:

Here is the screenshot for iPhone 6 plus:

As we see in landscape mode, it can hold too much information, such as the concept of split screen. These kinds of differences can't be solved only via Autolayout, and that's where the magic of size classes comes in. We will not go deep into its theory; let's build a simple demo together.

Getting ready

Size classes require Autolayout to be enabled in your app, so if you decide to opt out of Autolayout, you can't use size classes. When you work in size classes, you will note that there are three kinds of size classes:

- **Regular**: Think of it as BIG, such as the width and height in iPad or the width of iPhone 6 Plus in landscape mode.
- **Compact**: Think of it as LITTLE like the iPhone height in landscape orientation or the iPhone width in portrait.
- **Any**: This is used when your layout doesn't change in any screen size.

If you still feel a little bit confused, don't worry, everything will get clear in the demo.

How to do it...

1. Let's create a new Xcode project with the **Single View Application** template named `PlayWithSizeClasses`.

2. Open `Main.Storyboard`; at the bottom, you will find a button saying **View as: iPhone 6s (wC, hR)**. Click on it; a view like the following screenshot will open:

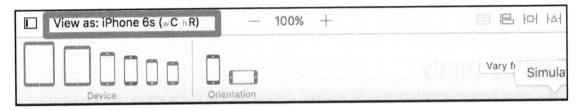

wC, hR means compact width and regular height. In all iPhones, the width is compact and height is regular. Clicking on any device will update the view sizes in the storyboard to simulate the device size.

3. Now, let's add a UIView with a red background and with the width equal to and the height half of the super view (main view). The constraints of the red view should be like this:

```
RedView.leading = superview.leading
RedView.top = superview.top
RedView.width = superview.width
RedView.height = 0.5 * superview.height
```

4. Add another green UIView below the red one with same dimensions. The constraints of the green view will look like this:

```
GreenView.leading = superview.leading
GreenView.top = RedView.bottom
GreenView.width = superview.width
GreenView.height = 0.5 * superview.height
```

5. Now, let's see how it looks but without running it in a simulator or device. We can use **Preview** for that. Click on **Assistant Editor** and then click on the top left of the assistant editor window, a popup will appear. Then, select **Preview**:

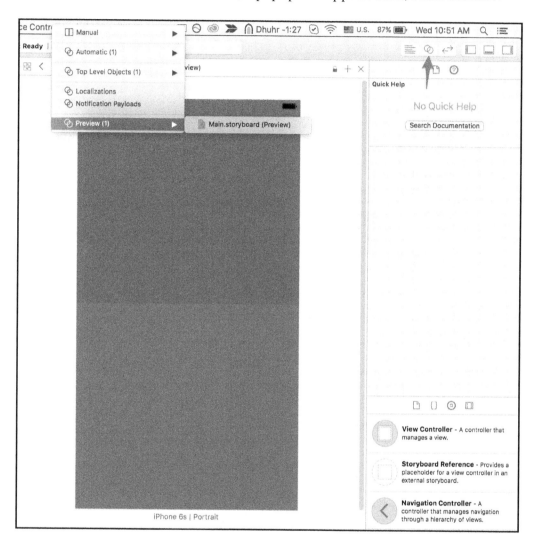

A screen representing iPhone 6s in portrait mode is displayed. If you tried to hover over iPhone 6s text, a button with an arrow icon will appear to switch to landscape mode. At the bottom-left corner, you will find a + icon button, where you can add multiple devices to preview your design:

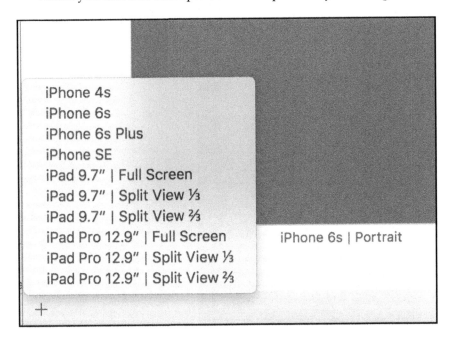

6. iPad also can be previewed, as we see in the menu. It can be previewed in full screen or in split view mode. The split view mode simulates the multitasking feature in iPad when two apps can be opened together when the screen splits.
7. Now, try to switch to landscape mode in the preview screen. Your app will look like this:

iPhone 6s | Landscape

It seems good, but it would be better if we could let both views share the same height and align horizontally, not vertically. It means we would keep the red view on the left and the green view at the right. To achieve this, we need to change the constraints of the red view. The `leading` and `top` constraints will be the same; we will only change the `width` and `height` constraints, like this:

```
RedView.width = 0.5 * superview.width
RedView.height = superview.height
```

8. The same will happen to the green view, but all constraints will be changed, like this:

```
GreenView.leading = RedView.trailing
GreenView.top = superview.top
GreenView.width = 0.5 * superview.width
GreenView.height = superview.height
```

9. Here comes the magic of size classes; they will enable us to specify different constraints based on the size class.

10. Let's do this. Select the red view and open the width constraint. At the bottom, you will find a + button to add new customization. Click on it, and choose compact width and compact height, which means the landscape size class for all iPhones. A new item will be added for wC hW, and then uncheck it to uninstall this constraint in the landscape mode to add a new one:

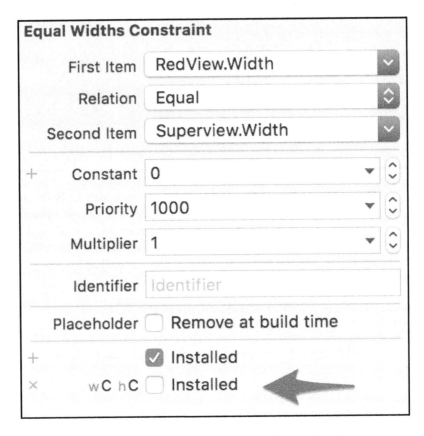

11. Now, in storyboard, change the current size class to landscape:

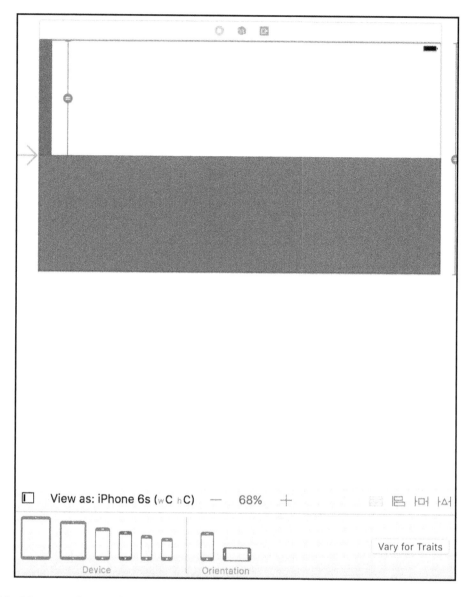

12. Now, in the landscape mode, we don't have a width constraint. Let's add a new width constraint as we did before with this rule:

```
RedView.width = 0.5 * superview.width
```

13. After adding it, make the constraint installed for **wC**, **hC** only, as shown in the following screenshot:

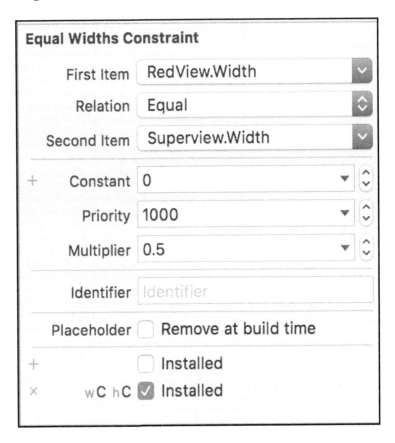

14. Now, in the preview window, you can see the red view with correct width dimension:

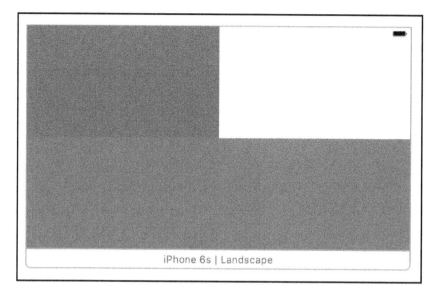

15. Follow the same steps to update the rest of constraints for the red and green views with same steps; the final result will be like this:

16. Size classes help us in customizing the font based on size class. Let's see it in action; add a `UILabel` as a subview of the red view, and center it horizontally and vertically. Change its title to `"I'm Red View"`. Do the same for the green view and change its title to `"I'm Green View"`. Change the text color for both to white color.

17. The labels will look great in all screen sizes if you try to test them in iPhones and iPads. However, the font size seems small when you test them in iPad, doesn't it? The size class for iPad is wR, hR (regular width and regular height); click on the label that we created, and open the Attribute Inspector tab. In the font attribute, you will find a **+** button at the left, click on it and choose wR, hR. Now, you will be able to add a customized font only for this specific size class. Add a new font with bold style and size 35:

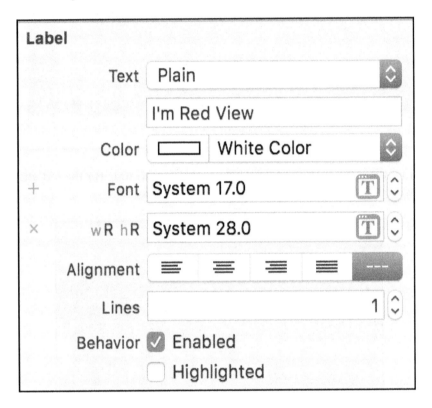

18. Now, try to test your screen in iPad; you will see it like this:

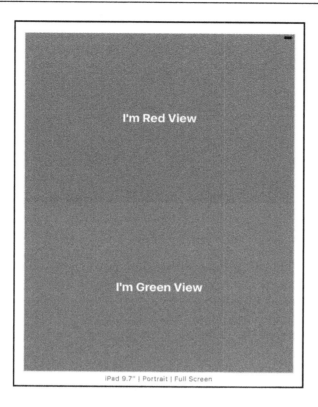

iPad 9.7" | Portrait | Full Screen

How it works...

The size classes feature is incredibly awesome when it comes to designing your screen, which has different customization based on the size class of your screen. When you work in your app, design it first to work in all screen sizes: iPhones, iPads, and with all different orientations. Then, think about the customization you need and start to add it just like what we did with the red and green views. To summarize what size classes can do, take a look at this list:

- **Add or remove view**: Yes, you can tell the layout to add or remove a specific view based on its size classes. For example, what if we wanted to remove the label `I'm Green View` in iPads? Before size classes, there was no way to do this without hardcoding it. With size classes, it's so simple. Let's check it out; select the label and open the Attribute Inspector tab. You will find a check mark that says Installed with a + icon button; click on it and add a rule for wR, hR and uncheck it. You will see that the label will disappear in the iPad mode:

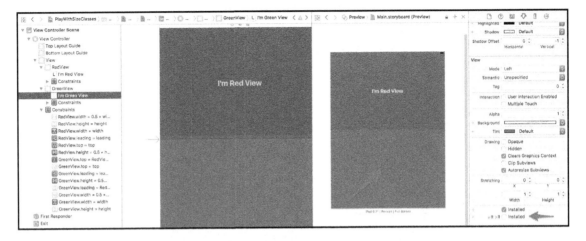

- **Add, remove, and edit constraints**: We removed and added constrains when we updated the layout of the red and green views for portrait and landscape modes. However, what about editing constraints? You can customize the constant value of your constraint based on its size class. If you try to open any constraint now, you will see at the left of the `Constant` parameter a + button to add any customizations.
- **Updating fonts**: We saw that already when we changed the font size of labels for iPad screens.

Embedding view controllers using container view

We will talk about something very simple in this section, but it has a high impact when working with storyboard and interface builder. In storyboard, you can create a container view, which acts as a holder or container for another view controller in your storyboard. You may ask why we need to do this when we can add the layout of this view controller just directly as a subview. The most benefit you can get out of this is when you have a view, which is reusable, in different locations in your app; you can create it in a different view controller and have it embedded whenever and wherever you want, without needing to duplicate any screen or any layout.

How to do it...

1. Let's create a new Xcode project to see this in action. Create a new project with template **Page-Based Application**.

2. Try to run the project; you will see something like this:

3. You will see a page view controller that displays a white subview and a month title. You can navigate between the pages using swipe and curl animation.

4. What will you do if this view controller is the subview of other view controllers in your app, or it's a reusable component? We will reuse it using container view.

5. Let's create a new view controller with a green background. Drag the arrow from the `RootViewController` to the new view controller to make it the initial view controller.

6. Drag a container view from **Object Library**, and add constraints, as follows:

```
Container.leading = superview.leading
Container.top = superview.top
Container.width = superview.width
Container.height = 0.5 * superview.height
```

7. Now, pressing the *Ctrl* key, drag the container view to the `RootViewController` and choose **Embed** from the list:

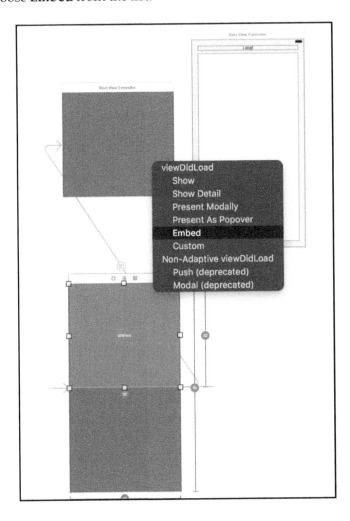

8. Now, build and run; you will see that the view is embedded like this:

How it works...

Using container view is very simple, as we saw in the preceding demo; however, it's very important and can solve a lot of problems and save a lot of time. The previous component is reusable in many screens; you will just embed it with a container view. Another advantage of using container view is that you separate the logic of the embedded view away from the parent view. The green view controller doesn't know anything about the `RootViewController` nor its subviews or its logic. This will help in building simple view controllers without huge logic and its component is encapsulated with its own logic.

There's more...

What if you want to do some setup for the embedded view controller or pass some data to it before being embedded? Segues are here to solve this problem with the prepareForSegue function. Container views use a special type of segue called Embed segue. Let's take a look at how we will use it to configure the root view controller:

1. In our previous demo, you will see a segue coming out from the container view to the RootViewController. Try to select it and give it the identifier embedRoot.

2. Create a custom view controller class to the green view controller, and name it StartViewController.

3. Go to storyboard file, and change the class of the green view controller to StartViewController from **Identity Inspector**.

4. Now, go to the StartViewController.swift file and override the prepareForSegue function:

```
override func prepare(for segue: UIStoryboardSegue, sender:
  AnyObject?) {
   if segue.identifier == "embedRoot"{
       let rootViewController = segue.destinationViewController
        as! RootViewController
       // do any setup here for rootViewController
       print(rootViewController)
   }
}
```

5. Now, build and run; an instance of RootViewController will be printed, and you can configure or pass any data to it.

5
Working with UITableView

In this chapter, we will cover the following topics:

- Working with scroll view
- Using TableView sections, headers, and footers
- Using custom cells
- Resizing table view cells dynamically
- Editing table view

Introduction

In iOS, it's very rare to find an app that is not using UIScrollView or UITableView. These two components are very important and are considered a must to know and master components. In the first section, we will give some information about UIScrollView and how to use it. Then, in the rest of the sections, we will talk about UITableView. We will talk about managing sections and how to add a header and footer to table sections or to the table itself. We will see how to create custom cells and resize them dynamically based on cell contents. UITableView provides us with APIs as well to edit it by adding or removing cells with/without animations and by dragging or dropping cells. This chapter is important to read and apply the demos yourself, as these components are heavily used in most apps.

Working with scroll view

Scroll view is a subclass of `UIView` that helps you add multiple views so that the sum of their height is larger than the height of super view. It lets you scroll between subview horizontally, vertically, or both at the same time; user can scroll with swipe and pan gestures. Scroll view provides the functionality to zoom its content by allowing a user to pinch zoom the content. This native component has an impressive set of APIs that provides you with flexibility and features to manage scrolling, zooming, and content size. Before getting into the `UITableView`, `UICollectionView`, or `UITextView` native components, you have to be experienced with `UIScrollView` because it is the superclass for all these views.

Getting ready

Before getting started with our example, I want to point out some properties in `UIScrollView` that are used heavily while dealing with it. The following is a list of the most important properties that you should be aware of:

1. **contentSize**: It's the size of the content view. For example, your scroll view bounds can be `(0, 0, 200, 400)`, which means that the `width` is 200 and `height` is 400. The content size can be, for example, `(500, 1000)`, which means the scroll view can scroll horizontally to 500 and vertically to 1000. Only 200 * 400 view is visible all the time, but it can be moved/shifted based on scrolling.

2. **contentOffset**: Content offset is how far the view has been moved horizontally or vertically. The following image helps you get an idea about it:

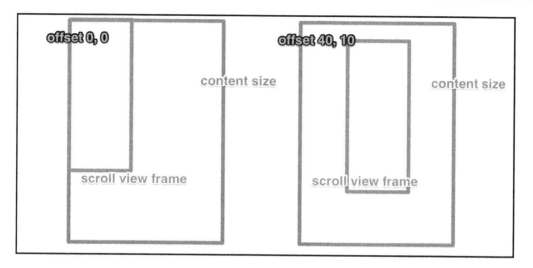

3. **contentInset**: It acts as adding inset (padding) to the content view. The inset can be added to the top, bottom, left, or right using:

```
UIEdgeInsetsMake(top, left, bottom, right)
```

To be experienced in using `UIScrollView` is not something you can get by just reading the book or the documentation; you have to experience it manually by writing sample apps to get your hands dirty with it.

How to do it...

1. Create a new Xcode project with **Single View Application** template and with the `ScrollViewDemo` name.
2. Open `Main.storyboard` to build a login screen where the user will be able to enter his credentials and we will later come across a situation where we will need the scroll view.
3. Open `ViewController` screen in storyboard to add a scroll view. From Object Library, drag a scroll view that fills the whole screen with the following constraints:

```
ScrollView.trailing = superview.trailing
ScrollView.top = superview.top
ScrollView.leading = superview.leading
ScrollView.bottom = superview.bottom
```

4. Add an empty view that identifies the boundary of the scroll view that has the same frame of scroll view. Add all these constraints to the view:

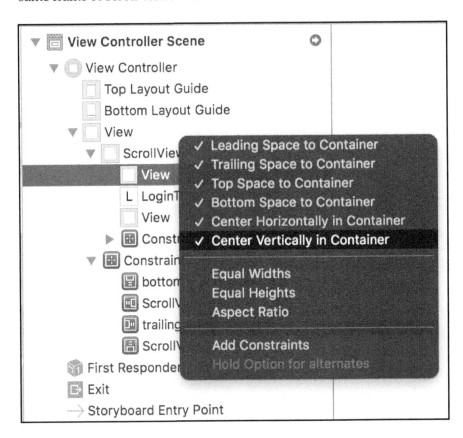

5. Drag a UILabel from **Object** library and add it as a subview to the scroll view. Center it horizontally and at y position = 30. Add Autolayout constraints to it like this:

```
LoginTitle.CenterX = ScrollView.CenterX
LoginTitle.top = ScrollView.top + 30
```

6. Now, let's add a `UIView` that acts as a container to the credentials fields. Drag a `UIView` from **Object** library, change its background color to gray, and add it at the bottom of the screen with the following constraints:

```
LoginContainer.trailing = ScrollView.trailing - 16
LoginContainer.bottom = ScrollView.bottom - 20
LoginContainer.leading = ScrollView.leading + 16
LoginContainer.height = ScrollView.height * 0.5
```

7. Now, add a username `UITextField` with placeholder text `Username` with, inside the container view, the following constraints:

```
Username.trailing = LoginContainer.trailing - 8
Username.top = LoginContainer.top + 23
Username.leading = LoginContainer.leading + 8
Username.height = 30
```

8. Add another password `UITextField` with placeholder text `Password` with the following constraints:

```
Password.trailing = LoginContainer.trailing - 8
Password.top = Username.bottom + 21
Password.leading = LoginContainer.leading + 8
Password.height = 30
```

9. At the bottom, add another `UIButton` to act as a login button with the following constraints:

```
Login.centerX = LoginContainer.centerX
Login.width = 113
Login.bottom = LoginContainer.bottom - 8
Login.height = 30
```

10. Now we have a login screen ready to work. Build and run the screen will look like this:

11. However, when you try to edit any text field, the keyboard will open the cover part of the screen, as follows:

12. Now we have multiple problems. We can't see what's behind the keyboard, like the login or the password text field. To solve this problem, we will ask for help from `UIScrollView`.

13. To listen for the keyboard showing, we will use `NotificationCenter` to listen for keyboard notifications. Add the following code to your `ViewController.swift`:

```swift
override func viewWillAppear(_ animated: Bool) {
  super.viewWillAppear(animated)
  listenToKeyboardNotifications()
}
override func viewWillDisappear(_ animated: Bool) {
  super.viewWillDisappear(animated)
  unlistenToKeyboardNotifications()
}
// MARK: - Keyboard Notifications & Animations -
private func listenToKeyboardNotifications(){
  //receive notification for keyboard
  NotificationCenter.default().addObserver(self, selector:
    #selector(ViewController.keyboardWasShown(notification:))
      , name: NSNotification.Name.UIKeyboardWillShow, object: nil)
}
private func unlistenToKeyboardNotifications(){
  //unregister receive notification for keyboard
  NotificationCenter.default().removeObserver(self, name:
    NSNotification.Name.UIKeyboardWillShow, object: nil)
}
```

14. When the keyboard shows, the `keyboardWasShown` function will be called, before implementing it. Let's add an `IBOutlet` to the `UIScrollView` with the name `currentScrollView`:

```swift
@IBOutlet weak var currentScrollView: UIScrollView!
Now let's implement keyboardWasShown function like this:
@objc private func keyboardWasShown(notification:NSNotification){
  var info : Dictionary = notification.userInfo!
  let kbSize = info[UIKeyboardFrameBeginUserInfoKey]
    ?.cgRectValue().size
  let contentInsets = UIEdgeInsetsMake(0.0, 0.0, (kbSize?.height)!,
    0.0)
  self.currentScrollView.contentInset = contentInsets
  self.currentScrollView.scrollIndicatorInsets = contentInsets
  self.perform(#selector(ViewController.scrollToBottom), with: nil,
    afterDelay: 0)
}
@objc private func scrollToBottom(){
```

```
let offset = CGPoint(x: 0, y:
  self.currentScrollView.contentSize.height -
    self.currentScrollView.bounds.height +
      self.currentScrollView.contentInset.bottom)
  self.currentScrollView.setContentOffset(offset, animated: true)
}
```

15. The function will get the keyboard height and add inset to the bottom with the same height of keyboard. Then, we scroll the scroll view to the bottom with animation by changing the content offset, as we mentioned in the previous section.

16. Now, try to build and run and you will see the magic. The scroll view will be animated and view will be displayed, as follows:

17. You can also scroll the screen to see the top title and the whole component while the keyboard is open.

How it works...

We started our demo by creating a login screen with text fields and a login button using techniques we learnt before in Chapter 4, *Working with Interface Builder*. Everything is straightforward but as we saw, when we run, the keyboard covers part of the screen and some components are not reachable/accessible. Scroll view will help greatly in situations like these and that's why all our subviews have been added inside a UIScrollView in storyboard.

To be notified when the keyboard starts showing, there are two ways. We can set a delegate of the UITextField to ViewController and override the beginEditing function; if you have multiple text fields, it will be painful. The second way is to register for the UIKeyboardWillShow notification that will be fired by the system when the keyboard is to be shown. As you may note, we register for the notification in viewWillAppear and unregister it in viewWillDisappear. We did that to avoid any conflicts or unexpected behavior when the keyboard shows in another screen and ViewController still resides in memory; in that case, it will be notified with this notification and may cause issues. So now, the notification will be shown only when this screen is visible to the user.

The keyboardWasShown function will be called once the keyboard starts to show with a NSNotification parameter, which has a property called userInfo that is a dictionary containing useful information about the notification. In userInfo, we retrieved the keyboard height and used it to add inset to the scroll view, so now the scroll view content size has been increased by the keyboard height.

ScrollView is now ready and it's contentSize has been increased. Still, the user has to scroll to see the hidden fields, which is kind of painful for him. We will scroll the view automatically using the contentOffset property that we mentioned before. The offset is calculated with the following formula:

```
let offset = CGPoint(x: 0, y: self.currentScrollView.contentSize.height -
self.currentScrollView.bounds.height +
self.currentScrollView.contentInset.bottom)
```

We don't have an offset horizontally and that's why it's zero. In y, the offset will be calculated by getting the content size height of the scroll and deducting from it the actual height of the scroll view and any inset (padding) we have added to the scroll view.

There's more...

In some situations, you may need to get notified with scrolling actions, current offset, or zooming information in your logic. In that case, you can use `UIScrollViewDelegate`. The delegate has many useful functions, such as `scrollViewDidScroll`, which is the ideal location to get the current offset to do any logic that depends on the offset. For the zooming functionality, the `scrollViewDidZoom` function will be called when user pinch zooms so that you get the correct scale value.

Using TableView sections, headers and footers

Starting from this section, we will talk about `UITableView`. One of the kings' UI controllers in iOS which is used heavily in most of iOS apps. It manages a list of cells with scrolling capability because its superclass is `UIScrollView`. `UITableView` helps you to display, organize, categorize, add, delete, and update cells with easy-to-use APIs. In this section, we will see how to organize your cells in sections. We will see how to add headers and footers to your section using the header titles or custom views.

Getting ready

Before getting started in a sample demo to see how to organize your sections and deal with headers and footers, ensure that you have used UITableView before even if in a simple demo, to see how to use its delegate and data source. We will now build a demo app showing how to manage cells in sections and add headers and footers.

How to do it...

1. Let's start, as usual, by creating a new project with the **Single View Application** template with the name `TableViewDemo`.
2. Click on the **View Controller** in the storyboard file and go to **Editor | Embed In | Navigation Controller** to add the current view controller as a root view controller to a `UINavigationController`.
3. Now, drag `UITableView` from the **Object Library** and place it as a subview.

4. Place the table at origin (0, 0) with the same size as the `ViewController` view.

5. Change its constraints to the following:

```
TableView.leading = superview.leading
TableView.top = superview.top
TableView.width = superview.width
TableView.height = superview.height
```

6. To let the table view know the information about the data to be displayed and trigger the actions of selection or any other actions, you will need to set the delegate and data source.

7. In storyboard, select the table view and, while holding the *Ctrl* key, drag it to **View Controller**:

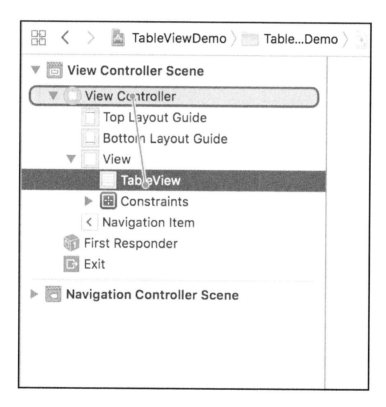

A popup will appear to set the delegate and data source:

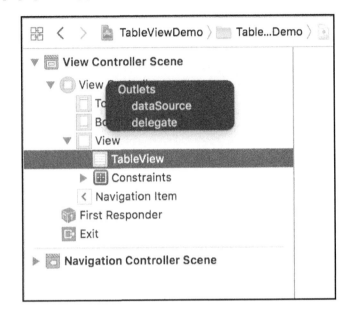

Now, click on delegate and data source to link both of them.

8. From the **Object Library**, drag `UITableViewCell` to add the cell that we will reuse. This cell will act as a template cell for the table view.

9. Select the cell that you have recently added. From **Attribute Inspector**, change the style of the cell to **Basic** and type `cell` in **Identifier**:

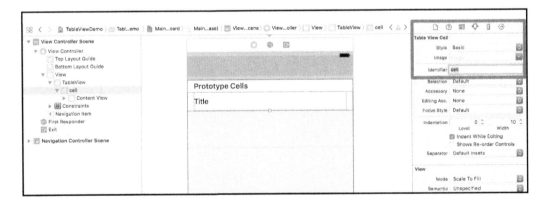

Now, a title label will appear to add any styling to it.

10. Now, we are almost ready in storyboard. All the configuration that we need is done in storyboard.

11. Now, open `ViewController.swift` to add the implementation of table view delegate and data source.

12. To implement `UITableViewDelegate` and `UITableViewDataSource`, we will use extensions.

13. Add the following extensions to `ViewController.swift`:

```
extension ViewController: UITableViewDelegate{
}

extension ViewController: UITableViewDataSource{
}
```

14. The `UITableViewDelegate` has no required method to implement and we will leave this extension empty.

15. For `UITableViewDataSource`, there are two required methods to implement. The following are their implementations:

```
extension ViewController: UITableViewDataSource {
  func tableView(_ tableView: UITableView, numberOfRowsInSection
    section: Int) -> Int {
    return 5
  }
  func tableView(_ tableView: UITableView, cellForRowAt indexPath:
    IndexPath) -> UITableViewCell {
    let cell = tableView.dequeueReusableCell(withIdentifier: "cell")
    cell?.textLabel?.text = "Cell #\(indexPath.row)"
    return cell!
  }
}
```

16. Now, we implemented the `numberOfRowsInSection` method to always return five cells. And in `cellForRow`, we ask the table view to dequeue a cell so that we can reuse it. Cell design is simple, as we will display the text `Cell` followed by the cell number.

17. Now, try to build and run; you will see something like this:

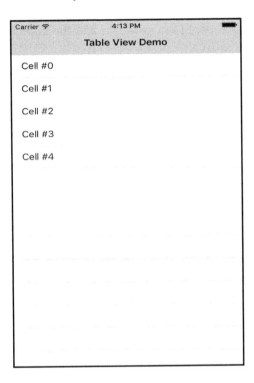

18. The table view is displayed with five cells, as we configured in the data source.

19. Now, let's see how sections can be added. Go to data source extension and implement the following method:

```
func numberOfSections(in tableView: UITableView) -> Int {
    return 3
}
```

20. Now, let's change the `numberOfRowsInSection` function to this:

```
func tableView(_ tableView: UITableView, numberOfRowsInSection
  section: Int) -> Int {
  switch section {
    case 0:
      return 3
    case 1:
      return 4
    case 2:
      return 5
```

```
      default:
         return 0
   }
}
```

21. Now, let's change the `cellForRow` method to display the section number beside the cell number:

```
func tableView(_ tableView: UITableView, cellForRowAt indexPath:
  IndexPath) -> UITableViewCell {
   let cell = tableView.dequeueReusableCell(withIdentifier: "cell")
   cell?.textLabel?.text = "Cell #\(indexPath.row), section
    #\(indexPath.section)"
   return cell!
}
```

22. Now, let's build and run. You will see sections like this:

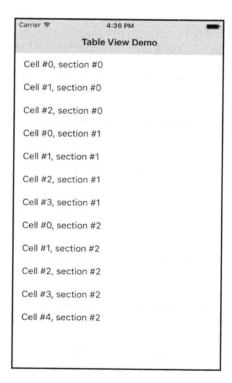

As you can see, we have three sections but, unfortunately, the sections are not organized.

23. Every section can have a header and footer. We will now add headers to the sections.

24. To separate the sections, we will use the `titleForHeaderInSection` function in `UITableViewDelegate`. Let's implement this function in the delegate extension:

```
extension ViewController: UITableViewDelegate{
    func tableView(_ tableView: UITableView, titleForHeaderInSection
    section: Int) -> String? {
      return "Section \(section)"
    }
}
```

25. Now build and run; sections are now separated by a header title:

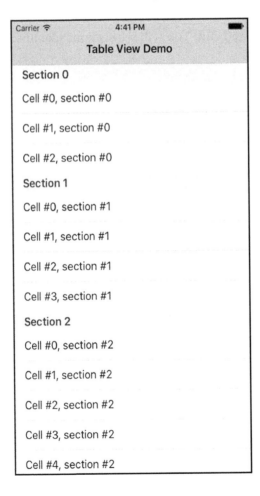

How it works...

As we saw in the previous demo, with just some simple implementations to the UITableViewDelegate or UITableViewDataSource function, we can add cells, sections, and headers to the added sections. Any UITableView requires you to tell it which object is the delegate and which object is the data source. The table view will know literally nothing about these objects, except that they are conforming to the UITableViewDelegate and UITableViewDataSource protocols. In the data source, you must implement the numberOfRows and cellForRow functions so that table view can display something on the screen. By default, there is only one section in the table view and you can change it as we saw in the demo by implementing the numberOfSections function. Every section in the table view has a header and footer. The header is displayed above the section and its title can be managed by overriding the titleForHeaderInSection function. It's the same for footer--it's displayed below the section and its title can be managed by overriding the titleForFooterInSection function.

There's more...

The table view can have a header and footer; they belong to the table itself and are totally different from the headers and footers of sections. The table header is very useful to add a custom view that will be displayed before the cells and, at the same time, it can be scrolled within the cells. In this header, you can add a view to filter the cells or sort them with a specific category.

If you want to add a view to act as table view header in storyboard, just drag and place it before your prototype cells. Programmatically, you can do this by setting the tableHeaderView or tableFooterView properties.

Custom section header and footer

In the demo, we saw how to add a header or footer to the section. The method we used is not customizable and all you can do is set the title. To customize the look and feel of the section header or footer, you need to provide a custom view. Let's do this in our previous demo to add a header, but with red background color and a centered label.

In the extension that conforms to `UITableViewDelegate`, let's override the following functions:

```
extension ViewController: UITableViewDelegate{
    func tableView(_ tableView: UITableView, viewForHeaderInSection
     section: Int) -> UIView? {
        var frame = tableView.bounds
        frame.size.height = 30.0
        let view = UIView(frame: frame)
        view.backgroundColor = UIColor.red()
        let label = UILabel(frame: view.bounds)
        label.text = "Section \(section)"
        label.textColor = UIColor.white()
        label.textAlignment = .center
        view.addSubview(label)
        return view
    }
    func tableView(_ tableView: UITableView, heightForHeaderInSection
     section: Int) -> CGFloat {
        return 30.0
    }
}
```

The `heightForHeaderInSection` function tells the table view the expected height of the header. The `viewForHeaderInSection` function asks the delegate about the view that will be displayed in the header. We create a custom view with red background and a center-aligned label inside. Now let's build and run; you will see the new headers like this:

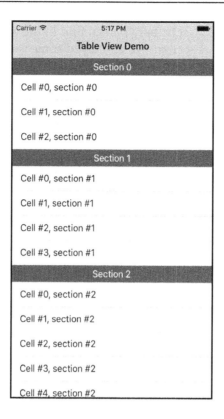

Using custom cells

UITableView provides us with native styles for the UITableViewCell, like the basic one that we saw in the previous demo. Another style you can use is the Detailed style, which displays a details label at the left or right of the cell. Another one, that is the Subtitle style, displays a subtitle label below the main label. You can still add your customization to table view cells, as the native ones are rarely used, especially in apps published in the App Store.

Getting ready

We will use the demo we created in the previous section as a starting point to build the demo of this section. We will add custom cells and use them instead of the basic ones.

In the demo, we will use some Assets that you can find in the Xcode project of this section in the code files. In the previous section, we displayed some sample cells with sample sections. We will use these to build a screen that displays food categories and sample foods inside each category.

How to do it...

1. Open the storyboard file, go to the table view, and select the prototype cell.
2. Change its **Style** from **Attribute Inspector** tab to **Custom**.
3. Change the cell height to 70 pixels.
4. From the **Object Library**, drag a `UIImageView` to add it as a subview to the custom cell. Add it at location (0, 0) with the same size as the custom cell.
5. Add Autolayout constraints to the image view as follows:

```
FoodImage.leading = Superview.leading
FoodImage.top = Superview.top
FoodImage.trailing = Superview.trailing
FoodImage.bottom = Superview.bottom
```

6. Open the **Attribute Inspector** tab and change the image name to `Sushi`. Change the mode to **Aspect Fill** to make the image fill the size, but keeping the aspect ratio:

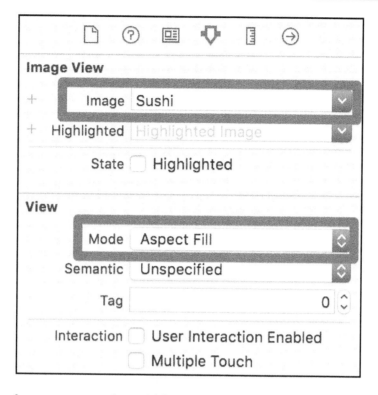

7. Now, drag a `UILabel` from **Object Library** and place it at the center of the custom cell.

8. Change the text color to white and add Autolayout constraints, as shown:

```
Label.centerY = Superview.centerY
Label.centerX = Superview.centerX
```

9. Now, the custom cell is almost ready. As it's a custom cell, we will create a new custom class for it.

10. Add a new Swift file called `FoodsTableViewCell` and make the class a subclass of `UITableViewCell`:

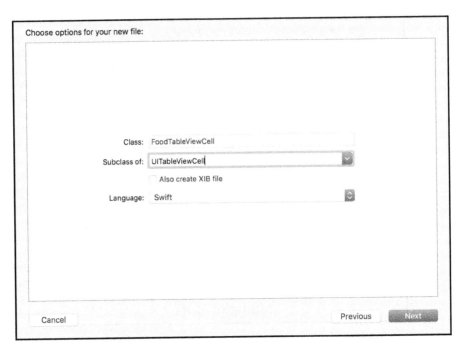

11. Now, return to your storyboard and select the custom cell. Open its **Identity Inspector** and change the class to `FoodTableViewCell`:

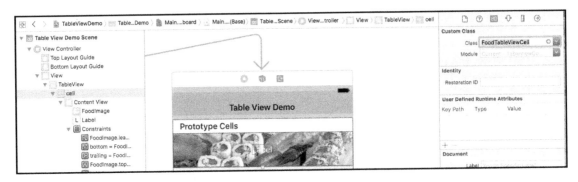

12. As we learnt before, link two IBOutlets to the image view and label the newly created custom class:

```
@IBOutlet weak var foodNameLabel: UILabel!
```

```
@IBOutlet weak var foodImageView: UIImageView!
```

13. Now, our custom cell is totally ready; let's edit our delegate and data source methods.

14. In the delegate methods extension, remove the custom section header and return to the native one, like this:

```
extension ViewController: UITableViewDelegate{
  func tableView(_ tableView: UITableView, titleForHeaderInSection
    section: Int) -> String? {
    switch section {
      case 0:
        return "Sweets"
      case 1:
        return "Lebanese Food"
      case 2:
        return "Sea Food"
      default:
        return ""
    }
  }
}
```

15. Now we have three sections: Sweets, Lebanese Food, and Sea Food.

16. Now, let's edit the data source method like this:

```
extension ViewController: UITableViewDataSource{
  func tableView(_ tableView: UITableView, numberOfRowsInSection
    section: Int) -> Int {
    return 3
  }
  func numberOfSections(in tableView: UITableView) -> Int {
    return 3
  }
  func tableView(_ tableView: UITableView, cellForRowAt indexPath:
    IndexPath) -> UITableViewCell {
    let cell = tableView.dequeueReusableCell(withIdentifier: "cell")
      as! FoodTableViewCell
    switch indexPath.section {
      case 0: // Sweets
        switch indexPath.row {
          case 0:
            cell.foodNameLabel.text = "Cheese Cake"
            cell.foodImageView?.image = UIImage(named: "CheeseCake")
          case 1:
            cell.foodNameLabel.text = "Donuts"
            cell.foodImageView?.image = UIImage(named: "Donuts")
```

```
        case 2:
          cell.foodNameLabel.text = "Arabic Sweets"
          cell.foodImageView?.image = UIImage(named: "ArSweets")
        default:
          print("No more cells in this section")
        }
      case 1: // Lebanese food
        switch indexPath.row {
        case 0:
          cell.foodNameLabel.text = "Shawerma"
          cell.foodImageView?.image = UIImage(named: "Shawerma")
        case 1:
          cell.foodNameLabel.text = "Homos"
          cell.foodImageView?.image = UIImage(named: "Homos")
        case 2:
          cell.foodNameLabel.text = "Mix Grill"
          cell.foodImageView?.image = UIImage(named: "MixGrill")
        default:
          print("No more cells in this section")
        }
      case 2:
        switch indexPath.row {
          case 0:
            cell.foodNameLabel.text = "Shrimps"
            cell.foodImageView?.image = UIImage(named: "Shrimps")
          case 1:
            cell.foodNameLabel.text = "Sushi"
            cell.foodImageView?.image = UIImage(named: "Sushi")
          case 2:
            cell.foodNameLabel.text = "Smoked Salmon"
            cell.foodImageView?.image = UIImage(named: "Salmon")
          default:
            print("No more cells in this section")
          }
      default:
        print("No more sections")
      }
      return cell
    }
  }
```

17. We added three sections and each section has three cells. In cell for row, we cast the cell to the custom cell class that we have created to access the outlets.

18. Now build and run, you will see that the table view becomes more awesome, as follows:

19. The table view looks perfect now but, as we see, the label is not easy to read as the white color conflicts with the image colors. In real apps, these images come from the backend so you don't have control over their colors.

20. To solve this problem and to make the label works fine with all images, we will add a dim background behind the label.

21. Drag a `UIView` from **Object Library** and place it before the `UILabel`. Change its size to be the same as that of the custom cells and those used in the image view.

22. From the **Attribute Inspector** tab, change the background color of the view to black color and **alpha** value to 0.35:

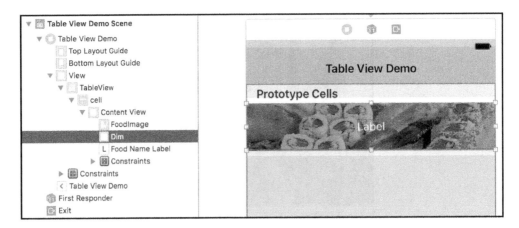

23. Now build and run; it will look perfect now:

How it works...

Building custom cell is pretty easy and so, it is important to design an awesome table that looks unique and stunning. Using storyboard, everything becomes easier as you can build custom cell and prepare the prototype to be used in the data source methods.

Building custom `UITableViewCell` classes is a very important thing to do to encapsulate your IBOutlets or any actions you need so that you can customize their values easily in the `cellForRow` method.

Resizing table view cells dynamically

In the previous demos, we saw that all the cells have the static cell height that can be configured from the storyboard. In this section, we will learn to resize table view cells dynamically, that is, based on the content height you have in your cell. Use this feature only if you want your cell to be resized based on the content height. Autolayout will help us greatly in this section and I recommend revising/reading the Autolayout chapter before starting this section.

How to do it...

1. Create a new Xcode project with the name `Dynamic Cells` and a Single View template.
2. Add a `UITableView` with the delegate and data source set. Add a prototype cell with a basic style, as we did in section one. Implement the delegate and data source and display only four cells.
3. In `ViewController.swift`, add the following titles to be displayed:

```
let titles = ["This is very simple title",
            "Long text goes here\nLong text goes here\nLong text goes
here\nLong text goes here\nLong text goes here\nLong text goes here",
            "Some text goes here, Some text goes here, Some text goes
here, Some text goes here, Some text goes here",
            "Long text goes here\nLong text goes here\nLong text goes
here\nLong text goes here\nLong text goes here\nLong text goes hereLong
text goes here\nLong text goes here\nLong text goes here\nLong text goes
here\nLong text goes here\nLong text goes hereLong text goes here\nLong
text goes here\nLong text goes here\nLong text goes here\nLong text goes
here\nLong text goes here"]
```

4. Now, in the `cellForRow` method, change it to read the title from the titles array we added earlier:

```
func tableView(_ tableView: UITableView, cellForRowAt indexPath:
  IndexPath) -> UITableViewCell {
    let cell = tableView.dequeueReusableCell(withIdentifier: "cell")
    cell?.textLabel?.text = titles[indexPath.row]
    return cell!
}
```

5. When you build and run, you will see that the titles have been displayed like this:

Not all the text has been displayed in cells and that's what we will do now.

6. Go to storyboard and select the cell label. Go to **Attribute Inspector** and change the number of lines to `Zero` and the line break mode to **Word Wrap**.

7. Link an IBOutlet to the table view in `ViewController.swift`:

```
@IBOutlet weak var demoTableView: UITableView!
```

8. Add the following code in the `viewDidLoad` function:

```
demoTableView.estimatedRowHeight = 43
demoTableView.rowHeight = UITableViewAutomaticDimension
```

9. Now build and run, you will see the following:

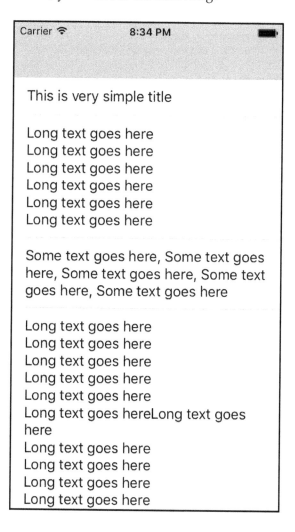

How it works...

Dynamic resizing table view cells is very important, especially when you work with dynamic height content in your table view. Autolayout makes life easier while dealing with dynamic height cell. You can build your UI in your custom cell and use Autolayout to identify the cell dimensions or boundaries so that, when your content changes and affects the subviews frames, the cell height will be changed automatically. All will work fine, but you have to do the following programmatically:

```
tableView.estimatedRowHeight = 43
tableView.rowHeight = UITableViewAutomaticDimension
```

Setting the `rowHeight` property to the `UITableViewAutomaticDimension` constant allows the self-sizing concept to work in table view. The `estimatedRowHeight` provides the estimated row height or the default height for your rows to improve the performance of loading the table view and correct the table view cells height after calculating the cell size based on constraints.

Editing table views

Table views are not meant only for displaying data (read-only); users can be engaged in managing the table views to insert, update, delete, and reorder the table view cells. Thanks to `UITableView`, these kinds of operations are not difficult to implement and with just simple lines of code, you can bring all these awesome features to your app. In this section, we will see how to trigger the editing mode in table view to delete or reorder cells. We will see how to insert new rows at runtime to the table view with animations as well.

Getting ready

In the demo project that we will implement, we are building a simple Todo app. We will have a screen where the user can see a list of open tasks and options to add new tasks, delete specific tasks, and reorder tasks based on priority. This demo will be very interesting.

How to do it...

1. First, let's create a new Xcode project with **Single View Application** template.
2. Add a table view and configure its delegate and data source, as we learnt in the previous sections.
3. Add a prototype table view cell in the storyboard with a basic style and set its identifier to toDoCell.
4. Let's create the data structure of the Task. This data structure will encapsulate the task information that we will use in the app. Create a new class in a new Swift file as a subclass to NSObject with the name Task. The class will look like this:

```
class Task: NSObject {
  var name: String
  init(taskName: String) {
    self.name = taskName
  }
}
```

5. We have only added the name property till now; you can add more properties such as details and createdAt date later.
6. Now, open the ViewController.swift file and add the following property:

```
var tasks = [Task]()
```

 This property is a collection of Task data structure that we created earlier. It will hold the current displayed tasks.

7. Now, let's update the data source functions to let them read the data from the tasks array:

```
extension ViewController: UITableViewDataSource{
  func tableView(_ tableView: UITableView, numberOfRowsInSection
    section: Int) -> Int {
    return tasks.count
}
func tableView(_ tableView: UITableView, cellForRowAt indexPath:
  IndexPath) -> UITableViewCell {
    let cell = tableView.dequeueReusableCell(withIdentifier:
    "toDoCell")
    let task = tasks[indexPath.row]
    cell?.textLabel?.text = task.name
```

```
        return cell!
    }
}
```

8. The `numberOfRows` function will return the number of tasks we have in the `tasks` list.

9. In `cellForRow`, we get the specific task from the list and bind its name.

10. If you tried to build and run now, you would see an empty table view:

The list is empty as we don't have any tasks yet.

Inserting cells with animation

Now, let's add a button to add a new task to the list.

1. Drag a **Bar Button Item** from **Object Library** and place it to the right of the top navigation bar. Also, change the item type from the **Attribute Inspector** tab to **Add**:

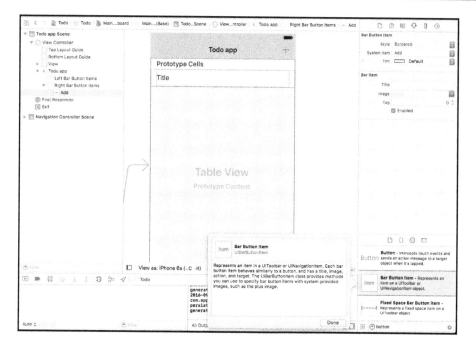

2. Now, open the **Assistant Editor** to link an action method to the bar button item:

```
@IBAction func didClickOnAddButton(_ sender: AnyObject) {
}
```

3. Now, add an IBOutlet to the table view in `ViewController.swift`, as follows:

```
@IBOutlet weak var tasksTableView: UITableView!
```

4. Now, let's add a function that will display a pop-up alert with a text field to ask the user to enter the task name:

```
func displayAlertToAddTask(){
    let title = "New Task"
    let doneTitle = "Create"
    let alertController = UIAlertController(title: title, message:
      "Write the name of your task.", preferredStyle: .alert)
    let createAction = UIAlertAction(title: doneTitle, style: .default)
      { (action) -> Void in
        let taskName = alertController.textFields?.first?.text
        let newTask = Task(taskName: taskName!)
        self.tasks.append(newTask)
        self.tasksTableView.insertRows(at: [IndexPath(row:
          self.tasks.count - 1, section: 0)], with: .top)
```

```
    }
    alertController.addAction(createAction)
    createAction.isEnabled = false
    self.currentCreateAction = createAction
    alertController.addAction(UIAlertAction(title: "Cancel", style:
     .cancel, handler: nil))
    alertController.addTextField { (textField) in
        textField.placeholder = "Task Name"
        textField.addTarget(self, action: #selector(ViewController
        .taskNameFieldDidChange(textField:)) ,
        for: .editingChanged)
    }
    self.present(alertController, animated: true, completion: nil)
}
```

5. The function will display a popup with a text field. Before proceeding, let's add the following property at the top of your file:

```
var currentCreateAction:UIAlertAction?
```

6. Now, let's build and run the app; click on the add button:

7. Once you type something in the text field, the **Create** button will be enabled to add the task. Once the task is created, it will be inserted into the table view with an animation:

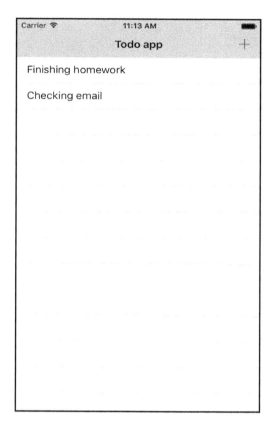

Now, the functionality to add new rows (tasks) is ready.

Removing cells with animation

Now, let's see how to edit the table view to delete cells:

1. In the same way that we added the **Add** button, let's add another **Bar Button Item** beside the **Add** button. Change the item type to **Edit**:

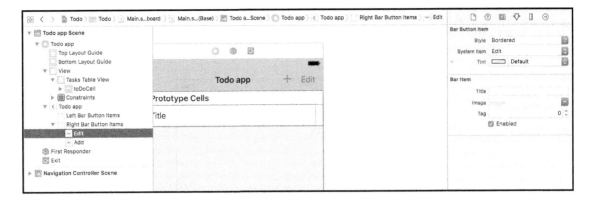

2. Link the **Edit** button action method to the `ViewController.swift`:

```
@IBAction func didClickOnEditButton(_ sender: AnyObject) {
  isEditingMode = !isEditingMode
  self.tasksTableView.setEditing(isEditingMode, animated: true)
}
```

3. At top of the file, add the following property:

```
var isEditingMode = false
```

4. Now, when you click on the **Edit** button, the table view will enter the edit mode.

5. Now, we need to define the actions that will be displayed in the edit mode. In this demo, we need an action to delete the task. Let's override the following function in `UITableViewDelegate`:

```
extension ViewController: UITableViewDelegate{
  func tableView(_ tableView: UITableView, editActionsForRowAt
   indexPath: IndexPath) -> [UITableViewRowAction]? {
    let deleteAction = UITableViewRowAction(style: .destructive,
     title: "Delete") { (deleteAction, indexPath) -> Void in
      //Deletion will go here
      self.tasks.remove(at: indexPath.row)
      tableView.deleteRows(at: [indexPath], with: .fade)
    }
    return [deleteAction]
  }
}
```

6. Now build and run, you will see the edit button and when you click on it, edit mode will be enabled. Clicking on the **Delete** button will remove the cell from the list:

Once the task is deleted, it will be removed from the table with fade animation.

Dragging and dropping to reorder cells

Now, let's implement the reordering of cells:

1. To enable the reordering of cells, you need exactly three steps. The first step is to enable the showing of the reordering control in cells. To do this, just do the following in the `cellForRow` method:

   ```
   cell?.showsReorderControl = true
   ```

2. The second step is to override the `canMoveRowAt` function in the data source:

   ```
   func tableView(_ tableView: UITableView, canMoveRowAt indexPath:
   ```

```
IndexPath) -> Bool {
  return true
}
```

3. This will ask you if the row at the given `indexPath` can be moved or not. As all the rows in our app can be moved, just return `true` for all.

4. The third step is to override the `moveRowAt` function, which is the function that performs the moving in your data model. The data model in our app is the `tasks` array, so we need to swap the values in the array:

```
func tableView(_ tableView: UITableView, moveRowAt sourceIndexPath:
IndexPath, to destinationIndexPath: IndexPath) {
    let taskToMove = self.tasks[sourceIndexPath.row]
    self.tasks.remove(at: sourceIndexPath.row)
    self.tasks.insert(taskToMove, at: destinationIndexPath.row)
}
```

5. Now, let's run the app. In the edit mode, you will see that you can reorder the cells like a charm:

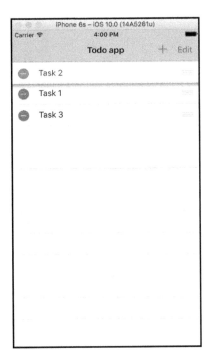

How it works...

In the previous demo, we built a very simple Todo app that allows users to create new tasks (insert rows in table view), delete tasks (delete rows from table view), and change the order of tasks (reorder table view cells).

We started with inserting rows to table view, displayed `UIAlertViewController` with a text field to get the task name first, and added a target method, that is `taskNameFieldDidChange`, to track the changes in the text field. This will give us an opportunity to disable the `Create` button when the field is empty. Once the user clicks on `Create`, we update our data model before triggering the table view to add a new row. So, we inserted the new task object to the tasks array, then we called the `insertRows` function to insert new rows to the table view.

To enable the editing mode in table view, just call `setEditing` and pass true. Then, the `editActionsForRowAt` function in `UITableViewDelegate` will be called to ask you about the edit actions that will be displayed when a user swipes the cell or edits it. In this function, we created an instance of `UITableViewRowAction` for the delete action. The instance takes a completion handler as a parameter to be called once the user clicks on this action. In that case, we remove the task from the data model first and then, call `deleteRows` to delete the rows from the table view.

Lastly, we worked in reordering the rows of table view. Reordering is very simple and straightforward and to accomplish this, you need exactly three steps:

1. Enable showing the reordering control in the `cellForRow` function by calling `cell?.showsReorderControl = true`.
2. Override the `canMoveRowAt` function to tell the table view which row can be moved.
3. Override the `moveRowAt` function to perform the moving in your data model.

There's more...

There's more that we can do in Todo app, such as adding a feature to complete a task. You can add two sections in the screen, one section for open tasks and one for completed ones. In the editing mode, you can add more action in the editing actions with the name `Complete`, which actually marks the task as completed and moves it to a completed section. The user can use the reordering feature to drag the cell from open to the completed section and vice versa. You already know how to do this and have all the information to accomplish that.

6

Animations and Graphics

In this chapter, we will cover the following topics:

- Drawing text, images, lines, rectangles, and gradients
- Animating shapes drawn with UIBezierPath
- Animating UIViews

Introduction

You will not see apps (successful ones) in the App Store using native components without customization. You need your app to look great, unique, appealing, attractive, and eye-catching. This can't be achieved without getting your hands dirty with drawing, animation, and getting the skills of how to build custom components. In this chapter, we will see how to draw simple shapes and animate them. We will draw lines, shapes, and text and animate them. We will see how to add gradients or shadows to shapes. Lastly, we will discuss the various ways of animating views or layers.

Drawing text, images, lines, rectangles, and gradients

In this section, we will learn to draw simple shapes, gradients, or even images. You will need to draw shapes, lines, and images to create custom components or to use in drawing apps where the user can draw shapes and generate an image of their drawing.

Getting ready

When you need to do any custom drawing in iOS, you will need the help of the Core Graphics framework. This framework is full of cool APIs that you can use to build awesome things. In this section, we will see how to use it to sketch custom drawings in custom UIView. In the following demo, we will draw a custom face with eyes, a nose, and a mouth.

How to do it...

1. Create a new Xcode project with the **Single View Application** template with name the Drawing.

2. Now, let's create a new custom view. Create a new class named CustomView, which is a subclass of UIView.

3. Add the following function, where custom drawing will be done. Xcode might create it for you, but it will be commented, so uncomment it if it's already there:

```
override func draw(_ rect: CGRect) {
  // Drawing code
}
```

4. All your custom drawings will be done inside this function. Let's start drawing. We will prepare a background color for our drawing. Add the following code to change the fill color to yellow:

```
override func draw(_ rect: CGRect) {
  // Drawing code
  if let context = UIGraphicsGetCurrentContext(){
      let yellow = UIColor.yellow
      context.setFillColor(yellow.cgColor)
      context.fill(self.bounds)
  }
}
```

5. Now, go to storyboard and drag a **UIView** to the center of the first view controller. Add constraints to center it vertically and horizontally. Change its size to any size you want, for example 300 pixels width and 100 pixels height. The most important step is to change its class from **Identity Inspector** to **CustomView**. Changing the class type will help us write custom code for the custom view. Now, build and run; you will see a screen like this:

6. Now we want to draw a face, we will first draw a black circle at the center of the view. So, update the drawRect method as follows:

```
override func draw(_ rect: CGRect) {
  // Drawing code
  if let context = UIGraphicsGetCurrentContext(){
    let yellow = UIColor.yellow
    context.setFillColor(yellow.cgColor)
    context.fill(self.bounds)
    // Drawing the face.
    context.setStrokeColor(UIColor.black.cgColor)
    context.setLineWidth(3.0)
    let radius = min(rect.width, rect.height) * 0.75 / 2
    context.addArc(center: CGPoint(x: rect.midX, y:
    rect.midY), radius: radius, startAngle: 0,
      endAngle: CGFloat(2 * M_PI), clockwise: false)
  }
}
```

7. Now build and run; you will see the face ready:

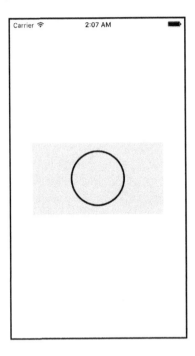

8. Now we want to add eyes; to do this, we will draw two small circles filled with red color. Add the following code after the drawing code for the face:

```
/// Drawing Eyes
// Left eye
context.addArc(center: CGPoint(x: rect.midX - radius /
  2, y: rect.midY - radius / 2), radius: 4.0,
    startAngle: 0, endAngle: CGFloat(2 * M_PI),
      clockwise: false)
// Right eye
context.addArc(center: CGPoint(x: rect.midX + radius /
  2, y: rect.midY - radius / 2), radius: 4.0,
    startAngle: 0, endAngle: CGFloat(2 * M_PI),
      clockwise: false)
// Filling
context.setFillColor(UIColor.red().cgColor)
context.fillPath()
```

9. Now the eyes are ready; build and run and you will see the face like this:

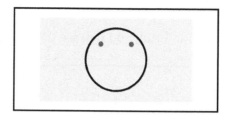

10. Now, let's draw the nose; the nose will be drawn by drawing a rectangle at the center of the circle. To draw the nose, just add the following code after the eye drawing:

```
let noseSize = CGSize(width: 4, height: 16)
context.addRect(CGRect(x: rect.midX - noseSize.width /
    2, y: rect.midY - noseSize.height / 2, width:
    noseSize.width, height: noseSize.height))
```

11. The face will be like this now:

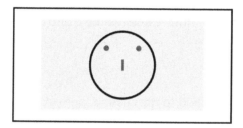

12. Now, let's draw the mouth; the mouth will be controlled later with a slider. Add the following code to draw the mouth:

```
let startPoint = CGPoint(x: rect.midX - radius / 2, y:
rect.midY + radius / 2)
let endPoint = CGPoint(x: rect.midX + radius / 2, y:
    startPoint.y)
context.move(to: startPoint)
let cp = CGPoint(x: rect.midX, y: (startPoint.y) *
    (satisfaction + 0.5))
context.addQuadCurve(to: endPoint, control: cp)
// Filling
context.strokePath()
```

13. Add the following variable at the top of your file:

```
var satisfaction: CGFloat = 0.5
```

14. Now, if you try to build and run, you will see the following:

15. Now we need to control the smile on the face. Go to the storyboard and add a new **UISlider** by dragging it from **Object Library**. Place it below the custom view.

 By default, the minimum value will be 0 and the maximum will be 1. The current one will be 0.5.

16. Link an IBoutlet method to the custom view in ViewController.swift, like this:

```
@IBOutlet weak var customView: CustomView!
```

17. Link an IBAction method to the slider to ViewController.swift to get the changed value of the slider:

```
@IBAction func didChangeSliderValue(_ sender: UISlider) {
    customView.satisfaction = CGFloat(sender.value)
}
```

18. Now we need to update the smile on the face based on the slider value. We have already updated the satisfaction value and need to redraw the face with the new value. Update the property to fire redrawing once the property is changed:

```
var satisfaction: CGFloat = 0.5{
        didSet{
            self.setNeedsDisplay()
        }
}
```

The `setNeedsDisplay` notifies the system that the view needs to be redrawn.

19. If you build and run now, you will see the face with a neutral smile, which corresponds to value 0.5:

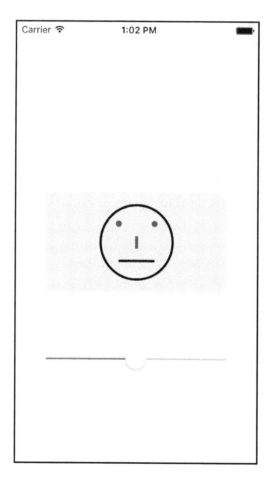

If you tried to change the slider value to 0.8 for example, it would be like this:

However, if you tried to change it to a value below 0.5, it would be like this:

20. Now, let's draw some text that tells us the status of the face (Happy, Sad, Neutral). To do this, let's add the following code at the end of our drawing method:

```
var status: NSString
    switch satisfaction {
    case let val where val == 0.5:
    status = "Neutral"
    case let val where val < 0.5:
      status = "Sad"
    default:
      status = "Happy"
    }
    status.draw(at: CGPoint(x: 5, y: 5), withAttributes:        nil)
```

The text will be drawn at position (5, 5)

21. Now try to build and run; you will see the text drawn at the top left of your custom view:

In the sad mode, it will be like this:

22. Now, let's draw a gradient as a background color for the view. Add the following code after drawing the face:

```
// Gradient color
let colorSpace = CGColorSpaceCreateDeviceRGB()
let componentCount : Int = 2
let components : [CGFloat] = [
    0.0, 1.0, 0.0, 1.0,
    0.0, 0.0, 1.0, 1.0
]
let locations : [CGFloat] = [0, 1.0]
let gradient = CGGradient(colorSpace: colorSpace,
```

```
    colorComponents: components, locations: locations,
      count: componentCount)
    context.drawLinearGradient(gradient!, start:
      CGPoint.zero, end: CGPoint(x: rect.maxX, y:
      rect.maxY), options: .drawsBeforeStartLocation)
```

The code will draw a gradient with green and blue colors:

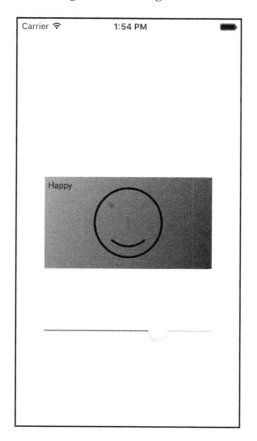

How it works...

We started our demo app by creating a custom UIView and overriding the drawRect
method. This step is the first step that you should start with when you decide to create
custom component or a a custom drawing. Before starting drawing with CoreGraphics,
you have to get a graphics context to draw in; we call the
UIGraphicsGetCurrentContext() function to get the current one.

Then, we fill the custom view with a yellow background color. The fill function takes the area that you want to fill, but you have to set the fill color before by calling `setFillColor`.

In drawing the face, we first set the stroke color to black to draw a black-bordered circle by calling `setStrokeColor`. You can customize the thickness of the line you draw by calling the `setLineWidth` function. To draw a circle in `CoreGraphics`, you have to draw an arc. The arc has a center point, starting/ending angles, and a radius. All of them will define how the system will draw the arc. Here is an image illustrating the factors we just explained:

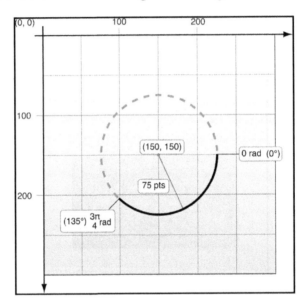

In the same way, wecreated the eyes of the face. We created two circles, but we filled them with red color. For the nose, we have a similar method to `addArc`, which is called `addRect`, to draw a rectangle.

To draw a smile, we used something called a **Quad curve**, which is defined by 3 points: the current point, end point, and a control point. Refer to the following image to get a better understanding of the curve:

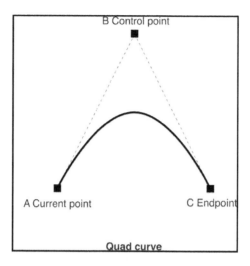

Drawing text is pretty easy. You just need to get your text, call the `draw(at:, withAttributes:)` function and pass the location of the text and attributes. In attributes, you can define customizations such as text color, font, and so on.

To draw a gradient in `CoreGraphics`, you have to create a `CGGradient` instance before drawing. To define a `CGGradient`, you need to provide the following information:

1. **The color space**: It's always been used as RGB color space and you can get that by calling `CGColorSpaceCreateDeviceRGB()`.
2. **Color components**: You can prepare them as an array of color or an array of `CGFloat` values to define the color. Each color needs 4 float values to define the **RGBA (Red, Green, Blue, Alpha)** of the color.
3. **Components count**: This refers to the number of colors that your gradient consists of.

Once you've prepared your gradient, you can notify the context to draw your gradient by calling `drawLinearGradient` and passing the gradient and start/end positions of your gradient.

There's more...

Drawing is such fun, especially if you let your users draw themselves in the app using touches and swipes on the screen. As drawing is something unique, or something you may want to share with your friends or save as a picture, we will see how to construct an image from your drawings and save it in your camera roll:

1. Go to the storyboard and add a new **UIButton** with the text Save. Link an IBAction to ViewController.swift, as follows:

```
@IBAction func didClickOnSaveButton(_ sender: AnyObject) {
   let image = self.customView.screenshot
   UIImageWriteToSavedPhotosAlbum(image, nil, nil, nil)
}
```

2. Now add the following extension at the top of your file:

```
extension UIView{
   var screenshot: UIImage{
     UIGraphicsBeginImageContext(self.bounds.size);
     let context = UIGraphicsGetCurrentContext();
     self.layer.render(in: context!)
     let screenShot =
     UIGraphicsGetImageFromCurrentImageContext();
     UIGraphicsEndImageContext();
     return screenShot!
   }
}
```

3. Before running your app, we need to define why we need to save photos in camera roll in the Info.plist file. Add the NSPhotoLibraryUsageDescription key to the Info.plist file and type any description.
4. Now build and run; you will see the image saved in your Photos app.

Animating shapes drawn with UIBezierPath

In iOS, you can use UIBezierPath to draw vector-based paths and use these paths to create shapes. With UIBezierPath, you can draw lines, curves, ovals, ellipses, and any complex shapes by combining them with subpaths. In this section, we will see how to create paths with UIBezierPath and build shape layers to animate them.

Getting ready

In the upcoming demo, we will draw a custom circular progress bar that can be animated with a percentage given like 50%, 80%, and so on.

How to do it...

1. Let's create a new Xcode project with the **Single View Application** template with the name `BezierPath`.

2. The circular progress bar will consist of two layers: a fixed layer that will be added as a background for the progress bar and a progressive layer that will be animated.

3. Now let's create a function that creates a circular layer so that we can reuse it for both layers. Add the following function in `ViewController.swift`:

```
private func getShapeLayerForRect(rect:CGRect, strokeColor
    sColor:UIColor) -> CAShapeLayer{
    let radius = rect.width / 2 - progressLineWidth / 2
    let newRect = CGRect(x: progressLineWidth / 2, y:
    progressLineWidth / 2, width: radius * 2, height:
        radius * 2)    let path = UIBezierPath(roundedRect: newRect,
    cornerRadius: radius).cgPath
    let shape = CAShapeLayer()
    shape.path = path
    shape.strokeColor = sColor.cgColor
    shape.lineCap = kCALineCapRound
    shape.lineWidth = progressLineWidth
    shape.fillColor = nil
    return shape
}
```

We created a circular Bezier path and then we created a shape layer, its path coming from the Bezier path we have just created.

4. Now, let's add the fixed and progressive layer in the `viewDidLoad` function:

```
override func viewDidLoad() {
    super.viewDidLoad()
    // Do any additional setup after loading the view, typically from a
nib.
    self.view.backgroundColor = UIColor.yellow
    let radius = 100
    let rect = CGRect(x: 0, y: 0, width: radius * 2,
```

```
        height: radius * 2)
let fixedLayer = getShapeLayerForRect(rect: rect,
    strokeColor: UIColor.black.withAlphaComponent(0.5))
fixedLayer.bounds = fixedLayer.bounds.offsetBy(dx: -
    50, dy: -100)
let progressiveLayer = getShapeLayerForRect(rect:
    rect, strokeColor: UIColor.black)
  progressiveLayer.bounds = fixedLayer.bounds
  progressiveLayer.strokeEnd = 0
  self.progressiveLayer = progressiveLayer
  self.view.layer.addSublayer(fixedLayer)
  self.view.layer.addSublayer(progressiveLayer)
}
```

5. Build and run; you will only see the fixed layer. The progressive layer is hidden because it's `strokeEnd` is set to 0:

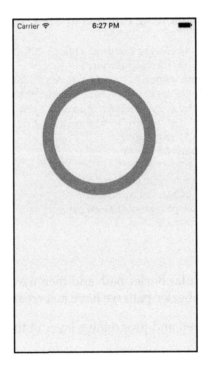

6. Now, let's add a button at the bottom of the screen and, when you click on it, we will animate the progress bar. The action method of the button will be like this:

```
@IBAction func didClickOnDownloadButton(_ sender:
    AnyObject) {
  self.progressiveLayer?.strokeEnd = 0.75
  let animation = CABasicAnimation(keyPath:
      "strokeEnd")
  animation.fromValue = 0
  animation.toValue = 0.75
  animation.duration = 4
  animation.timingFunction =
      CAMediaTimingFunction(name:
        kCAMediaTimingFunctionEaseInEaseOut)
  self.progressiveLayer?.add(animation, forKey:
      "progress")
}
```

7. Now build and run; you will see a view like this:

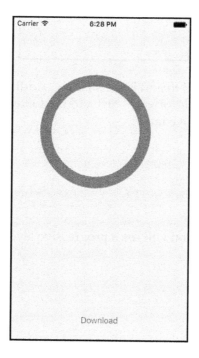

8. Clicking on the button will animate the progress bar to 75%:

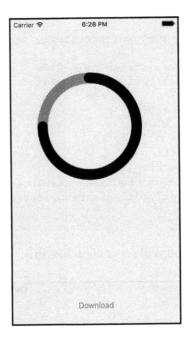

9. The last thing we need to add is the shadow. Adding shadow to shape layers is pretty easy and straightforward. Just add the following lines once you have created your progressive layer:

```
progressiveLayer.shadowColor = UIColor.black.cgColor
progressiveLayer.shadowRadius = 9.0
progressiveLayer.shadowOpacity = 0.9
progressiveLayer.shadowOffset = CGSize(width: 0,
   height: 0)
```

10. Now build and run; you will see a progressive layer with an awesome shadow:

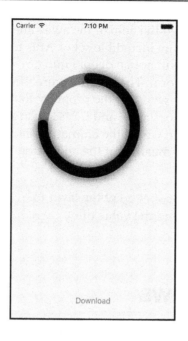

How it works...

In our demo, we started by creating two layers. A fixed layer with the gray as background color and a progressive layer with black as the background color. We first created a circular Bezier path and used this path to define the bath of CAShapeLayer, which is a special type of layer for shapes. This CAShapeLayer has many useful properties; we used the strokeColor property to define the color of stroke path and the lineCap property to define the style of the ending line of the shape, which we set as round corners.

As the progressive layer is hidden at first, we set it's strokeEnd to 0, which means no path is drawn as yet. Later, we will animate the progressive layer by updating its strokeEnd value in animation.

To animate layers in iOS, you need the help of the awesome `CoreAnimation` animation framework. It provides you with an incredible set of APIs to animate layer properties and control the animation style. We will not go deeply into `CoreAnimation` because, if we did; we would need a separate book for it. To create an animation, we created an instance of `CABasicAnimation` using the `keyPath` of the property that you want to animate, which is `strokeEnd`. Then, you set the `fromValue` and `toValue` to animate to; you can animate from any value to any value. Then we set the animation duration and timing function. The timing function `EaseInEaseOut` means that the animation will accelerate at the beginning and then decelerate slowly.

Before we animate, we set the `strokeEnd` of the layer to `0.75` because the animation only animates the presentation layer and the value of `strokeEnd` will fall back to its original value after the animation.

Animating UIViews

In the previous section, we saw how animation works with `CoreAnimation`. iOS provides us with another mechanism for animation, which is the animation with UIKit framework. Animating `UIViews` can be done by animating their layers with `CoreAnimation` or animating the view itself using the animation APIs provided in the UIKit framework, especially in the `UIView` class.

How to do it...

To animate `UIViews`, perform the following steps:

1. Create a new Xcode project with the **Master-Details** template and name it `UIViewAnimation`.
2. The project will be created with the navigation controller template, where you will find a master screen where you can add new cells representing the current time and you will see a details screen when you click on it.
3. We will change the native animation of the navigation controller that you see when you push and pop between view controllers.
4. Now, let's create a new Swift file. Name the file `NavigationFlipAnimator` to create a class with the name `NavigationFlipAnimator` and extend it from `NSObject`.
5. The class will act as an animator for the navigation controller classes. That's why we will let the class conform to the

`UIViewControllerAnimatedTransitioning` protocol.

6. Now, add the following code to `NavigationFlipAnimator`:

```
var navigationOperation:
    UINavigationControllerOperation = .push
func transitionDuration(using transitionContext:
    UIViewControllerContextTransitioning?) ->
      TimeInterval {
   return 0.5
}

func animateTransition(using transitionContext:
    UIViewControllerContextTransitioning) {
  if let fromView =
     transitionContext.viewController(forKey:
       UITransitionContextViewControllerKey.from)?.view,
         let toView =
            transitionContext.viewController(forKey:
              UITransitionContextViewControllerKey.to)?.view{
    let direction: UIViewAnimationOptions =
       self.navigationOperation == .push ?
         .transitionFlipFromLeft :
           .transitionFlipFromRight
    UIView.transition(from: fromView, to: toView,
        duration: 1.0, options: direction, completion: {
          (finished) in
     transitionContext.completeTransition(true)
    })
  }
}
```

7. Now the animator is ready to animate the views. Let's tell the navigation controller to user this animator instead of the native one.

8. Now, open `MasterViewController` to add an extension to it to conform to the `UINavigationControllerDelegate` protocol.

9. Add the following extension at the bottom of the `MasterViewController` file:

```
extension MasterViewController:
    UINavigationControllerDelegate{
  func navigationController(_ navigationController:
     UINavigationController, animationControllerFor
       operation: UINavigationControllerOperation, from
         fromVC: UIViewController, to toVC:
           UIViewController) ->
             UIViewControllerAnimatedTransitioning? {
    let animator = NavigationFlipAnimator()
    animator.navigationOperation = operation
```

```
        return animator
    }
}
```

10. Now go to the `viewDidLoad` function and add the following line of code:

```
self.navigationController?.delegate = self
```

11. Everything is ready; let's run the app now. When you click on a time record, the view will be flipped to display the details like this:

12. Also, once you click on back on the details screen, the view will be flipped to the other way to go back to the master screen:

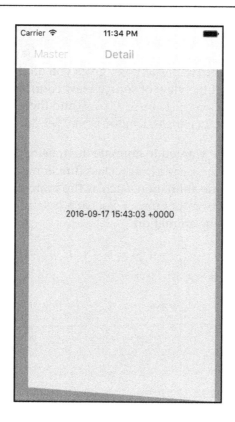

How it works...

UIKit provides us with awesome APIs to animate `UIViews` that are very easy to use and simpler than `CoreAnimation`. In the previous demo, we saw how we provided totally new animation instead of the native animation for `UINavigationController`. To provide custom transitioning animation for view controllers, you have to create a new animator controller. The animator controller can be any class in your app, but the most important thing about this class is that it conforms to the `UIViewControllerAnimatedTransitioning` protocol. This protocol requires you to override two important methods. The first method is `transitionDuration(using transitionContext: UIViewControllerContextTransitioning?)`, which asks you to provide the animation transition time between `FromViewController` and `ToViewController`. In our example, we returned half a second for that animation.

The second function is `animateTransition(using transitionContext:
UIViewControllerContextTransitioning)`, where you have to do your action
transition animation. The `transitionContext` gives you all the information you need to
animate the views. We first got the view of source view controller using the key
`UITransitionContextViewControllerKey.from` and then got the view of destination
view controller using the key `UITransitionContextViewControllerKey.to`.

Once we got the two views, we wanted to animate them using flip animation. The `UIView`
class provides us with a `UIView.transition` class function to perform a transition
between two views with specific animation, such as flip animation. Once we finished the
animation, we called `transitionContext.completeTransition(true)` to let UIKit
know that we had completed the animation.

7
Multimedia

In this chapter, we will cover the following topics:

- Working with audio capabilities
- Playing videos
- Capturing photos and videos
- Using filters with CoreImage

Introduction

Multimedia is one of the important categories that people are interested in with mobile apps. On a daily basis, there is a 100% chance that you might have played music or videos, captured photos or videos, or opened your Photos app to share one of your images on social media or applied some filters to them. When you check the App Store, you can see a huge bunch of apps to edit photos and videos. These apps offer an awesome experience and let you play with your pictures by letting you apply filters or processing images to output incredible, or funny photos. Some of these apps, such as Snapchat, apply filters not only to photos, but also to videos. These kind of apps have had a great impact on multimedia and many apps are competing to provide the most appealing and attractive experience for users.

Working with audio capabilities

In this section, we will talk about audio capabilities in iOS. Now, we have a lot of remarkable APIs to provide the best experience when dealing with audio files. You can play back audio files, record audio, or even recognize speech. In this section, we will see how to play back audio files, record voices, and use the new Speech framework in iOS 10 to recognize speech in many different languages. We will build a demo to see how to work with all of these awesome features.

Getting ready

The only thing that you should be ready with is an audio file to play. In our demo, we are using a sample audio file to play in the app.

How to do it...

1. Create a new Xcode project with the **Single View Application** template and the name `PlayingWithAudio`.
2. Add a `UIButton` method at the top of screen with the title `Play Audio`.
3. Link the action of this button to the `ViewController.swift` file, like this:

   ```
   @IBAction func didClickOnPlayAudio(_ sender: AnyObject) {
   }
   ```

4. Add the following import statement at the top of the file:

   ```
   import AVFoundation
   ```

5. Add the following property to the `ViewController` class for the video player:

   ```
   var player: AVAudioPlayer?
   ```

6. Now let's implement the logic of playing an audio file. Edit the `didClickOnPlayAudio` function to be like this to play an audio file:

   ```
   @IBAction func didClickOnPlayAudio(_ sender: AnyObject) {
       let filePath = Bundle.main.path(forResource: "Song",
         ofType: "mp3")
       let fileURL = URL(fileURLWithPath: filePath!)
       do{
           self.player = try AVAudioPlayer(contentsOf: fileURL)
   ```

```
        self.player?.play()
    }catch{
        print("Error in playing audio file: \(error)")
    }
}
```

The code simply creates a variable that holds the path to the audio file that we want to play. As the file resides in the app bundle, we have used the NSBundle.main.path to get a path to a specific resource. Then, we used AVAudioPlayer to play the file located there.

7. Now build and run the app. After you click on the play button, you should hear the audio file playing in the background.

8. You will note that, once you play the audio, you will not be able to pause it. We will update the function now, check whether the audio is playing to pause it and, if not, it will play it again.

9. First, let's link an IBOutlet to the play button:

```
@IBOutlet weak var playButton: UIButton!
```

10. Now change the didClickOnPlayAudio function as follows:

```
@IBAction func didClickOnPlayAudio(_ sender: AnyObject) {
    if player == nil{
        let filePath = Bundle.main.path(forResource:
            "Song", ofType: "mp3")
        let fileURL = URL(fileURLWithPath: filePath!)
        do{
            self.player = try AVAudioPlayer(contentsOf:
                fileURL)
            self.player?.play()
        }catch{
            print("Error in playing audio file: \(error)")
        }
    }
    else if let player = self.player{
        if player.isPlaying {
            player.pause()
            self.playButton.setTitle("Play Audio", for:
                .normal)
        }
        else{
            player.play()
            self.playButton.setTitle("Pause", for: .normal)
        }
    }
}
```

```
        }
```

We have edited the function to keep tracking the player's status; it doesn't make sense to keep creating an audio player each time and that's why we added a condition to check whether we have a player or not. Then, we check whether the player is playing and, in that case, we pause the audio; otherwise, we play the audio.

Now build and run; you will be able to play and pause the audio.

How it works...

In the previous demo app, we created a very basic audio player to play and pause audio files. Before starting to play any media file, you need to have a file path to the media file. As our file is located in the application's main bundle, we get the file path by calling `Bundle.main.path(forResource: "Song", ofType: "mp3")`. This function returns the file path for any resource file you have in the main bundle; you need to path the file name and file extension. Once you get the file path, iOS provides you with a helper class to play the audio file, which is AVAudioPlayer that plays audio files using the file path URL.

You will note in the example, that we created a strong reference to the audio player by setting it to the player parameter. We did that because the AVAudioPlayer will be deallocated from memory if we don't have a strong reference to it, which causes unexpected results, such as not hearing any playing media files. AVAudioPlayer has a great bunch of helpful APIs to play, pause, or stop the audio. To play, we called the `play()` function, which starts playing the audio from the current position. Then, we checked whether the player was playing any audio to pause it instead of calling play again; the `isPlaying` property indicates whether the audio file is playing or not.

There's more...

In iOS, you can do more and more when dealing with audio capabilities. In this section, we will talk about a new framework introduced in iOS 10, which is the Speech framework.

Recognizing speech

The framework communicates with Apple's servers or tries to use an on-device recognizer if available. We will build a demo to see how to use the framework to recognize speech.

We will use the same project to add the feature of recognizing speech:

1. Open the storyboard and, at the bottom, let's add a button with the title Start Recording with the following constraints:

   ```
   Record.height = 49
   Record.leading = Superview.leading + 16
   Record.trailing = Superview.trailing - 16
   Record.bottom = Superview.bottom - 8
   ```

2. Link IBOutlet and IBAction to the button in the ViewController.Swift file:

   ```
   @IBOutlet weak var recordButton: UIButton!

   @IBAction func didClickOnRecordButton(_ sender: AnyObject) {
   }
   ```

3. Now, let's add a UITextView above the record button with the following constraints:

   ```
   TextView.height = 230
   TextView.leading = Superview.leading + 16
   TextView.trailing = Superview.trailing - 16
   TextView.bottom = Record.top - 8
   ```

4. Now, the UI will look like this:

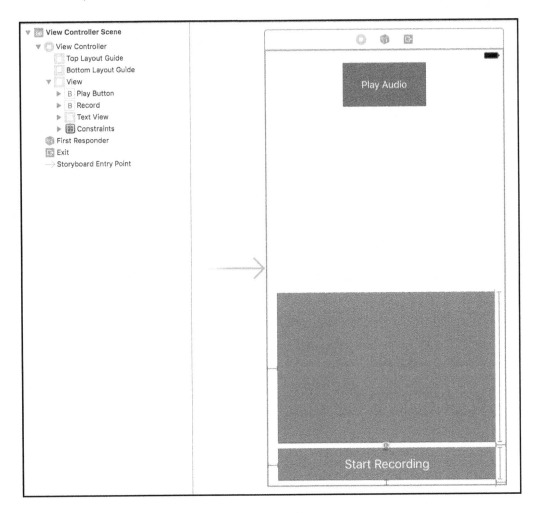

5. Link an IBOutlet in ViewController.swift for the text view:

```
@IBOutlet weak var speechTextView: UITextView!
```

6. Let's get back to ViewController.swift; add the following import statement at the top of the file:

```
import Speech
```

7. Now the `Speech` framework is read. Add the following properties:

```
private var speechRecognizer: SFSpeechRecognizer!
private var recognitionRequest:
    SFSpeechAudioBufferRecognitionRequest!
private var recognitionTask: SFSpeechRecognitionTask!
private let audioEngine = AVAudioEngine()
private let defaultLocale = Locale(identifier: "en-US")
```

8. Add the following extension to make `ViewController` conform to `SFSpeechRecognizerDelegate` protocol:

```
extension ViewController: SFSpeechRecognizerDelegate{
    public func speechRecognizer(_ speechRecognizer:
        SFSpeechRecognizer, availabilityDidChange available:
          Bool) {
      if available {
        self.recordButton.isEnabled = true
        self.recordButton.setTitle("Start Recording", for:
            [])
      } else {
        self.recordButton.isEnabled = false
        self.recordButton.setTitle("Recognition is not
            available", for: .disabled)
      }
    }
}
```

9. Now add the following function to prepare the recognizer:

```
private func prepareRecognizer(locale: Locale) {
    speechRecognizer = SFSpeechRecognizer(locale: locale)!
    speechRecognizer.delegate = self
}
```

The function creates a recognizer instance with a given locale (language).

10. Update the `viewDidLoad` function to call `prepareRecognizer`:

```
override func viewDidLoad() {
  super.viewDidLoad()
  // Do any additional setup after loading the view,
      typically from a nib.
  self.recordButton.isEnabled = false
  prepareRecognizer(locale: defaultLocale)
}
```

11. Now override the `viewDidAppear` function to ask for authorization from the user to access speech recognition:

```
override func viewDidAppear(_ animated: Bool) {
  super.viewDidAppear(animated)
  SFSpeechRecognizer.requestAuthorization { authStatus
      in
  /*
  The callback may not be called on the main thread.
      Add an operation to the main queue to update the
        record button's state.
  */
    OperationQueue.main.addOperation {
      switch authStatus {
        case .authorized:
          self.recordButton.isEnabled = true
        case .denied:
          self.recordButton.isEnabled = false
          self.recordButton.setTitle("User denied
              access to speech recognition", for:
                .disabled)
        case .restricted:
          self.recordButton.isEnabled = false
          self.recordButton.setTitle("Speech
              recognition restricted on this device",
                for: .disabled)
        case .notDetermined:
          self.recordButton.isEnabled = false
          self.recordButton.setTitle("Speech
              recognition not yet authorized", for:
                .disabled)
      }
    }
  }
}
```

12. Now update the `didClickOnRecordButton` function to check, first, whether `audioEngine` is running or not and, based on that, we can stop it or start recording:

```
@IBAction func didClickOnRecordButton(_ sender:
    AnyObject) {
  if audioEngine.isRunning {
    audioEngine.stop()
    recognitionRequest?.endAudio()
    self.recordButton.isEnabled = false
    self.recordButton.setTitle("Stopping", for:
```

```
         .disabled)
  } else {
    try! startRecording()
      self.recordButton.setTitle("Stop recording", for:
        [])
  }
}
```

13. Now let's implement the recording function:

```
private func startRecording() throws {
  // Cancel the previous task if it's running.
  if let recognitionTask = recognitionTask {
    recognitionTask.cancel()
    self.recognitionTask = nil
  }
  let audioSession = AVAudioSession.sharedInstance()
    try
        audioSession.setCategory(AVAudioSessionCategoryRecord)
    try
        audioSession.setMode(AVAudioSessionModeMeasurement)
    try audioSession.setActive(true, with:
      .notifyOthersOnDeactivation)
    recognitionRequest =
      SFSpeechAudioBufferRecognitionRequest()
    guard let inputNode = audioEngine.inputNode else {
      fatalError("Audio engine has no input") }
    guard let recognitionRequest = recognitionRequest
        else { fatalError("Unable to create a
          SFSpeechAudioBufferRecognitionRequest object")
        }
  // Configure request so that results are returned before audio
    recording is finished
  recognitionRequest.shouldReportPartialResults =
      true
  // A recognition task represents a speech recognition session.
  // We keep a reference to the task so that it can be cancelled.
  recognitionTask =
      speechRecognizer.recognitionTask(with:
        recognitionRequest) { result, error in
      var isFinal = false
    if let result = result {
      self.speechTextView.text =
          result.bestTranscription.formattedString
      isFinal = result.isFinal
    }
    if error != nil || isFinal {
      self.audioEngine.stop()
```

```
        inputNode.removeTap(onBus: 0)
        self.recognitionRequest = nil
        self.recognitionTask = nil
        self.recordButton.isEnabled = true
        self.recordButton.setTitle("Start Recording",
            for: [])
    }
}
let recordingFormat =
    inputNode.outputFormat(forBus: 0)
inputNode.installTap(onBus: 0, bufferSize: 1024,
    format: recordingFormat) { (buffer:
        AVAudioPCMBuffer, when: AVAudioTime) in
    self.recognitionRequest?.append(buffer)
}
audioEngine.prepare()
try audioEngine.start()
self.speechTextView.text = "(listening...)"
}
```

14. Before we start running, let's add the following keys to the `Info.plist` file so that users will get a usage description in an alert before using speech and recognition:

```
NSSpeechRecognitionUsageDescription
NSMicrophoneUsageDescription
```

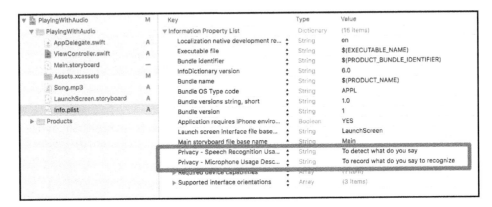

15. Now build and run the app; the app will first ask for permission to access speech recognition:

16. Once you click on the **Start Recording** button, it will ask you for permission to access the **Microphone**:

17. You will note that the messages we set in the `Info.plist` file are being displayed on the alerts.

18. Now the view will be ready for recording:

19. Now, try to speak and you will note that the speech recognizer is working and that what you're saying is displayed on the text view:

As you see, the power of the new framework is that it lets you use the feature to recognize what the user is saying to convert it to text so that you can use it in the app.

We first create an instance of SFSpeechRecognizer using the locale (language) that you want to use. The default locale that we have used in the app is **en-US**, which is the default device locale. You can use a different locale from the currently supported locales, and you can access them by calling SFSpeechRecognizer.supportedLocales().

Then, we asked the user for authorization to access Speech Recognition by calling SFSpeechRecognizer.requestAuthorization, which will tell you the current authorization status.

In the `startRecording()` function, we set a reference to share the audio session by calling `AVAudioSession.sharedInstance()` and then we set the category mode to `AVAudioSessionCategoryRecord` to record and silence any playback audio. Then, we asked for a recognition request by calling `SFSpeechAudioBufferRecognitionRequest`. The request will be used to create a recognition task by calling `speechRecognizer.recognitionTask`. In the completion handler, we will get a reference to `SFSpeechRecognitionTask`, from which you can get the transcript by calling `result.bestTranscription.formattedString`.

Playing videos

In this section, we will deal with videos instead of audio files. Playing videos is one of the most common tasks in iOS apps to play movies, shows, ads, or even tutorials for your app. We will look at the various ways of playing videos and how can you play a video in the picture in picture mode for iPad multitasking.

Getting ready

We will use some sample video files from `http://www.sample-videos.com/`, which has a huge list of different sizes, resolutions, and formats of videos that you can use in testing, and all of them are free.

How to do it...

Perform the following steps to add a video:

1. Let's, as usual, create a new Xcode project with the **Single View Application** template called `PlayingWithVideos`.
2. For the demo app, we have downloaded the 1280 * 720 (5 MB) file to use in testing.

Ensure that you have copied the video file in the Xcode project, as we will read the file from the main bundle.

3. We will use `AVPlayerViewController` to display the video file. To embed a view controller in the `ViewController` screen that we have, we will use the `Container` view that we talked about earlier.

4. Go to **Object Library** and drag a **Container** view with the following constraints:

```
Container.leading = Superview.leading
Container.trailing = Superview.trailing
Container.height = 250
Container.top = Superview.top
```

5. When you add the **Container**, you will note that it's embedding another sample view controller. Remove this as we will embed an `AVPlayerViewController`.

6. Now, from **Object Library**, drag an `AVPlayerViewController` to the storyboard. Then, click on the container and, while holding the ctrl key, drag the **Container** view to the `AVPlayerViewController`. A list like the following will be shown; select **Embed**:

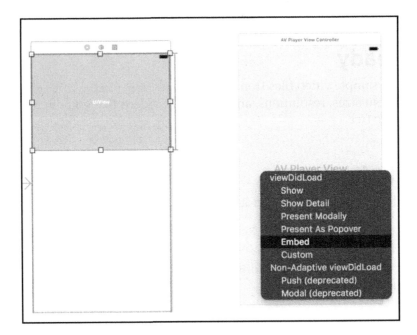

7. The storyboard should look like this when you embed the **AVPlayerViewController**:

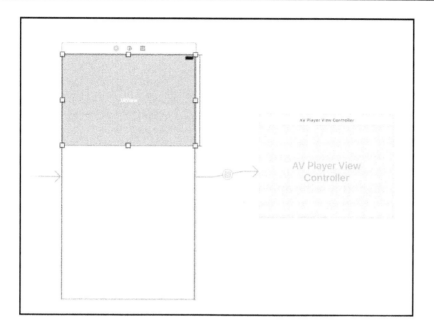

8. Now, select the embed segue and change its identifier to **showPlayerController**.
9. Now let's write some code. Open `ViewController.swift` and add the following import statement:

   ```
   import AVKit
   ```

10. Then, add the following property to have a reference to the player view controller:

   ```
   var playerViewController: AVPlayerViewController?
   ```

11. To get a reference to the view controller once it's been created from the storyboard, we will override the `prepareForSegue` function:

   ```
   override func prepare(for segue: UIStoryboardSegue,
       sender: Any?) {
     if segue.identifier == "showPlayerController"{
       self.playerViewController = segue.destination as?
           AVPlayerViewController
       preparePlayerViewController()
     }
   }
   ```

12. After getting a reference to the player view controller, we will prepare it to play the sample video file by calling `preparePlayerViewContoller()`:

```
private func preparePlayerViewController(){
   if let playerVC = self.playerViewController{
      let itemURL = Bundle.main.url(forResource:
         "SampleVideo", withExtension: "mp4")
      playerVC.player = AVPlayer(url: itemURL!)
   }
}
```

13. Now build and run the app; you will see something like this:

Now the video player has been added and you can use the native controls to pause, resume, seek, navigate to fullscreen, and see the timer. What if we want to display custom controls or embed the video view as a subview?

14. To do this, we will now display the video but in a totally different way --using layers.

15. Add the following property to `ViewController.swift`:

```
var playerLayer: AVPlayerLayer?
```

16. Now let's add a button at the bottom of the screen with the title `Play` and link an `IBAction` to it, like this:

```
@IBAction func didClickPlay(_ sender: AnyObject) {
  if let layer = self.playerLayer{
    layer.player?.play()
  }
}
```

17. Now, add the following function and call it from the `viewDidLoad` function:

```
private func addVideoLayer(){
  let itemURL = Bundle.main.url(forResource:
      "SampleVideo", withExtension: "mp4")
  let player = AVPlayer(url: itemURL!)
  let playerLayer = AVPlayerLayer(player: player)
  playerLayer.position = CGPoint(x: 0, y: 300)
  playerLayer.frame = CGRect(x: 0, y: 300, width:
      self.view.bounds.width, height: 200)
  self.playerLayer = playerLayer
  self.view.layer.addSublayer(playerLayer)
}
```

18. Now build and run; you will see another player layer like this:

How it works...

In the previous demo, we saw the various ways of showing video content in an iOS app. The first way was very easy and provides everything that a user could need to play video, such as pausing, resuming, seeking, or navigating to fullscreen. In this way, we use AVPlayerViewController that we have embedded inside a container view. The only thing that the AVPlayerViewController instance needs is setting the player property to an AVPlayer instance, which we have created with the file URL.

The second way provides more customization and handling for everything. We create a player layer and add it as a sublayer. The AVPlayerLayer class is a special type of CALayer that you can instantiate and add as a sublayer to play video content. The most important thing is to set the frame of the layer before adding it as a sublayer.

There's more...

A new feature has been added in iPad, which is multitasking. With multitasking, you can work with two apps at the same time and both of them will be in the foreground state. We have three types of multitasking in iPad, which will be covered further on.

Slide Over

You can interact with a secondary app without leaving the current app. By swiping left from the right edge of your iPad, you can pick the secondary app to overlay your primary app (in RTL language, the secondary app appears on the left side by swiping from the left edge). Thanks to `Size` classes in the interface builder, you see how the Calendar app in the following screenshot has adapted itself to the new width:

In earlier chapters, we talked about `Size` classes and Xcode 8 gives you the ability to configure your view while being in the size classes mode. In the following screenshot, you will see the different size classes in iPad mode:

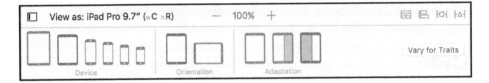

Split View

After you select your secondary app to slide over your primary app in the **Slide Over** mode, you will see a button at the center, outside the **Slide Over** area. When you tap on this button, you tell the system to enter the **Split View** mode. In the **Split View** mode, the two apps will be displayed and adapted to the new width and the user can interact with two apps at the same time:

As you see, a divider will be displayed between the two apps and users can drag this divider to resize the two apps, as follows:

Users can drag the divider all the way to the left to dismiss the secondary app. In the same way, users can drag the divider all the way to the right and, in that case, the primary app will go into the background and the secondary app will become the primary app.

Picture-in-Picture

In the **Picture-in-Picture** (PiP) mode, you can add a floating window of a playing video while the two apps are in the foreground. This video comes from a third app and this app is in the background. If you tried to open our demo app on an iPad, you would see a new button in the video controls that allows you to enter the PiP mode:

When you click on it, the floating window will appear and can be accessed while opening any other app:

Capturing photos and videos

Most of the apps that we develop require a way to pick or capture a photo or video to use in the app. All social networking apps have the feature of sharing images and they ask you to upload images or videos from **Camera** or **Photos**. Similarly for other types of apps such as, chatting, and image editing apps. This kind of feature is very simple to implement in iOS and, in this section, we will see how to provide options for users to pick images.

How to do it...

To provide options for users to pick an image, perform the following steps:

1. Create a new Xcode project with the **Single View Application** template and name it `ImageVideoPicker`.
2. Add a button at the center of the screen to pick a photo or video. Change the title of the button to `Pick photo / video`.
3. Add `IBAction` to the button in `ViewController.swift`, like this:

```
@IBAction func didClickOnPickButton(_ sender:
    AnyObject) {
}
```

4. We will ask the user to choose whether to pick a photo/video from the saved photos or by capturing from camera before picking.
5. First, let's add the code that will display an action sheet to the user to select an action from:

```
@IBAction func didClickOnPickButton(_ sender:
    AnyObject) {
let actionSheetController = UIAlertController(title:
    "Pick media", message: "From where to you want to
      pick your photo or video", preferredStyle:
        .actionSheet)
let photosAction = UIAlertAction(title: "Photos",
    style: .default) { (action) in
  self.openPickerWithSourceType(type:
      .photoLibrary)
}
let cameraAction = UIAlertAction(title: "Camera",
    style: .default) { (action) in
  self.openPickerWithSourceType(type: .camera)
}
let cancelAction = UIAlertAction(title: "Cancel",
    style: .cancel, handler: nil)
  actionSheetController.addAction(photosAction)
  actionSheetController.addAction(cameraAction)
  actionSheetController.addAction(cancelAction)
  self.present(actionSheetController, animated: true,
      completion: nil)
}
```

6. The preceding code will display an action sheet to ask the user to pick an action. The `openPickerWithSourceType` function will be called when a user selects an option. The function will look like this:

```
func openPickerWithSourceType(type:
    UIImagePickerControllerSourceType){
  let imagePickerViewController =
    UIImagePickerController()
  imagePickerViewController.mediaTypes = [kUTTypeImage
    as String, kUTTypeMovie as String]
  imagePickerViewController.sourceType = type
  self.present(imagePickerViewController, animated:
    true, completion: nil)
}
```

7. Now we are almost ready; but if you tried to run the app, it would crash, as some descriptions are yet to be added to the `Info.plist` file.

8. Open the `Info.plist` file and add the following keys with any description you want:

```
<key>NSCameraUsageDescription</key>
<string>Capturing images</string>
<key>NSMicrophoneUsageDescription</key>
<string>Capturing Videos</string>
<key>NSPhotoLibraryUsageDescription</key>
<string>Picking images or videos</string>
```

9. Now try to build and run and then click on the pick button:

10. If you tried to select **Camera** for example, a screen like this would be presented to capture a photo or video:

11. To handle the canceling or choosing of media, you have to conform to
    UIImagePickerControllerDelegate protocol. Add the following line to the
    openPickerWithSourceType function:

    ```
    imagePickerViewController.delegate = self
    ```

12. Now add the following extension to conform to the protocol:

    ```
    extension ViewController: UIImagePickerControllerDelegate,
      UINavigationControllerDelegate{
        func imagePickerController(_ picker:
            UIImagePickerController,
              didFinishPickingMediaWithInfo info: [String : Any])
      {
        print(info)
        let type = info[UIImagePickerControllerMediaType] as!
            String
        if type == kUTTypeImage as String{
          print("Done picking image")
          let image =
              info[UIImagePickerControllerOriginalImage] as!
                UIImage
        }
        else{
          print("Done picking video")
    ```

```
        if let videoURL =
            info[UIImagePickerControllerMediaURL]{
          print(videoURL)
        }
      }
      picker.dismiss(animated: true, completion: nil)
    }
    func imagePickerControllerDidCancel(_ picker:
        UIImagePickerController) {
      picker.dismiss(animated: true, completion: nil)
    }
  }
```

How it works...

Picking images or videos is pretty easy in iOS thanks to the `UIImagePickerController` class; it offers plenty of APIs to customize the source type or media type of the chosen media. In the sample demo that we just created, we first created an instance of `UIImagePickerController` and then we set the media types. The `mediaTypes` property is an array of all media types that you want to deal with; in our demo, we set it to **[kUTTypeImage as String, kUTTypeMovie as String]**, which means images and videos.

After we identified the media types, we set the source type. We have the camera source type, which means we will get photos or videos from the camera. The `photoLibrary` source type allows you to pick an image or a video from the photos library of the device. To get callbacks after capturing or selecting media, we conformed to `UIImagePickerControllerDelegate` protocol. The delegate has two methods: `didFinishPickingMediaWithInfo` and `imagePickerControllerDidCancel`. The first method will be called when the user picks their chosen media and then a dictionary that has all the media information will be passed. The second method will be called when a user clicks on cancel and, in this case, we should dismiss the image picker controller.

Using filters with CoreImage

You may have the Instagram app in your device or will at least have come across a few photo editing apps and edited some photos by applying filters to enhance or change the look of your photo. Nowadays, photo editing apps are invading the App Store with unique and funny filters that you can use. In this section, we will see how to deal with the CoreImage framework to apply built-in filters to photos.

How to do it...

To apply built-in filters to photos, perform the following steps:

1. Create a new Xcode project with the **Single View Application** template and name it `ImageFilters`.

2. Add `UIImageView` with the following constraints and set any image of your choice:

   ```
   ImageView.leading = Superview.leading
   ImageView.trailing = Superview.trailing
   ImageView.top = Superview.top
   ImageView.height = Superview.height * 0.5
   ```

3. Then, add `UIPickerView` with the following constraints:

   ```
   PickerView.leading = Superview.leading
   PickerView.trailing = Superview.trailing
   PickerView.bottom = Superview.bottom
   PickerView.height = Superview.height * 0.5
   ```

4. The design should be something similar to this:

5. Now set the delegate and **data** source of **UIPickerView** to the **ViewController**, like this:

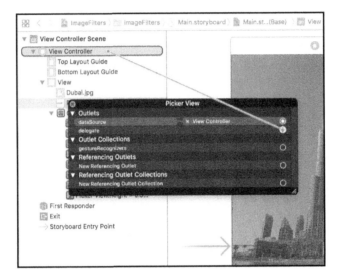

6. Now add the following IBOutlets for the image view and picker view:

```
@IBOutlet weak var imageView: UIImageView!
@IBOutlet weak var filtersPickerView: UIPickerView!
```

7. Let's add the following properties to have reference to the original image and the list of filters:

```
private var filters: [String]!
private var originalImage: UIImage!
```

8. Now let's prepare the filters that we will use in the demo project. Edit the viewDidLoad function like this:

```
override func viewDidLoad() {
    super.viewDidLoad()
    // Do any additional setup after loading the view,
        typically from a nib.
    self.originalImage = imageView.image
    self.filters = prepareFilters()
    self.filters.insert("Original", at: 0)
}
```

9. Here is the prepareFilters() function that will be called to prepare filters:

```
func prepareFilters() -> [String]{
  let names = CIFilter.filterNames(inCategory:
      kCICategoryBuiltIn).filter { (name) -> Bool in
    if ["CININePartStretched", "CININePartTiled",
        "CIDroste"].contains(name){
      return false
    }
    guard let filter = CIFilter(name: name) else
        {fatalError()}
    guard let categories =
        filter.attributes[kCIAttributeFilterCategories]
          as? [String] else {fatalError()}
    if categories.contains(kCICategoryGradient) {
      return false
    }
    let versionStr =
        filter.attributes[kCIAttributeFilterAvailable_iOS] as?
          String ?? "0"
    let versionInt = Int(versionStr)
    if versionInt == 10 {
      return true
    } else {
      return false
    }
  }
  return names
}
```

Here, we prepared a list of filters that are available in iOS. We filter them to pick only the ones that can be directly applied to the image and don't require additional settings that are out of our scope.

10. Filters are now ready; let's implement the picker delegate and data source:

```
extension ViewController: UIPickerViewDelegate{
  func pickerView(_ pickerView: UIPickerView, titleForRow
      row: Int, forComponent component: Int) -> String? {
  return filters[row]
  }
  func pickerView(_ pickerView: UIPickerView,
      didSelectRow row: Int, inComponent component: Int) {
    if row == 0 {
      imageView.image = self.originalImage
      return
    }
    DispatchQueue.global(qos: .default).async {
      self.applyFilter(name: self.filters[row], handler:
          { (image) in
```

```
                    DispatchQueue.main.async(execute: {
                      self.imageView.image = image
                    })
                })
            }
        }
    }
    extension ViewController: UIPickerViewDataSource{
        func numberOfComponents(in pickerView: UIPickerView) ->
            Int {
            return 1
        }
        func pickerView(_ pickerView: UIPickerView,
            numberOfRowsInComponent component: Int) -> Int {
            return self.filters.count
        }
    }
```

11. Now add the following function that will apply the filter:

```
func applyFilter(name: String, handler: ((UIImage?) ->
    Void)) {
    let inputImage = CIImage(image: self.originalImage)!
    guard let filter = CIFilter(name: name) else
        {fatalError()}
    let attributes = filter.attributes
    if attributes[kCIInputImageKey] == nil {
      print("\(name) has no inputImage property.")
      handler(nil)
      return
    }
    filter.setValue(inputImage, forKey: kCIInputImageKey)
    filter.setDefaults()
    // Apply filter
    let context = CIContext(options: nil)
    guard let outputImage = filter.outputImage else {
      handler(nil)
      return
    }
    let size = self.imageView.frame.size
    var extent = outputImage.extent
    let scale: CGFloat!
    // some outputImage has infinite extents
    if extent.isInfinite {
      scale = UIScreen.main.scale
      extent = CGRect(x: 0, y: 0, width: size.width,
          height: size.height)
    } else {
```

```
    scale = extent.size.width /
        self.originalImage.size.width
  }
  guard let cgImage =
      context.createCGImage(outputImage, from: extent)
        else {fatalError()}
  let image = UIImage(cgImage: cgImage, scale: scale,
      orientation: .up)
  handler(image)
}
```

This function applies a filter with a given name to the original image that we have. We first get an instance of `CIFilter` using the given name. We add the original image as attribute input to the filter and then we will get the output, which is the filtered image.

12. Now, everything should be ready; try to play around with the filters. Here is the filtered image when you filter it with the X-Ray filter:

Here's the image when you filter it with the Thermal filter:

How it works...

We started building our demo by creating the UI of the demo by adding `UIImageView` and `UIPickerView` to pick the filter that you want to apply. Building UI will become very straightforward when you master using the storyboard and Autolayout. After creating the UI, we will start loading the filters.

In loading filters, we called the `CIFilter.filterNames(inCategory: kCICategoryBuiltIn)` function, which loads all the filters available in the CoreImage framework and are built-in, not plugged-in. We filtered this list by calling the `filter(name)` function. We first excluded these filters `["CINinePartStretched", "CINinePartTiled", "CIDroste"]` because they are complex and need more configuration; you may have a look at them later. Then, we excluded the filters whose categories have the `kCICategoryGradient` category, as it also needs more configuration with color. Then, we excluded the filters that are not compatible with iOS 10 so that we can display only the new filters that come in iOS 10, and also for simplicity.

Then, we implemented the delegate and data source of `UIPickerView` to display the list of filters and handle the selection of the filter. When a user selects a filter, we get the selected filter and apply it to the image.

To apply a filter, you have to create an instance of the filter using its name, for example, `CIFilter(name: name)` and then set its properties. The most important property is the input image, which is the source image that will be filtered:

```
filter.setValue(inputImage, forKey: kCIInputImageKey)
filter.setDefaults()
```

After setting all the properties and settings, just call let `outputImage = filter.outputImage` to get the output image and update the UI. You will note that the messages

8
Concurrency

In this chapter, we will cover the following topics:

- Using Dispatch queues
- Using Operation queues
- Using Operation subclassing

Introduction

Concurrency is always considered a nightmare for many developers. I partially agree with these developers and think that concurrency is a big headache if you don't understand it well and don't know how to use it. In this chapter, we will try to get your hands dirty working with concurrency. We will understand what's going on and see how simple it is with the APIs that iOS provides, to work with it and harness its capabilities. Concurrency is a two-sided weapon; it can be helpful and harmful at the same time. It helps you to write efficient, fast executing, and responsive apps, but at the same time, misusing it will ruin your app memory. That's why, before starting to write any concurrency code, think why you need concurrency and which API you need to use to solve this problem? In iOS, we have different APIs that can be used. In this chapter, we will talk about two of the most commonly used APIs: Operation and Dispatch queues.

Using Dispatch queues

In this section, we will talk about the most commonly used API in concurrency, which is the **General Central Dispatch (GCD)** queues. GCD manages concurrent code and executes operations asynchronously at the Unix level of the system. GCD manages tasks in something called **queues**. A queue, as we know, is a data structure that manages items in the order of **First In First Out (FIFO)**. Queues in programming mimic the actual queues that we see in real life, which follow the first come first served concept. In Dispatch queues, the tasks in your iOS app will be submitted to queues in the form of blocks of code.

Getting ready

Before getting started with a demo, there is something that needs to be highlighted. Dispatch queues have two types of queues. Let's look at the difference between them in brief:

- **Serial Queues**: In serial queues, you can execute only one task at a time. All the submitted tasks will respect each other and will be executed serially. You can, of course, keep executing tasks concurrently using multiple serial queues. Serial queues can be used when you have a shared resource and you want to guarantee a serialized access to the resource to avoid any race conditions.
- **Concurrent Queues**: In concurrent queues, you can execute multiple tasks in parallel. The tasks (blocks of codes) start in the order in which they are added in the queue. However, their executions occur concurrently and they don't have to wait for each other to start. Concurrent queues guarantee that tasks start in the same order, but you will not know the order of execution, execution time, or the number of tasks being executed at a given point.

When you decide to work with GCD, you have to know which type of queue you will use. You can create any number of serial queues and the system already provides you with a ready-to-use serial queue that is the main Dispatch queue. The main Dispatch queue executes tasks in the application's main thread. All tasks related to updating the app UI and updating the UIViews will be submitted there. Also, because it's a serial queue, only one task will be executed at a time and that's why performing any heavy job in the main queue will block your UI.

On the other hand, in concurrent queues, the system provides us with four concurrent queues, called General Dispatch Queues. The queues are global and can be differentiated only by their priority levels. We have **High**, **Default**, **Low**, and **Background** queues, and they are ordered based on their priorities. The High queue has the highest priority. Let's see how to use the GCD in action.

How to do it...

To see GCD in action, perform the following steps:

1. Create a new Xcode project with the **Single View Application** template and with the name GCDDemo.

2. Open **Main.storyboard** and add an image view with the following constraints in the view controller:

   ```
   ImageView.leading = Superview.leading
   ImageView.top = Superview.top
   ImageView.width = Superview.width * 0.5
   ImageView.height = Imageview.width
   ```

3. In the same way, add 3 more image views to be like a grid:

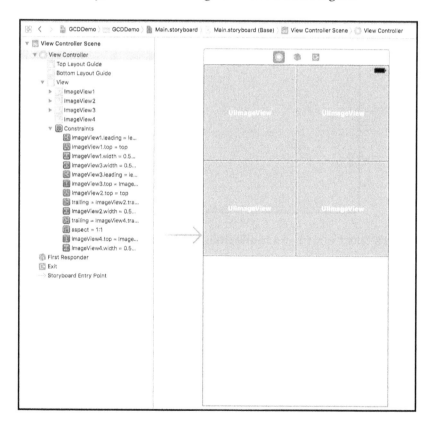

4. Now let's add a slider that will just be used to check whether we did any operation that blocked the UI or not.

5. The final UI of the screen will look like this:

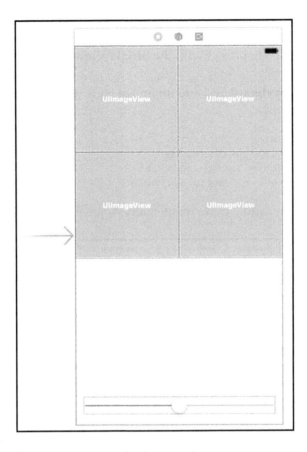

6. Now, let's take IBOutlets to the image views:

```
@IBOutlet weak var imageView1: UIImageView!
@IBOutlet weak var imageView2: UIImageView!
@IBOutlet weak var imageView3: UIImageView!
@IBOutlet weak var imageView4: UIImageView!
```

7. Add the following URLs for the image that we will present:

```
let url1 =
    "http://www.blirk.net/wallpapers/1280x720/kitten-wallpaper-17.jpg"
let url2 =
    "http://www.blirk.net/wallpapers/1280x720/kitten-wallpaper-16.jpg"
let url3 =
    "http://www.blirk.net/wallpapers/1280x720/kitten-wallpaper-15.jpg"
let url4 =
    "http://www.blirk.net/wallpapers/1280x720/kitten-wallpaper-14.jpg"
```

8. Add the `loadImages()` function and call it from `viewDidAppear` to start loading images from the remote server:

```
override func viewDidAppear(_ animated: Bool) {
    super.viewDidAppear(animated)
    loadImages()
}
func loadImages(){
    do{
        let data1 = try Data(contentsOf: URL(string: url1)!)
        self.imageView1.image = UIImage(data: data1)
        let data2 = try Data(contentsOf: URL(string: url2)!)
        self.imageView2.image = UIImage(data: data2)
        let data3 = try Data(contentsOf: URL(string: url3)!)
        self.imageView3.image = UIImage(data: data3)
        let data4 = try Data(contentsOf: URL(string: url4)!)
        self.imageView4.image = UIImage(data: data4)
    }
    catch{
        print(error)
    }
}
```

9. If you try to run the app now, you will see that the slider is blocked till the four images finish loading:

10. Here, we are waiting for the images to load and, when you try to move the slider, it will not respond, as the UI is blocked:

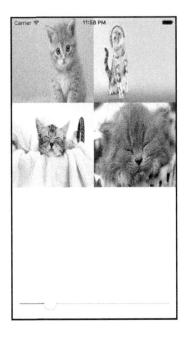

11. To fix issues like these and stop blocking the UI, we will use GCD. Update the `loadImages()` function as follows:

```
func loadImages(){
    let queue = DispatchQueue.global(qos: .default)
    queue.async {
        let data = try! Data(contentsOf: URL(string: self.url1)!)
        DispatchQueue.main.async {
            self.imageView1.image = UIImage(data: data)
        }
    }
    queue.async {
        let data = try! Data(contentsOf: URL(string: self.url2)!)
        DispatchQueue.main.async {
            self.imageView2.image = UIImage(data: data)
        }
    }
    queue.async {
        let data = try! Data(contentsOf: URL(string: self.url3)!)
        DispatchQueue.main.async {
            self.imageView3.image = UIImage(data: data)
        }
    }

    queue.async {
        let data = try! Data(contentsOf: URL(string: self.url4)!)
        DispatchQueue.main.async {
            self.imageView4.image = UIImage(data: data)
        }
    }
}
```

Simply, we created a new queue to perform all heavy tasks inside it without doing it in the main queue. For each `queue.async` call, we submit a task to the queue.

12. Now build and run; you will see that the images are loaded asynchronously and there is no blocking of the UI:

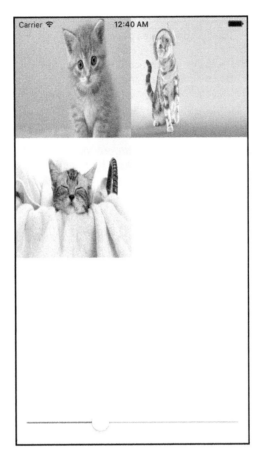

You will be able to play with the slider while loading the images, as all heavy operations have now been moved to separate threads.

How it works...

We started our app by adding four image views so that their images were allocated remotely and needed to be fetched. We first started by loading them in the main thread. As we saw in this approach, the response was terrible, as the UI became unresponsive and got blocked completely. To solve this issue, we used Dispatch queues.

The first thing that you need to get before working with Dispatch queues is a reference to the queue itself. We called `DispatchQueue.global(qos: .default)` to get a reference to one of the global queues, which is the default queue. This queue is a concurrent queue where all tasks will be run concurrently, but in the same order. After you get the reference to the queue, you can submit any task easily by calling `queue.async {}`. Inside the curly braces, you put your block of code that represents the task.

We added four tasks to fetch the four images from the server. Once we get the image from the server in the background, we need to update the UI. We can't update the UI in the default queue because all the UI related tasks should be executed in the main queue. To return to the main queue, you can simply call `DispatchQueue.main.async`, which submits a task to the main thread.

There's more...

In the preceding example, you can use a serial queue instead of a concurrent one. If you want to do that, you have to create a new queue with a type serial queue. You can't use the global serial queue because it's the main queue. To do this, you can do the same thing we did before, but change only the queue reference to be something like this:

```
let serialQueue = DispatchQueue(label: "serialQueue")
```

In this line, you created a new serial queue with name `serialQueue`. In the same way, you can create a new concurrent queue instead of using the global queue, as shown:

```
let concurrentQueue = DispatchQueue(label:"concurrentQueue", attributes:
.concurrent)
```

Using Operation queues

In `OperationQueue`, we will see another way to perform concurrency in iOS. `OperationQueue` is a higher-level abstraction of the queue model; on the other hand, GCD is a lower-level C API. `OperationQueue` is built on top of GCD but in a more object-oriented fashion. In this section, we will perform the same demo but with `OperationQueue`, and we will see how simple it is, as with GCD.

Getting ready

Before getting started with `OperationQueue`, let's talk about how it is different from GCD:

1. It doesn't follow FIFO and doesn't conform to First-In-First-Out like GCD. There are two reasons why it doesn't stick to FIFO. The first one is that you can set an execution priority to the operations so that the operation with the highest priority will be executed first, regardless of its order in the queue. The second thing is that you can add dependency between operations. Dependency means that some operations will not be executed unless some other operation is executed first, as some operation(s) depend on others.

2. All operations are executed concurrently. There are no serial queues in Operation queues and, by default, they run concurrently. Using the feature of dependency in Operation queues, you can do a workaround to support serial queues by adding dependency between each operation so that they wait for each other to be executed.

3. Tasks submitted to the Operation queue should be in the form of an `Operation` class. `Operation` class is an abstract class and you can't use it directly, but you have to use `Operation` subclasses. In iOS, we are provided with two concrete subclasses to `Operation`, which are `BlockOperation` and `InvocationOperation`. You can still create your own operation which extends the `Operation` class and add your custom work as well.

`Operation` class has some advantages that make it a great choice to use instead of GCD. I will list these advantages in brief:

- **Supports dependency**: We have already mentioned this in the preceeding paragraph.
- **Changing the execution priority**: The ability to change the priority of execution by setting the `queuePriority` property to one of these values:

```
public enum QueuePriority : Int {
    case veryLow
    case low
    case normal

    case high

    case veryHigh
}
```

- **Cancellation**: You can cancel any particular operation or ask the queue to cancel all operations inside. When you cancel an operation, the effect will depend on the state of the operation. If the operation has already been executed, the cancellation has no effect. If the operation is being executed, the system will not be able to cancel it, but it will mark the cancelled property to true in the operation. The last state is when the operation is yet to be executed; in that case, the operation will not be executed and will be removed from the queue.
- Each operation has three useful properties that you can use:
  - ready
  - finished
  - cancelled
  - The ready property will be set to true when the operation is about to be executed, the finished property is set to true once the operation execution is done, and the cancelled property will be set to true if the operation is cancelled.
- **Completion block**: A completion block is to be called once the finished property is set to true.

Now you have all the information you need to get started with Operation queues.

How to do it...

To get started with Operation queues, perform the following steps:

1. Let's use the same demo, but Operation queues instead of GCD.
2. Add the following function to call it instead of the loadImages() function:

```
func loadImagesWithOperationQueues(){
  let queue = OperationQueue()
  queue.name = "Loaidng Images Queue"
  let operation1 = BlockOperation {
    let data = try! Data(contentsOf: URL(string:
        self.url1)!)
      OperationQueue.main.addOperation {
      self.imageView1.image = UIImage(data: data)
    }
  }
  queue.addOperation(operation1)
  let operation2 = BlockOperation {
    let data = try! Data(contentsOf: URL(string:
        self.url2)!)
```

```
            OperationQueue.main.addOperation {
              self.imageView2.image = UIImage(data: data)
            }
        }
    queue.addOperation(operation2)
      let operation3 = BlockOperation {
        let data = try! Data(contentsOf: URL(string:
            self.url3)!)
        OperationQueue.main.addOperation {
          self.imageView3.image = UIImage(data: data)
        }
    }
    queue.addOperation(operation3)
    let operation4 = BlockOperation {
      let data = try! Data(contentsOf: URL(string:
          self.url4)!)
      OperationQueue.main.addOperation {
        self.imageView4.image = UIImage(data: data)
      }
    }
    queue.addOperation(operation4)
  }
```

3. Now build and run; similar behavior is observed:

4. Now, let's see how to use the completion handler. Edit the function to set the completionBlock property with a block to be called once the operation is done:

```
func loadImagesWithOperationQueues(){
  let queue = OperationQueue()
  queue.name = "Loaidng Images Queue"
  let operation1 = BlockOperation {
    let data = try! Data(contentsOf: URL(string:
        self.url1)!)
    OperationQueue.main.addOperation {
      self.imageView1.image = UIImage(data: data)
    }
  }
  operation1.completionBlock = {
    print("Image 1 completed")
  }
  queue.addOperation(operation1)
  let operation2 = BlockOperation {
    let data = try! Data(contentsOf: URL(string:
        self.url2)!)
    OperationQueue.main.addOperation {
      self.imageView2.image = UIImage(data: data)
    }
  }
  operation2.completionBlock = {
    print("Image 2 completed")
  }
  queue.addOperation(operation2)
  let operation3 = BlockOperation {
    let data = try! Data(contentsOf: URL(string:
        self.url3)!)
    OperationQueue.main.addOperation {
      self.imageView3.image = UIImage(data: data)
    }
  }
  operation3.completionBlock = {
    print("Image 3 completed")
  }
  queue.addOperation(operation3)
  let operation4 = BlockOperation {
    let data = try! Data(contentsOf: URL(string:
        self.url4)!)
    OperationQueue.main.addOperation {
      self.imageView4.image = UIImage(data: data)
    }
  }
  operation4.completionBlock = {
    print("Image 4 completed")
  }
  queue.addOperation(operation4)
}
```

The code creates a new instance of OperationQueue to submit the heavy tasks to it. Each operation is created as an instance of BlockOperation and is responsible for downloading the image and updating the UI to render the image. To add an operation in the main queue, we call OperationQueue.main.addOperation.

5. Now run the demo. You will see something like this in the console:

```
Image 2 completed
Image 3 completed
Image 1 completed
Image 4 completed
```

How it works...

First, we started to create a new queue to perform our concurrent tasks. The queue can be named by setting the name property. The name works as an identifier to the queue, and it is useful only in debugging or in error handling and helps us to know which queue has the issue. Then, we created four operations using the built-in BlockOperation operation class. Each operation is responsible for downloading an image in the background and updating the UI. Once your operation is ready, you just call the addOperation function, which submits the operation to the block immediately.

 The completionBlock property is very useful to track the completion of any operation you have in the queue.

Next, we have the image from the server and need to update the UI. You can't update the UI inside the created queue as updating the UI needs to be done only in the main queue. To get the main queue, just call OperationQueue.main, which returns reference to the main queue. Once you get the reference, you can submit a new operation with a block to update the image view.

Using Operation subclassing

Most often, operations that you need to perform are better encapsulated in a custom subclass of the `Operation` class. We have already worked with `BlockOperation` in the previous demo, but we saw a lot of redundancy in writing code and it's not customized. In this section, we will implement the same demo and see how we build a custom `Operation` class to perform the task that will be done concurrently.

How to do it...

To build a custom `Operation` class, perform the following steps:

1. In our Xcode project, add a new Swift file with a class, named `ImageDownloader`, which extends the `Operation` class:

2. In the `ImageDownloader.swift` file, add the following code:

```
class ImageDownloader: Operation {
    let imgURL: URL
    var downloadedImage: UIImage?
    init(imageURL: URL) {
        self.imgURL = imageURL
    }
    override func main() {
        if self.isCancelled {
            return
        }
        do{
            let data = try Data(contentsOf: self.imgURL)
            if self.isCancelled {
                return
            }
            self.downloadedImage = UIImage(data: data)
        }
        catch{
            print(error)
        }
    }
}
```

3. Now, go back to `ViewController.swift` and add the following functions:

```
func loadImagesWithCustomOperations(){
  let queue = OperationQueue()
  queue.name = "LoadingQueue"
  self.addImageOperationToQueue(queue: queue, imgURL:
      URL(string: self.url1)!, imageView:
        self.imageView1)
  self.addImageOperationToQueue(queue: queue, imgURL:
      URL(string: self.url2)!, imageView:
        self.imageView2)
  self.addImageOperationToQueue(queue: queue, imgURL:
      URL(string: self.url3)!, imageView:
        self.imageView3)
  self.addImageOperationToQueue(queue: queue, imgURL:
      URL(string: self.url4)!, imageView:
        self.imageView4)
}
func addImageOperationToQueue(queue: OperationQueue,
    imgURL: URL, imageView: UIImageView){
  let imageDownloader = ImageDownloader(imageURL:
      imgURL)
  imageDownloader.completionBlock = {
```

```
         OperationQueue.main.addOperation {
           if let img = imageDownloader.downloadedImage{
             imageView.image = img
           }
         }
       }
     }
     queue.addOperation(imageDownloader)
   }
```

4. Change the call of loading images in `viewDidAppear` like this:

```
override func viewDidAppear(_ animated: Bool) {
    super.viewDidAppear(animated)
    loadImagesWithCustomOperations()
}
```

5. Now build and run; the loading of the images is completed perfectly and concurrently now.

How it works...

In the preceding demo, we saw how we can use the `Operation` subclasses to create custom operations. Using custom operations instead of the native `Operation` classes, such as `BlockOperation`, is highly recommended to encapsulate the logic of the execution. To create a custom `Operation` class, just create a new class that extends the `Operation` class. The code that performs the execution of the operation is added inside the overridden main function. Feel free to add any properties to the custom operation, as we did by adding `imgURL` and `downloadedImage`. You will note that we checked the `isCancelled` property multiple times in the main function. This check is very important to stop any execution or to ignore the execution result if the operation is cancelled.

9
Location Services

In this chapter, we will cover the following topics:

- Detecting user location
- Displaying pins in map view
- Getting directions between locations
- Working with geofencing

Introduction

Every one of us, at some point in time, has used maps on a smartphone to search for locations or get directions. GPS and location services have become a guide in our life that facilitate us to reach any place we want or to search for locations. Now it's not a problem to travel to an unknown place and easily get to your destination without getting lost, thanks to GPS and location services apps. These services are not restricted to mobile phones; they're integrated in most car models that have navigation to help you reach the place you want safely instead of using your smartphone. In this chapter, we will give an introduction and the necessary information you need to use in any map or navigation related app.

Detecting user location

The first thing that a user needs to know when he opens the map is where he is on the map. Getting the user's current location helps him to get an idea of his location, nearby places, and points of interest. To respect the user's privacy, apps can't get the user's current location without the user granting them access to it. In this section, we will see how to ask for permission to access location services and display the current location to the user.

How to do it...

To help display the current location, perform the following steps:

1. Create a new Xcode project with the **Single View Application** template and with name the `LocationServicesDemo`.

2. In the view controller in storyboard, embed the view controller in **Navigation Controller**. Then, drag a navigation item from **Object Library**.

3. Add a **UIBarButtonItem** at the top right of the navigation item with the title `Locate Me`.

4. Now, add a map view that will be responsible for displaying maps. Drag a **MKMapView** from **Object Library** and place it to fill the screen, like this:

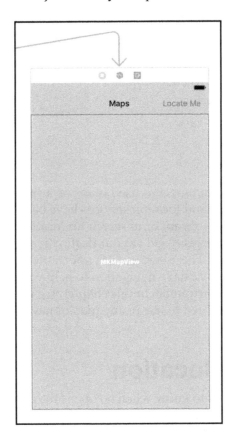

5. Now we need to ask for permission to access the user's location (if we don't have it) when the user clicks on the **Locate Me** button. Once we get permission, we will track the user's location to display a mark on the map.

6. Now link an `IBOutlet` to the map view, like this:

```
@IBOutlet weak var mapView: MKMapView!
```

7. Line an `IBAction` to the button to get the user's location:

```
@IBAction func didClickOnLocateMe(_ sender: AnyObject) {
}
```

8. First, let's add a function that will display an alert message to the user. We will use this function to display messages to enable location services, or a warning if the app is not authorized to get the user's location:

```
func showAlertWithMessage(message: String){
   let alertController = UIAlertController(title:
       "Alert", message: message, preferredStyle: .alert)
   let action = UIAlertAction(title: "Ok", style:
       .cancel, handler: nil)
   alertController.addAction(action)
   self.present(alertController, animated: true,
       completion: nil)
}
```

9. Now update the `didClickOnLocateMe` function to check whether location services are already enabled in the device or not. If not, we will display a warning alert:

```
@IBAction func didClickOnLocateMe(_ sender: AnyObject) {
   if CLLocationManager.locationServicesEnabled(){
     let status =
         CLLocationManager.authorizationStatus()
     switch status {
       case .denied, .restricted:
         self.showAlertWithMessage(message: "Your app is
             not authorized to use access user's location.
             Please check device Settings")
       case .notDetermined:
         self.showLocationPermissionAlert()
       default:
         /// App is authorized to get user location.
         self.startUpdatingLocation()
     }
   }
}
```

```
    else{
      showAlertWithMessage(message: "Location services is
         disabled. Please enable it from Settings.")
    }
  }
```

10. Now go to the top and add the following properties:

```
let locationManager = CLLocationManager()
var myLocationAnnotation: MKAnnotation!
```

11. If location services are already enabled, we will check the authorization status and, based on the status, we will show the permission to start updating. Add the following functions that are responsible for asking for permission or detecting a user's location:

```
func showLocationPermissionAlert(){
  self.locationManager.requestWhenInUseAuthorization()
  self.startUpdatingLocation()
}

func startUpdatingLocation(){
  self.locationManager.delegate = self
  self.locationManager.startUpdatingLocation()
}
```

12. Now add the following extension to make the `ViewController` class conform to the `CLLocationManagerDelegate` protocol:

```
extension ViewController: CLLocationManagerDelegate{
    func locationManager(_ manager: CLLocationManager,
didUpdateLocations locations: [CLLocation]){
        if let location = locations.first{
            if let annotation = self.myLocationAnnotation {
              self.mapView.removeAnnotation(annotation)
            }
            let annotation = MKPointAnnotation()
            annotation.coordinate = location.coordinate
            annotation.title = "You're here!"
            self.myLocationAnnotation = annotation
            self.mapView.addAnnotation(annotation)
        }
    }
}
```

13. Finally, open the `Info.plist` file and add the following key/value:

```
<key>NSLocationWhenInUseUsageDescription</key>
<string>Displaying your current location on map</string>
```

14. Now build and run; the following alert will be shown when you click on the **Locate Me** button and location services are not enabled:

15. Try to enable **Location Services** from the **Privacy** options in the **Settings** app of the device. Now try to click on the **Locate Me** button:

16. Once you click on **Allow**, an annotation will be displayed on the app. When you click on it, it will display a label saying **You're here**:

How it works...

To get access to a user's location, the location services should be enabled in the device so that GPS can keep detecting the current location and update apps. Thus, the first thing we did is check whether location services was enabled or not. The CLLocationManager class has a class method, locationServicesEnabled(), which returns true if its enabled, or false otherwise. If it's not enabled, we prompt the user to enable it from device **Settings**. Before asking for permission to access location, we need to read the current authorization status for our app. The CLLocationManager has another helper class function, authorizationStatus(), which returns one of the following values: notDetermined, restricted, denied, authorizedAlways, or authorizedWhenInUse.

If the status is denied or restricted, we will prompt the user, as the app is not authorized to access location services and he has to check permissions in the device settings. If the status is notDetermined, we will try to ask for permission to access location services. If it's something else, it means that the app is authorized and we can check for updates.

To let the locationManager show the permission alert, we call the following code:

```
self.locationManager.requestWhenInUseAuthorization()
```

It asks the system to request authorization to access the user's location while the app is in use. The usage description should be listed in Info.plist so that the system combines this description in the system alert. Once everything is ready, just call the following code to stay updated with location changes:

```
self.locationManager.delegate = self
self.locationManager.startUpdatingLocation()
```

To stay updated with location changes, the ViewController class should conform to the CLLocationManagerDelegate protocol to be the delegate of the locationManager. The didUpdateLocations function will be called and it will pass the list of locations for the current location. You can choose any location from the array; in the demo, we've used the first one. The location has information, such as coordinates, and this info will be used to display an annotation on the map. Using the coordinates, we will create a new instance of MKPointAnnotation and add it to the map. If we already have an annotation, we will remove it before adding a new one.

Displaying pins in map view

Pins (or annotations) are used to display markers on the map for specific locations, nearby places, or points of interest to the user. Each annotation represents a single point (coordinate) on the map which the user can select to get more information about the location. Annotations have another advantage, which is that they remain fixed on the map while the user scrolls or zooms the map; in that case, the annotation will move appropriately.

Getting ready

Before displaying annotations on the map, we need to highlight some points related to annotations and how they work. To display an annotation on the map, you need two separate things:

- **Annotation object**: An annotation object is any object that conforms to MKAnnotation protocol. This object manages the annotation data, such as coordinate, title, and subtitle.
- **Annotation view**: This is any object derived from MKAnnotationView, which manages the drawing of the visual representation of the annotation object on the map.

The annotation object, as we discussed, is a protocol and any object can conform to this protocol and be used as an annotation. Annotation objects are meant to be lightweight in memory to allow smooth scrolling and zooming to the map, especially if your app deals with a large number of annotations.

In the previous demo, we already displayed a pin to the current location. This pin is one of the standard annotation views that the MapKit framework provides us with. Although MapKit provides some standard views, we can still add our custom annotation views to the map. We will see, in demos, that we don't get involved in adding the annotation view on the map itself; instead, we use the map delegate that passes the view to the map when the map asks for a view to the annotation, then the map will take care of dealing with view hierarchy.

How to do it...

To customize, let's use the demo we built in the previous section. We will see how to customize the annotation object and the annotation view:

1. Add a new Swift source file for a new class, called `CustomAnnotation`.

2. Change the `CustomAnnotation` class to conform to the `MKAnnotation` protocol. The protocol requires you to define the coordinate property so that the map view can understand the location of the annotation:

```
import UIKit
import MapKit
class CustomAnnotation: NSObject, MKAnnotation{
    var coordinate: CLLocationCoordinate2D
    var title: String? = ""
    var color: UIColor
    override init() {
        coordinate = CLLocationCoordinate2D()
        color = UIColor.black
    }
    init(location: CLLocationCoordinate2D) {
        self.coordinate = location
        color = UIColor.black
    }
    init(location:CLLocationCoordinate2D, color: UIColor) {
        self.coordinate = location
        self.color = color
    }
}
```

The `CustomAnnotation` helps you to add any additional information or logic for your annotation.

3. Now, update the current location annotation creation in `ViewController.swift` to use the new custom annotation class:

```
let annotation = CustomAnnotation(location:
    location.coordinate)
annotation.title = "You're here!"
self.myLocationAnnotation = annotation
self.mapView.addAnnotation(annotation)
```

4. When you build and run, you will get the same behavior we got in the previous demo, but the difference is that you're using your custom annotation that can contain additional logic and information.

5. Now, let's customize the annotation view. To customize the annotation view, you need to override the `viewForAnnotation` delegate method of `MKMapViewDelegate`.

6. Add the following extension to override delegate methods:

```
extension ViewController: MKMapViewDelegate{
    func mapView(_ mapView: MKMapView, viewFor annotation:
        MKAnnotation) -> MKAnnotationView? {
      let annotationView = MKAnnotationView(annotation:
          annotation, reuseIdentifier: "CustomView")
      annotationView.image = UIImage(named: "car.png")
      return annotationView
    }
}
```

7. Set the `delegate` to `mapView` in the `viewDidLoad` function:

```
override func viewDidLoad() {
  super.viewDidLoad()
  // Do any additional setup after loading the view,
      typically from a nib.
  self.mapView.delegate = self
}
```

8. Now, when you build and run, the annotation view will be customized like this:

9. Now let's add more annotations to a different country, for example `Finland`, and animate the map to this region. The annotations will be shown using pin annotation.

10. Add the following function to add three annotations and call it from `viewDidAppear`:

```
func addTestAnnotations(){
   let annotation1 = MKPointAnnotation()
   annotation1.coordinate =
      CLLocationCoordinate2D(latitude: 60.1690368,
         longitude: 24.9370282)
   annotation1.title = "Stockmann"
   let annotation2 = MKPointAnnotation()
   annotation2.coordinate =
      CLLocationCoordinate2D(latitude: 60.1716389,

         longitude: 24.9405934)
   annotation2.title = "Aleksis Kiven"
   let annotation3 = MKPointAnnotation()
   annotation3.coordinate =
      CLLocationCoordinate2D(latitude: 60.17152,
         longitude: 24.9366044)
   annotation3.title = "Helsinki Music Centre"
   self.mapView.addAnnotations([annotation1,
      annotation2, annotation3])
   self.mapView.showAnnotations([annotation1,
      annotation2, annotation3], animated: true)
}
```

11. Now, update the `viewForAnnotation` to display the pin views for the three previous annotations:

```
extension ViewController: MKMapViewDelegate{
    func mapView(_ mapView: MKMapView, viewFor annotation:
MKAnnotation) -> MKAnnotationView? {
       if annotation.isKind(of: MKUserLocation.self){
         return nil
       }
       if annotation.isKind(of: CustomAnnotation.self){
         let annotationView = MKAnnotationView(annotation:
            annotation, reuseIdentifier: "CustomView")
         annotationView.image = UIImage(named: "car.png")
         return annotationView
       }else{
         var pinView: MKPinAnnotationView
         if let pv =
            mapView.dequeueReusableAnnotationView
```

```
            (withIdentifier:
            "PinView") as? MKPinAnnotationView{
        pinView = pv
        pinView.annotation = annotation
    }
    else{
        pinView = MKPinAnnotationView(annotation:
            annotation, reuseIdentifier: "PinView")
        pinView.pinTintColor = UIColor.red
        pinView.animatesDrop = true
        pinView.canShowCallout = true
    }
    return pinView
    }
}
}
```

12. Now build and run; you will see annotations like this:

13. As you can see, a view is displayed when you tap on the pin; it's the callout. We will see how to customize it.

14. Update the `viewForAnnotation` function to add the disclosure button and icon to the callout view:

```
func mapView(_ mapView: MKMapView, viewFor annotation:
    MKAnnotation) -> MKAnnotationView? {
  if annotation.isKind(of: MKUserLocation.self){
    return nil
  }
  if annotation.isKind(of: CustomAnnotation.self){
    let annotationView = MKAnnotationView(annotation:
        annotation, reuseIdentifier: "CustomView")
    annotationView.image = UIImage(named: "car.png")
    return annotationView
  }else{
    var pinView: MKPinAnnotationView
    if let pv =
        mapView.dequeueReusableAnnotationView(withIdentifier:
          "PinView") as? MKPinAnnotationView{
      pinView = pv
      pinView.annotation = annotation
    }
    else{
      pinView = MKPinAnnotationView(annotation:
          annotation, reuseIdentifier: "PinView")
      pinView.pinTintColor = UIColor.red
      pinView.animatesDrop = true
      pinView.canShowCallout = true
      let rightButton = UIButton(type:
          .detailDisclosure)
      pinView.rightCalloutAccessoryView = rightButton
      let imageView = UIImageView(image: UIImage(named:
          "icon.png"))
      pinView.leftCalloutAccessoryView = imageView
    }
    return pinView
  }
}
```

15. Override the following function to be notified when a user clicks on the disclosure button on the callout:

```
func mapView(_ mapView: MKMapView, annotationView view:
    MKAnnotationView, calloutAccessoryControlTapped
      control: UIControl) {
  print(view.annotation?.title)
}
```

16. Now build and run; you will see a callout view like this:

How it works...

In the previous demo, we saw how to customize the annotation object and annotation view. We started by customizing the annotation object that acts as a model object for the visual annotation view. Any custom annotation class should conform to the MKAnnotation protocol. The protocol has some properties to override; the mandatory and most important one is the coordinate property, which tells the map where exactly on the map the should annotation be placed. In the custom annotation, you include all additional information about the annotation of any specific logic. You can customize the annotation view by overriding the viewForAnnotation in the MKMapViewDelegate protocol. We changed the current location annotation view to an image view of a black car icon. MapKit provides the MKAnnotationView class to customize the look of the annotation by setting the image to customize annotation image.

Then, we added three different annotations to the map in different countries by passing the coordinates and titles of the three locations. To add any number of annotations to the map at once, you can call the `addAnnotations` function, and to update the visible region on the map to the region that combine these annotations, just call `showAnnotations`. These annotations have been added with the built-in `MKPointAnnotation` annotation class. We used this class to show you how to differentiate between annotations in `viewForAnnotation` so that we can give them different looks.

So, in that function, if the annotation class is of type `MKUserLocation` class, it means this pin is indicating the current user location and we passed nil, which means we don't want it to provide any custom look. If the class is of type `CustomAnnotation` class, we created a new instance of `MKAnnotationView` and we changed the image to the car image. If the annotation class is not one of those, we will display the normal `MKAnnotationView`. Because the annotation views are reusable, we ask the system first to dequeuer a reusable one so we can reuse and we do this by calling `dequeueReusableAnnotationView(withIdentifier: "PinView")`. If there is no available one, we create new one by initializing it like this `MKPinAnnotationView(annotation: annotation, reuseIdentifier: "PinView")` and pass the same identifier.

By default, a standard callout view will be displayed when you click on the annotation that is a view with a label to display the annotation title. The callout can be further customized by adding a subtitle, an image, and a control button. The title and subtitle can be set via the `MKAnnotation` protocol and by implementing these parameters. To set an image and a control button, you can use the `leftCalloutAccessoryView` and `rightCalloutAccessoryView` properties to customize the callout. Once the user taps on the accessory control, the `calloutAccessoryControlTapped` function will be called and the annotation view will be passed to retrieve the annotation and do any specific logic.

Getting directions between locations

Getting directions between source and destination locations is one of the common operations when dealing with maps and navigation apps. You can get directions from the current location or any other source location to the destination location and those directions will differ depending on the mode of transit, such as walking, driving, cycling, or public transport. In this section, we will learn how to get the direction between any two source and destination points and display them on the map.

How to do it...

To get directions between a source and destination, perform the following steps:

1. Let's continue using our demo to add a way to display directions between two locations.
2. Go to storyboard and open our view controller to add a **UIButton** at the bottom with the title `Directions`. Add constraints to the button to stick it to the bottom, like this:

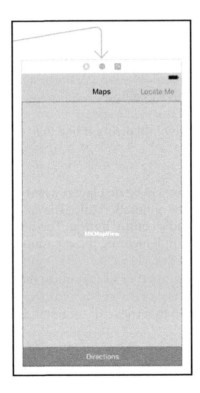

3. Add an `IBAction` function, `didClickOnDirections`, to the button in `ViewController.swift` like this:

```
@IBAction func didClickOnDirections(_ sender:
    AnyObject) {
}
```

4. Update the `didClickOnDirections` function like this:

```
@IBAction func didClickOnDirections(_ sender:
```

```
    AnyObject) {
  let mapItem1 = MKMapItem(placemark:
     MKPlacemark(coordinate:
        CLLocationCoordinate2D(latitude: 60.1690368,
           longitude: 24.9370282)))
  let mapItem2 = MKMapItem(placemark:
     MKPlacemark(coordinate:
        CLLocationCoordinate2D(latitude: 60.1716389,
           longitude: 24.9405934)))
  let directionRequest = MKDirectionsRequest()
  directionRequest.source = mapItem1
  directionRequest.destination = mapItem2
  directionRequest.transportType = .walking
  let directions = MKDirections(request:
     directionRequest)
  directions.calculate { (response, error) in
    if let routingError = error{
      print(routingError)
    }
    else{
      if let directionsResponse = response{
        for route in directionsResponse.routes{
          self.mapView.add(route.polyline, level:
             .aboveRoads)
        }
      }
    }
  }
}
```

The function will create a request to get directions between the two provided locations and then we will display the routes on the map.

5. Finally, we need to override the delegate MKMapViewDelegate function renderedForOverlay, which tells the delegate which renderer to use to style the polyline that will be drawn for the directions:

```
func mapView(_ mapView: MKMapView, rendererFor overlay:
     MKOverlay) -> MKOverlayRenderer {
  if overlay.isKind(of: MKPolyline.self){
    let renderer = MKPolylineRenderer(overlay: overlay)
    renderer.strokeColor = UIColor.blue
    renderer.lineWidth = 5.0
    return renderer
  }
  return MKOverlayRenderer()
}
```

6. Everything is done; let's run the app now. You will see that directions are drawn like this:

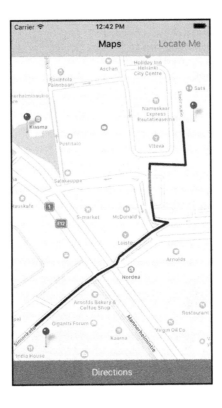

7. Try to change the transport type to automobile instead of walking; new directions will be drawn like this:

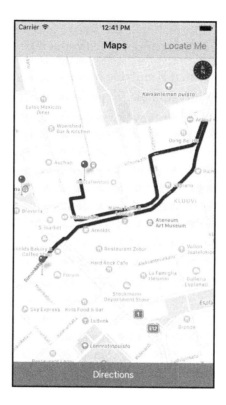

How it works...

Getting directions in MapKit is pretty easy. MapKit provides us with ready-to-use classes to fetch directions between source and destination easily. We started our demo by adding a button to fire the actions of getting the directions between two given locations. Each location should be encapsulated as an instance of MKMapItem.

Once you create the two instances of MKMapItem for the source and destination, you have to create a directions request that is an instance of MKDirectionsRequest. The request acts as a decoder for all the information needed to calculate the directions/routes between two locations. The most important information is the source and destination, then we set the transportType. We have four types supported as yet in iOS:

- The automobile type that is suitable for driving
- The walking type that is suitable for pedestrians
- The transit type that is suitable for public transportation
- The any type that is suitable for any transportation

After the request was ready to be calculated, we created a new instance of the MKDirections class using the request that we had already built. Then, we called the calculate function and passed a completion handler, because this function performs asynchronously and not on the main thread. The request is sent to Apple servers to be processed and, when we get the response, the handler is called by passing two parameters; an instance of MKDirectionsResponse and an error, if one exists.

The response encapsulates all information related to the routes we got from the Apple servers. In the response object, we have the routes property that contains all the routes found between the source and destination. Each object in that array is an instance of the MKRoute class that has all the information about a specific route between source and destination, such as distance, estimated time, transport type, names, and polyline. The polyline is used to draw the route on the map and we did that by calling the addRoute function in the map view. That function will try to draw the route on the map, but it will ask for a renderer class that is responsible for styling or determining the look and feel of the drawn route.

To provide this renderer, we overode the rendererForOverlay function in the MKMapViewDelegate delegate. In the function, we created a new instance of MKPolylineRenderer that is responsible for rendering the polyline. We customized the stroke color of the line to be blue and the line width.

Working with geofencing

Geofencing is the concept of being notified when a user enters or exits a specific region. This region can be, for example, a shopping mall to remind the user to buy some stuff or to perform any specific action. Many apps can be built on the concept of geofencing to remind or notify users when they enter or exit specific regions. In the following demo, we will build a sample screen that allows the user to register a new geofencing to the map. The user will be able to select a location on the map, a diameter of the region, when to be notified (upon entry or upon exit), and some notes to be displayed on the notification that will be fired when the user passes this region.

How to do it...

To add geofencing, perform the following steps:

1. Open storyboard, drag a **UIBarButtonItem** and add it to the right of the **Locate Me** button. Change its type to the **Add** type:

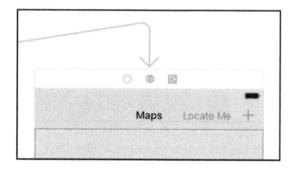

2. Add a new **View Controller** for adding geofencing to the map. Link a **Show segue** from the new plus button to the new view controller.
3. Add a **MKMapView** so that the user can use it to pick a location and make it at the bottom with half of the screen.
4. Add a **UISegmentedControl** at the top of the view with two segments. The first segment will be called **Upon Entry** and the second one **Upon Exit**. This will help the user to choose the type of geofencing.
5. Below the segmented control, drag a label and text field so that users can enter the distance radius of the region.
6. Lastly, add a **UITextView** so that users can write some notes that will be displayed on the notification.

7. The final look of the **View Controller** will be like this:

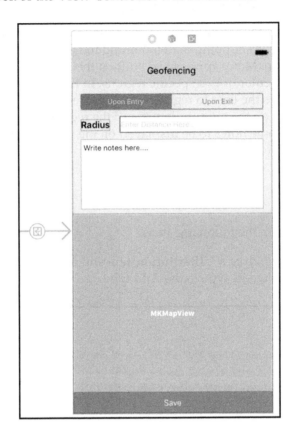

8. Create a new Swift file for a new view controller class, called GeofencingViewController, and then update the class of the newly added view controller from **Identity Inspector**.

9. Now add IBOutlets to the views that we created to read the information when a user clicks on **Save**:

```
@IBOutlet weak var segmentedControl:
    UISegmentedControl!
@IBOutlet weak var distanceTextField: UITextField!
@IBOutlet weak var notesTextView: UITextView!
@IBOutlet weak var mapView: MKMapView!
```

10. Add an `IBAction` to the **Save** button to save geofencing:

```
@IBAction func didClickOnSaveButton(_ sender:
    AnyObject) {
}}
```

11. The first thing we need to do is detect tapping on the map to draw an annotation on the selected location so that a user knows at which location they want to add geofencing.

12. In the `viewDidLoad` function, add the following code to add a `UITapGestureRecognizer` to the map view:

```
override func viewDidLoad() {
  super.viewDidLoad()
  // Tap gesture
  let tapGesture = UITapGestureRecognizer(target: self,
      action:
        #selector(GeofencingViewController.didTapOnMapView
          (gesture:)))
  tapGesture.numberOfTapsRequired = 1
  self.mapView.addGestureRecognizer(tapGesture)
}
```

13. Then, add the following action function that will be called when a user taps on the map to show a pin:

```
func didTapOnMapView(gesture: UITapGestureRecognizer){
  let point = gesture.location(in: self.mapView)
  let coordinate = self.mapView.convert(point,
      toCoordinateFrom: self.mapView)
  if let currentAnnotation = self.currentAnnotation{
    self.mapView.removeAnnotation(currentAnnotation)
  }
  self.currentAnnotation = MKPointAnnotation()
  self.currentAnnotation?.coordinate = coordinate
  self.mapView.addAnnotation(self.currentAnnotation!)
}
```

14. Add the following property to have a reference to the current annotation:

```
var currentAnnotation: MKPointAnnotation?
```

15. Now build and run; you will see that a pin will be dropped at each location you tap on:

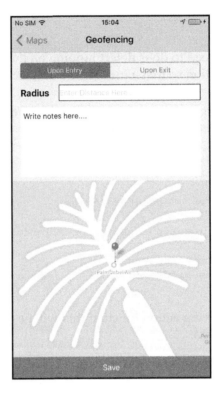

16. Now let's add the code that will draw a circle with the given distance around the pin added. Add the following line of code in `viewDidLoad` to be notified when a user changes the distance:

```
self.distanceTextField.addTarget(self, action:
    #selector(GeofencingViewController.didChangeDistanceValue
    (sender:)), for: .editingChanged)
```

17. Add the following functions to get the change of distance value and draw a circle:

```
func didChangeDistanceValue(sender: UITextField){
  if let text = sender.text{
    let distance = (text as NSString).doubleValue
    showCircleWithRadius(radius: distance)
  }
}
func showCircleWithRadius(radius: Double){
```

```
    if let annotation = self.currentAnnotation{
      if let circle = self.currentCircle{
        self.mapView.remove(circle)
      }
      if radius > 0{
        let circle = MKCircle(center:
            annotation.coordinate, radius: radius)
        self.mapView.addOverlays([circle])
        self.currentCircle = circle
      }
    }
  }
```

18. Add the following property to keep a reference to the current drawn circle:

```
var currentCircle: MKCircle?
```

19. As we learned in the previous section, we need to have a renderer before drawing on the map. So, let's set the delegate in the `viewDidLoad` function and override the following functions:

```
extension GeofencingViewController: MKMapViewDelegate{
    func mapView(_ mapView: MKMapView, rendererFor overlay:
        MKOverlay) -> MKOverlayRenderer {
      let renderer = MKCircleRenderer(overlay: overlay)
      renderer.strokeColor = UIColor.red
      renderer.fillColor =
          UIColor.red.withAlphaComponent(0.6)
      return renderer
    }
    func mapView(_ mapView: MKMapView,
        regionWillChangeAnimated animated: Bool) {
      self.view.endEditing(true)
    }
}
```

20. When you build and run, you will be able to see that the area has been drawn with a red circle, like the following screenshot:

21. Before adding the logic of saving the geofence, let's create a model class to encapsulate all geofence information together. Create a new Swift class with the name GeoFenceData:

```
class GeoFenceData: NSObject {

    var notes:String
    var radius:Double
    var latitude:Double
    var longitude:Double
    var notifyOnEntry:Bool
    var identifier: Int
    init(notes: String, radius: Double, latitude lat:
        Double, longitude lot: Double, notifyOnEntry: Bool,
            identifier: Int) {
        self.notes = notes
        self.radius = radius
        self.latitude = lat
        self.longitude = lot
        self.notifyOnEntry = notifyOnEntry
```

```
        self.identifier = identifier
    }
}
```

22. Now add the following function to register the geofencing to the location services system:

```
@IBAction func didClickOnSaveButton(_ sender:
    AnyObject) {
  if let annotation = self.currentAnnotation, let
      circle = self.currentCircle, let text =
        self.notesTextView.text{
    // All data are available.
    let maxId = UserDefaults.standard.integer(forKey:
        "GeoFenceId")
    UserDefaults.standard.set(maxId + 1, forKey:
        "GeoFenceId")
    let geoFence = GeoFenceData(notes: text, radius:
        circle.radius, latitude:
          annotation.coordinate.latitude, longitude:
            annotation.coordinate.longitude,
              notifyOnEntry:
                self.segmentedControl.
                  selectedSegmentIndex == 0,
                    identifier: maxId)
    startMonitoringGeoFence(fence: geoFence)
  }
}
func regionFromGeoFence(fence: GeoFenceData) ->
    CLCircularRegion{
  let region = CLCircularRegion(center:
      CLLocationCoordinate2DMake(fence.latitude,
        fence.longitude), radius: fence.radius, identifier:
          "Fence\(fence.identifier)")
  region.notifyOnEntry = fence.notifyOnEntry
  region.notifyOnExit = !fence.notifyOnEntry
  return region
}
func startMonitoringGeoFence(fence:GeoFenceData){
  if !CLLocationManager.isMonitoringAvailable(for:
      CLCircularRegion.self) {
    print("Geofencing is not supported on this
        device!")
    return
  }
  if CLLocationManager.authorizationStatus() !=
      .authorizedAlways {
    print("Your geotification is saved but will only be
```

```
              activated once you grant Geotify permission to
                 access the device location.")
        }
      else{
        let region = regionFromGeoFence(fence: fence)
        let locationManager = CLLocationManager()
        locationManager.startMonitoring(for: region)
      }
  }
```

23. Geofencing needs your app to always have permission to have access to the current location. In ViewController, change the calling of the requestWhenInUseAuthorization() function to requestAlwaysAuthorization(). Thus, we can keep the current location updated and trigger a user upon entry into or exit from a specific region.

24. Now, go to the Info.plist file to add a new description for location usage:

```
<key>NSLocationAlwaysUsageDescription</key>
<string>Geofencing</string>
```

25. Now build and run the app. Click on the **Locate Me** button to authorize access to user location, but as always access:

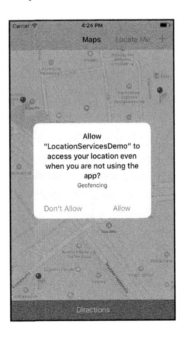

26. Now, if you tried to add any geofence regions, they would be added normally.

27. Open `AppDelegate.swift` to add some code to detect the entry into or exit from a region. Once we are notified of entry/exit of a specific region, we will trigger a local notification to the user with the notes written when registering for geofencing.

28. Add the following import statement to import the `UserNotification` framework:

```
import UserNotifications
```

29. Add the following property to have a reference to `CLLocationManager` to detect the geofencing:

```
let locationManager = CLLocationManager()
```

30. Then, add the following code in the `didFinishLaunchingWithOptions` function:

```
let center = UNUserNotificationCenter.current()
center.requestAuthorization(options: [.alert, .sound])
    { (granted, error) in
  // Check authorization here....
}
self.locationManager.delegate = self
```

31. The preceding code will ask the user to grant us permission to send notifications when we detect any entry or exit for registered regions. If you tried to run, an alert like the following will be presented:

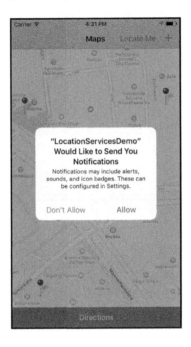

32. In the `AppDelegate` file, implement the `CLLocationManagerDelegate` delegate to be notified when a user enters or exits a registered region:

```
extension AppDelegate: CLLocationManagerDelegate{
    func locationManager(_ manager: CLLocationManager,
        didEnterRegion region: CLRegion) {
      didEnterOrExitRegion(region: region)

    }
    func locationManager(_ manager: CLLocationManager,
        didExitRegion region: CLRegion) {
      didEnterOrExitRegion(region: region)
    }
    func didEnterOrExitRegion(region: CLRegion){
      if let region = region as? CLCircularRegion{
        let id = (region.identifier as
            NSString).integerValue
        let notes = UserDefaults.standard.string(forKey:
            "Fence\(id)")
        if UIApplication.shared.applicationState == .active
```

```
        {
          print("Did Enter/Exit region. Notes: \(notes)")
        }
        else {
        // Otherwise present a local notification
        let content = UNMutableNotificationContent()
        content.body = notes!
        content.sound = UNNotificationSound.default()
        content.title = "Geo fence detection"
        let request = UNNotificationRequest(identifier:
            "Fence\(id)", content: content, trigger: nil)
        UNUserNotificationCenter.current().add(request,
            withCompletionHandler: { (error) in
          print("Did finish sending notification with
              error \(error)")
        })
      }
    }
  }
}
```

33. To test the geofencing, it requires simulating changing the location, which is quite painful and not logical to do manually. That's why in iOS, you can simulate the changing of locations between points by adding **GPX file**.

34. Create a new file and, from resources, choose **GPX file**:

35. Add the locations to the file in the following format. Feel free to add different locations based on your country and the registered geofencing regions:

```
<?xml version="1.0"?>
  <gpx version="1.1" creator="Xcode">
    <!-- Provide one or more waypoints containing a
      latitude/longitude pair. If you provide one waypoint,
      Xcode will simulate that specific location. If you
      provide multiple waypoints, Xcode will simulate
      a route visiting each waypoint.
    -->
    <wpt lat = "25.197197" lon = "55.2721824">
      <name> Burj Khalifa </name>
      <time>2016-11-12T13:18:00Z</time>
    </wpt>
    <wpt lat="25.118107" lon="55.198414">
      <name>Mall Of The Emirates</name>
      <time>2016-11-12T13:18:10Z</time>
    </wpt>
    <wpt lat="25.120555" lon="55.129897">
      <name>Palm Jumeriah</name>
      <time>2016-11-12T13:18:15Z</time>
    </wpt>
  </gpx>
```

36. Now, open the app and add a geofence to a region that will be passed during the route you defined in the GPX file, for example, the following, in the beautiful city of Dubai:

37. After saving the geofencing, put the app in the background and lock the phone or simulator; now click on the simulate button in Xcode, as follows:

38. You will see a notification like the following:

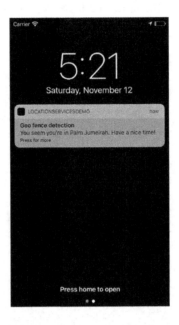

How it works...

In the previous demo, we started our demo by creating a simple UI to add a geofence for a specific region. To mark a specific region, we first let the user add a pin for a location and then type the radius of the region to detect. We used the UITapGestureRecognizer to detect taps on the map view. The didTapOnMapView function will be called once the user taps on the map view. To get the coordinate of the tapped location, you need to do two things. First, get the point of tap on the map view by calling gesture.location(in: self.mapView) and then convert this point to coordinates by calling self.mapView.convert(point, toCoordinateFrom: self.mapView). Then, we can simply add an annotation to that location and remove the old one (if we have one). Then, when the user types the radius, we draw a circle with the given radius and the center is the previously added pin. The MKCircle class is a custom overlay class provided by the MapKit framework for drawing circles. As we saw in the previous section, to customize the look and feel of the overlay, you have to override the rendererForOverlay function. In that function, we created a circle renderer that is an instance of MKCircleRenderer. We changed only the stroke and fill color of the circle.

From a UI perspective, we have done everything. Now we need to do the logic behind the geofencing. First, we create a new class to encapsulate all the information about the GeoFence data; then, we get a unique identifier for our region in the didClickOnSaveButton function. We start the identifiers by value 0 and then we auto-increment the value. The last used value is used in the UserDefaults storage. Also, the notes entered by the user will be saved in UserDefaults so that we can use them in the notification body that we will display to the user. Before starting to monitor the region, we create a region that is an instance of CLCircularRegion and then we ask the location manager to start monitoring this area by calling startMonitoring(for: region).

Geofencing needs your app to have permission to always have access to the current location, even if your app is in background; we need to change the permission to always. In the ViewController class, we already have the code that requests access to the current location. If you checked the code, you will see that we call the requestWhenInUseAuthorization() function that authorizes getting the current location while the app is in use. We changed it to requestAlwaysAuthorization() to keep the current location updated and trigger the user upon entry into or exit from a specific region.

Now, we registered geofencing regions, but we need to be notified once the user enters or exits a region. First, we want to ask the user to grant the app access to send him local notifications. We conformed to the CLLocationManagerDelegate protocol to implement the didEnterRegion and didExitRegion functions. In both cases, we get the notes from UserDefaults using the identifier of the region; if the app is not in the active state, we display a local notification with notes that the user typed when creating the geofencing region.

10
Security and Encryption

VIn this chapter, we will cover the following topics:

- Using Touch ID for user authentication
- Working with Keychain
- Encryption

Introduction

When you deal with user information, there is nothing more important than respecting the user's privacy, and ensuring that all information shared by the user is in a secure location and no one except your system can access it. Right now, we deal with many apps that know a lot or almost everything about life, such as photos, videos, notes, payments, messages, call history, and so on. Dealing with sensitive data recklessly leads to serious problems to your users, and you will be in trouble. Making everything secure is not an easy solution or a final solution. You can say that yes, my app is now secure or no one can hack my system at any rate. All giant companies always do research and tests for their system and are up to date on all new ways to block attacks or to protect users' information. In iOS, users feel more secure than with other systems, thanks to Apple's restrictions for users and developers. It does its best to protect users from any kind of attacks. I can't say it's the best, but it does its best to minimize all kinds of hacking of a user's privacy.

In this chapter, we will learn to utilize the features of iOS, such as using Touch ID to authenticate users or using system keychain to save sensitive information.

Using Touch ID for user authentication

The fingerprint, also known as **Touch ID** from a developer's perspective, is one of the greatest features in new Apple devices, starting from iPhone 5s, and now in modern android devices as well. Most people think that Touch ID is used for authenticating the user to unlock their devices only but, actually in iOS, you can use it to unlock the device, make payments, authenticate a user for apps that support Touch ID, and download apps from the App Store. In this recipe, we will see how to integrate Touch ID in an iOS app to authenticate the user instead of having them retype their credentials.

Getting ready

Apple provides developers with a framework, called **Location Authentication**. It handles all heavy tasks for you and takes care of the access sensor and authenticating the user, and gets back to you with a result and error, if any. It's very important to know that the framework doesn't share or expose any information or data, that represents or has a relation to, a user's fingerprint; this is something that helps developers and users to have no concerns about their sensitive information.

How to do it...

1. Create a new Xcode project with the **Single View Application** template and with name the `TouchIDDemo`.
2. The demo app will be very simple; we will have a screen with only one button that will notify the authenticating user.

3. Open `Main.storyboard` and change the layout of the screen to be as follows:

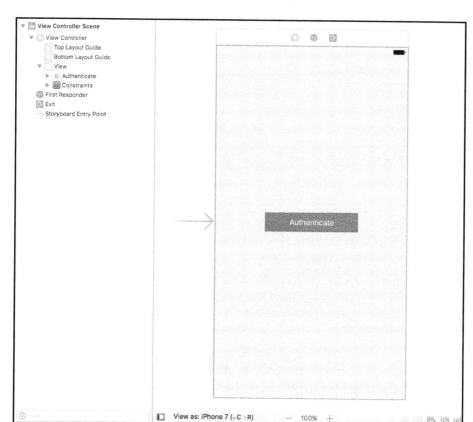

4. Link an `IBAction` to the button in `ViewController.swift` to perform the logic of Touch ID authentication:

```
@IBAction func didClickOnAuthenticate(_ sender: Any) {
}
```

5. Add the following `import` statement at the top of the source file:

```
import LocalAuthentication
```

6. In the `action` function, first add the following code to check whether Touch ID is available on the device:

```
@IBAction func didClickOnAuthenticate(_ sender: Any) {
   let context = LAContext()
   var error: NSError? = nil
   if context.canEvaluatePolicy
     (LAPolicy.deviceOwnerAuthenticationWithBiometrics,
       error: &error){
   }
   else{
       self.showAlertWithMessage(msg: "Touch ID is not
         available in your device!")
   }
}
func showAlertWithMessage(msg: String){
   let alertController = UIAlertController(title:
     "Authentication Error", message: msg,
       preferredStyle: .alert)
   let action = UIAlertAction(title: "OK", style:
     .cancel, handler: nil)
   alertController.addAction(action)
   self.present(alertController,
     animated: true, completion: nil)
}
```

7. Now, we need to update the code to authenticate the user, and display the result based on the response we get from the system:

```
@IBAction func didClickOnAuthenticate(_ sender: Any) {
   let context = LAContext()
   var error: NSError? = nil
   if context.canEvaluatePolicy
     (LAPolicy.deviceOwnerAuthenticationWithBiometrics,
       error: &error){
     context.evaluatePolicy
       (LAPolicy.deviceOwnerAuthenticationWithBiometrics,
         localizedReason: "Please authenticate to proceed
           using the app.", reply: { (success, error) in
             if let error = error{
                 print(error)
                 self.showAlertWithMessage
                   (msg: "A problem has occured
                     while verification.")
             }
             else{
                 if success{
```

```
                        self.showAlertWithMessage(msg:
                            "Thanks!\nYou're the device owner
                              and we can proceed now.")
                }
                else{
                    self.showAlertWithMessage(msg:
                        "Authentication has been failed
                          as you're not the device owner.")
                }
            }
        })
    }
    else{
        self.showAlertWithMessage(msg: "Touch ID is not available in
your device!")
    }
}
```

8. Now, let's run this on the simulator where there is no Touch ID available:

9. Now, run the app on a device that supports Touch ID:

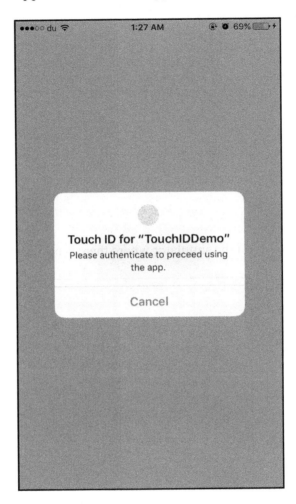

10. Now, try to the run the app on a device where you're not the owner (try another finger):

11. Now, let's try with the authenticated user; the alert will look like this:

How it works...

The demo app is very simple and it didn't require too much code/logic to be added to your project. However, we have integrated a great feature to the app, which is the capability to authenticate your app users with their fingerprint, thanks to Touch ID in Apple devices. This helps you to add a great layer of security to your app and build higher trust between you and the users.

First, we started importing the LocalAuthentication framework, which is responsible for all the magic that has happened to authenticate users. The first step is getting a reference to an instance of LAContext, which has all the APIs we need to communicate with Touch ID. Before doing any logic, we have to ensure that the device the app operates on has Touch ID. The canEvaluatePolicy function does this and returns false if the device doesn't support this kind of policy. If Touch ID is supported, we ask the system to authenticate our user by calling evaluatePolicy, and we pass the reason as a string to the function to be displayed in the Touch ID authentication alert. The function takes a block as a parameter that will be called once authentication first occurs.

The block has two parameters, an error reference if an error occurs, and a flag that indicates the success or failure of user authentication. Based on these parameters, we display the correct message to the user.

Working with Keychain

When you work in mobile apps, you will come across situations when you need to store sensitive information, such as passwords, keys, tokens, user sessions, and so on. Saving this information in plain format or in a place where other apps or the user himself can access it is a disaster and can compromise the security of your device.

From my point of view, I don't recommend saving any sensitive information on the device. However, if you really want to go ahead with it then, before saving anything, you have to ask yourself, do I really need to do this? It's very important to save all important information on the server side and, if it is absolutely necessary to save anything locally, it has to be encrypted and saved in a secure place, such as **Keychain**.

Getting ready

Keychain is a secure place however nothing is 100% secure and you can assume that anyone can hack it and you have to be ready to save sensitive information inside (if needed to). Keychain assures that all data saved in it has to be encrypted first, which is something to relieve you from worrying about encryption/decryption algorithms. Keychain is well-managed to control all the secure data inside, and only privileged apps can access its data.

In this chapter, we will see how simple it is to save/retrieve data in/from Keychain, thanks to the open source Keychain wrappers that are available in GitHub, so that you don't have to get your hands dirty with more logic.

How to do it...

1. Install **Carthage** in your system; you can download the latest version, `Carthage.pkg`, from the following URL:
   `https://github.com/Carthage/Carthage/releases`
2. If you are already familiar with Carthage and it's already installed in your system, you can skip to step 5.

3. To install a third-party library, we will use a dependency manager tool to organize these dependencies. In the previous chapters, we talked about an awesome tool, which is Cocoapods. To learn something new in this chapter, we will install a third-party library using another tool, which is Carthage.

4. Create a new Xcode project with the **Single View Application** template and with name the `KeychainDemo`.

5. Once Carthage is installed, you can start adding frameworks to your project. Create a new file called the Cart file, which lists the frameworks that you will use in your project. With any text editor, create a new file with the name `Cartfile` and save it in the same directory as you have the Xcode project.

6. We will install the following framework in our project: `https://github.com/kishikawakatsumi/KeychainAccess`

7. In most of the good frameworks provided by third parties, the authors usually mention an installation guide that has information about how to install the library with Cocoapods or Carthage. In the library that we mentioned before, you will see that you need to add the following line to `Cartfile` to install the library with Carthage:

```
github "kishikawakatsumi/KeychainAccess
```

8. Open the terminal and navigate to the folder that has the Xcode project and `Cartfile`. Then, run the following command:

```
carthage update
```

9. The terminal should have something like this:

```
Hossams-MacBook-Pro:            hossamghareeb$ cd /Users/hossamghareeb/Documents/                                 'KeychainDemo
Hossams-MacBook-Pro:KeychainDemo hossamghareeb$ carthage update
*** Cloning KeychainAccess
*** Downloading KeychainAccess.framework binary at "v3.0.1"
*** xcodebuild output can be found in /var/folders/rt/zrqm2v3d12d2rz4j0sjc2zvh0000gn/T/carthage-xcodebuild.STDG74.log
```

10. Now, open the Xcode project and choose the **Build Phases** tab:

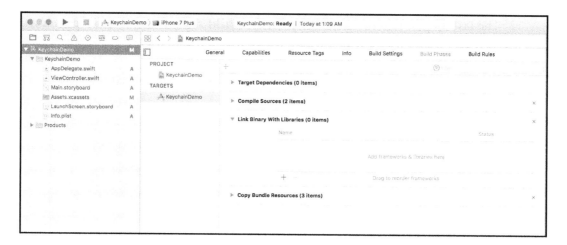

11. Under the **Link Binary With Libraries** section, click on the **+** button and click on **Add Other** from the list. Then, navigate to the `Carthage` folder to select the frameworks that you want to add:

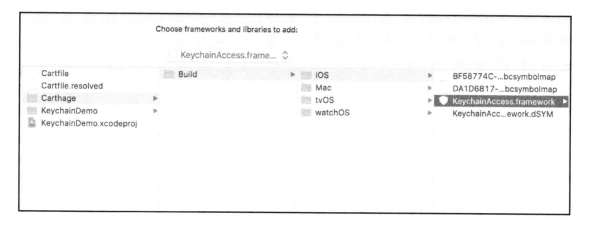

12. The last thing is to add a **Run Script** in the **Build Phases** tab. At the top, you will see a + button; click on it and choose **New Run Script Phase**:

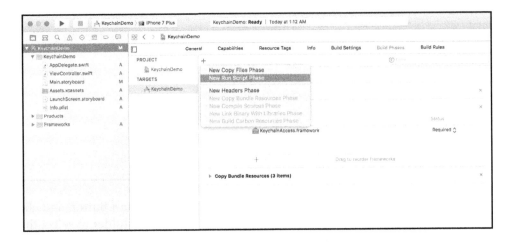

13. Under **Shell**, add the following script:

```
/usr/local/bin/carthage copy-frameworks
```

14. Then, add the following URL under **Input Files**:

```
$(SRCROOT)/Carthage/Build/iOS/KeychainAccess.framework
```

15. The final look for the **Build Phases** tab should be like this:

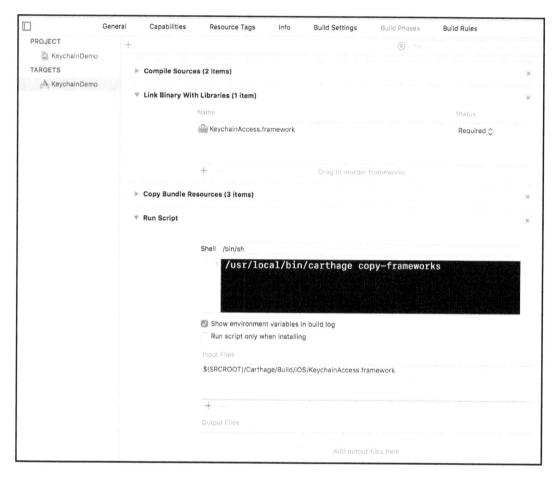

16. Now, clean and build the project and ensure that there are no build errors. If you get any errors, review the preceding steps.

17. In Xcode, select the project from the left panel and click on the **Capabilities** tab. At the **Keychain Sharing** capability, switch it **ON**:

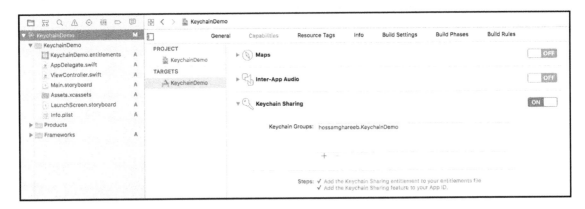

18. Now, open the `ViewController.swift` file and edit it to be like this:

```swift
import UIKit
import KeychainAccess
class ViewController: UIViewController {
    override func viewDidLoad() {
        super.viewDidLoad()
        // Do any additional setup after
          loading the view, typically from a nib.
        let keyChain = Keychain(service:
          "hossamghareeb.keychainDemo")
        keyChain["session"] =
          "13u989843-3232023-323234-fdij8nk-jlk48a-hknut"
        if let session = keyChain["session"]{
            print(session)
        }
    }
}
```

19. When you build and run, you will see that the session value we saved is retrieved and logged in the debug area:

How it works...

In the previous simple demo, we learnt how to deal with Keychain and the most important part is how to install a third-party library with Carthage. Cartfile is where all the magic happens; you can list all the third-party libraries that you want to add to your project and the libraries will be ready for you to add via Xcode with a simple command. After we installed the library, we saw how simple it is to add information, such as user session, to the Keychain and to retrieve it easily with the same key.

Encryption

In the preceding section, we saw how to save data securely in Keychain. However, when saving information in Keychain or wherever you want, there is a chance that someone can get this information and that it will be exposed. The best practice when saving any sensitive information in your app or in the server side is for it to be encrypted and, when someone sees the encrypted message, they should not be able to decrypt it again. In this section, we will talk about the cryptographic hash functions.

Getting ready

The cryptographic hash function is a special type of hash function that can be used in cryptography. Using this hash function, you can convert any data (message) to another form of data (digest). These hash functions are meant to be one way and infeasible to be inverted. Let's see the properties of cryptographic hash functions:

- The same messages always return the same digest (hash value)
- Infeasible to revert the digest and get the message
- Infeasible to find two messages with the same digest

We will not go deeper in to how this works and how to generate the digest from a message. In this section, we will see how to generate hashed values from messages so that we can save them instead of plain text.

We will use the `CommonCrypto` library from Apple, which is a library specialized in encryption and cryptographic hash functions. The library is a low-level library and it will be challenging working with it directly in Swift. Thanks to third-party libraries, there is an awesome Swift wrapper library for `CommonCrypto` that we can use in our demo project:

`https://github.com/soffes/Crypto`

How to do it...

1. Let's continue using our previous demo to add a way to hash the session before saving it to Keychain.

2. As we learnt in the preceding section, let's install the library using Carthage. Add the following to the `Cartfile` we have:

```
github "soffes/Crypto"
```

3. Now, run the `carthage update` command.

4. After the library is installed, open the **Build Phases** tab and add **CommonCrypto.framework** and **Crypto.framework** from the build directory under **Link Binary With Libraries**:

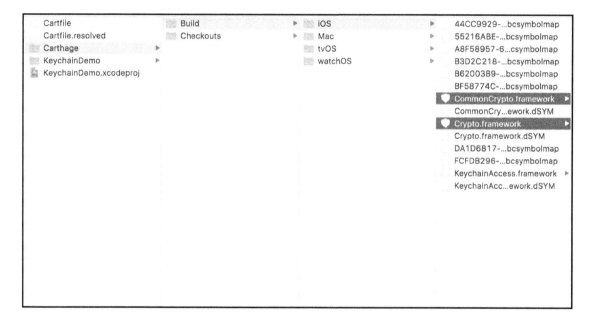

5. Then, add the following links for **Input Files** under the **Run Script** we have:

```
$(SRCROOT)/Carthage/Build/iOS/CommonCrypto.framework
$(SRCROOT)/Carthage/Build/iOS/Crypto.framework
```

6. Now, the final look of the **Build Phases** tab will be like this:

7. In `ViewController.swift`, simply change the code to the following:

```swift
import UIKit
import KeychainAccess
import Crypto

class ViewController: UIViewController {
```

```
override func viewDidLoad() {
  super.viewDidLoad()
  // Do any additional setup
    after loading the view, typically from a nib.
  let session =
    "13u989843-3232023-323234-fdij8nk-jlk48a-hknut"
  let digest =
    HMAC.sign(message: session, algorithm:
      .sha512, key: "secretKey")
  let keyChain = Keychain(service:
    "hossamghareeb.keychainDemo")
  keyChain["session"] = digest
  if let session = keyChain["session"]{
    print(session)
  }
 }
}
```

How it works...

There is not much to be mentioned here. As you see, the encryption is done like a charm using the `CommonCrypto` framework and thanks to the awesome Swift wrapper `Crypto` library. We simply converted the session to digest with the hash function `SHA512` by calling the `HMAC.sign` function and passing the type of algorithm. The library supports different kinds of algorithms that you can play with. I suggest having a good read about all algorithms to understand the differences between them.

11
Networking

In this chapter, we will cover the following topics:

- Using NSURLSession API for network connections
- Parsing JSON data
- Social sharing

Introduction

We don't live offline nowadays. It's become very rare nowadays to find an app that has no backend to pull data from, or to be updated by users' actions or by any data that seems important. A lot of apps have a user system where users can log in and register themselves to use the app. Each user has different information or data that needs to be saved. This data needs a server to be saved in and, pulled from any client side (a mobile app or website). Even if you don't have a server, you need a place to fetch data from and keep your app up to date. You don't need an app update in Appstore if you want to update anything in the data you deal with. Some heavy tasks need a server to take care of them, thanks to its power and its accessibility to all information that the tasks need. Networking is one of the core skills that every iOS developer should know, as it's used heavily in most of the apps these days. In this chapter, we will give you a good introduction to networking in iOS and how to establish connections between your app and the server side. You will also learn how to parse the JSON response received from the server, and how to convert it to model objects that can be used in your app.

Using NSURLSession API for network connections

The NSURLSession is one of the greatest APIs that has been added to the iOS framework and is to be used in setting up connections between the app and the backend, and fetching contents from your server. In this section, we will talk in details (but not boring detail) about NSURLSession: how to deal with it, and what kind of tasks it can do. We will build a demo project for this chapter and, in each section, we will add a feature related to the topic in the project.

Getting ready

With Apple, by default, NSURLSession supports the following URL schemes:

- File Transfer Protocol: (ftp://)
- Hypertext Transfer Protocol: (http://)
- Encrypted Hypertext Transfer Protocol: (https://)
- File URLs: (file://)
- Data URLs: (data://)

In the app, you can have multiple sessions, and each session can deal with a group of related data connections. Any kind of operation done via NSURLSession is called a task, which is a subclass of an abstract class, called NSURLSessionTask. We have three concrete session task classes, as follows:

- **Data tasks**: These are implemented via the NSURLSessionDataTask class. This kind of task is used to fetch data from a server in the form of NSData. Think of it as a HTTP GET request.
- **Upload tasks**: These are implemented via the NSURLSessionUploadTask class. This kind of task is used to upload data (in the form of files) to a server. It supports background uploads while the app is not running. Think of it as a HTTP PUT or POST request.
- **Download tasks**: These are implemented via the NSURLSessionDownloadTask class. This kind of task is used to download data (in the form of files) from a server. It supports background downloading while our app is not running.

All tasks within a URL session follow or share a common session configuration. Each session has a configuration, which defines the connection behavior, timeout, caching, number of simultaneous connections, whether it uses the cellular network or not, and so on. The session configuration is of the type NSURLSessionConfiguration class, and we have three types of configurations:

- **Singleton shared session**: It's a special kind of session, which has no configuration object. It's not a customizable session and can be used only for basic requests. To use this session, you can simply call the sharedSession class method in the NSURLSession class.

- **Default session**: This uses the disk global cache, cookie storage, and credentials. To use this configuration, you can simply call defaultSessionConfiguration in the NSURLSessionConfiguration class.

- **Ephemeral session**: This is like a default session, but it doesn't write caches, cookies, or credentials to disk. You can use this configuration by calling ephemeralSessionConfiguration in the NSURLSessionConfiguration class.

- **Background session**: It lets you upload or download content in the background while your app is not running. You can use this configuration by calling backgroundSessionConfiguration in the NSURLSessionConfiguration class.

Now, you almost have the whole information to let you start working with networking with no hassle. Of course, we can't cover everything, as we don't talk about theory here. You can visit **Apple URL Session Programming Guide,** where they talk in detail about URL session:

https://developer.apple.com/library/content/documentation/Cocoa/Conceptual/URLLoadingSystem/URLLoadingSystem.html. For testing purposes, we will use the following website, which has open source APIs for sample contacts or users we can fetch and display in the app:

https://randomuser.me/

How to do it...

1. Create a new Xcode project with the **Single View Application** template and name it NetworkingDemo.

2. Let's add a button at the center of the screen so that when a user clicks on it, we will trigger a server connection to fetch some data.

3. Open `Main.storyboard` and add a button at the center, with the title **Connect**:

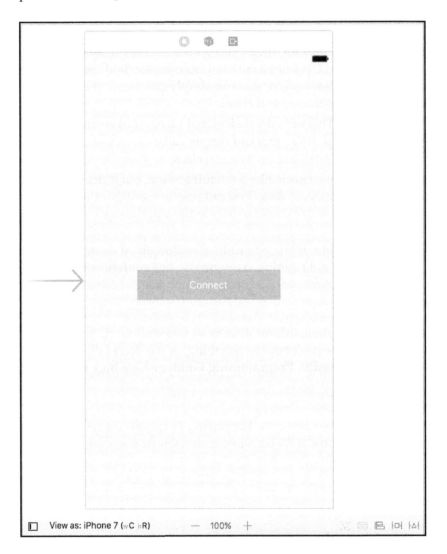

4. Link an `IBOutlet` and `IBAction` to the button, as follows:

```
@IBOutlet weak var connectButton: UIButton!
@IBAction func didClickOnConnectButton(_ sender: Any) {
}
```

5. Now, create a new Swift file for a new class called `ContactsManager`. This class will be responsible for fetching contacts information from a server.

6. In the `ContactsManager.swift` file, add the following code:

```swift
import UIKit

typealias CompletionHandler = (_ success: Bool) -> ()

class ContactsManager: NSObject {
    func fetchContacts(handler: @escaping CompletionHandler){
        let session = URLSession.shared
        let url = URL(string: "https://randomuser.me/api/")
        let dataTask = session.dataTask(with: url!,
          completionHandler: { (data, response, error) in
            if let error = error {
                print(error.localizedDescription)
                handler(false)
            } else if let httpResponse = response as?
              HTTPURLResponse {
                if httpResponse.statusCode == 200 {
                    let responseString = NSString(data:
                      data!, encoding:
                        String.Encoding.utf8.rawValue)
                    print(responseString)
                    handler(true)
                }
                else{
                    handler(false)
                }
            }
        })
        dataTask.resume()
    }
}
```

7. The preceding code will be responsible for fetching data from the server. Return to the `ViewController.swift` file and update the action function, as follows:

```swift
@IBAction func didClickOnConnectButton(_ sender: Any) {
    UIApplication.shared.
      isNetworkActivityIndicatorVisible = true
    let contactsManager = ContactsManager()
    self.connectButton.setTitle
      ("Connecting....", for: .normal)
    self.connectButton.isEnabled = false
    contactsManager.fetchContacts { (success) in
        DispatchQueue.main.async {
```

```
          UIApplication.share
            d.isNetworkActivityIndicatorVisible = false
          print(success)
          self.connectButton.setTitle
            ("Finishing connection", for: .normal)
        }
      }
    }
```

8. Now, build and run the project; the app will look like this:

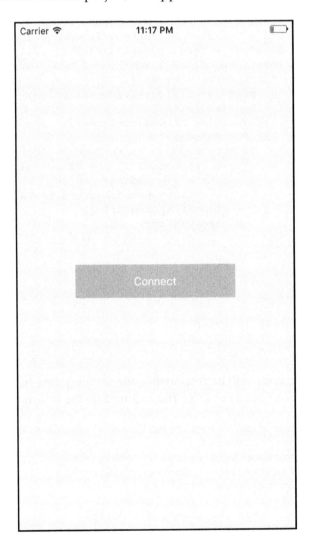

9. Once you click on the **Connect** button, the network indicator will be visible at the top and the title of the button will be changed to **Connecting...**:

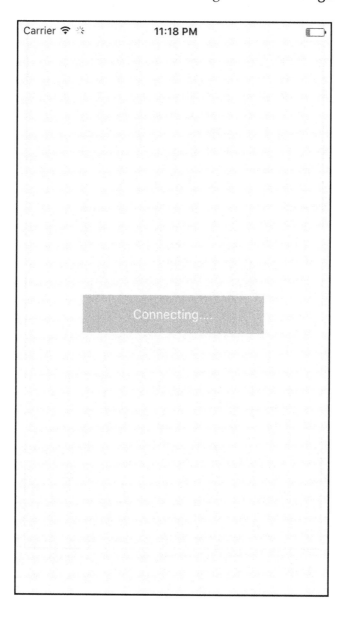

10. After your request gets executed, the screen will look like this:

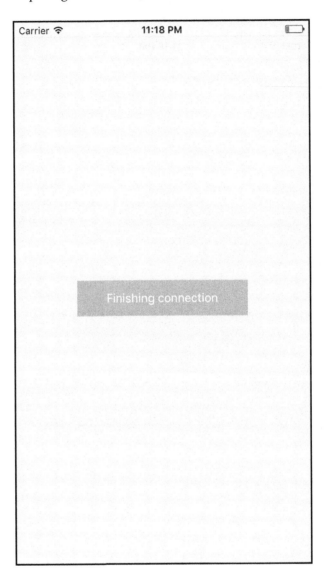

11. In the console, you will see that the JSON response is printed out:

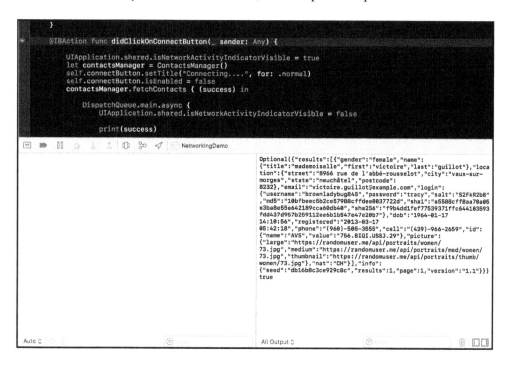

How it works...

We started our simple demo by adding a `UIButton` so that we have something to trigger the connection to the server. To make our app more organized, we created a model class called `ContactsManager`. This manager acts as a model class that is responsible for all interactions with backend and that deals with responses. The model will convert this response to a friendly form of data structure to be used directly in a view controller. At the top of the file, we declared a closure called `CompletionHandler` so that we can use it as a callback when the function finishes the request asynchronously. In the `fetchContacts` function, we first created a `URL` to the server that we wanted to connect to. We get a reference to the default `URLSession` by calling `URLSession.shared`. Once we have a reference to the session that we are going to use, we can simply create a task by calling `session.dataTask(with: url, compltionHandler: )`, which returns a task to be used. The handler will be called given the data returned, the URL response, and an error if anything wrong happened. Calling `dataTask.resume()` will start executing the task.

In the response, we check first whether we have an error, then we log the error and call the handler with a success value equal to false. If we have no error and the response status code is equal to 200, we convert the response data to NSString to log it in a readable way.

In the action function, we started by displaying the network activity to the user so that the user will know that the app performs a connection to the server to fetch data. Then, we changed the title of the button and disabled it so that the user will not be able to click on the button while it performs the API request to the server. An instance of ContactsManager has been created, and the fetchContacts function was called to fetch the contacts. Since the URLSession works asynchronously and not in the main thread, we used DispatchQueue to perform any UI tasks when the function finishes calling the request. We hid the network activity and changed the button title.

Parsing JSON data

In the previous demo, we saw how we can use URLSession to fetch data from an API in the form of a JSON response. In the demo, we printed the JSON response in the console. However, it doesn't work like that in real apps. In normal scenarios, we parse this JSON response and convert it to model objects, which are friendly enough and encapsulated so that they can be used directly in view controllers to update the UI or to do any logic. In this section, we will continue working on the same demo, but instead of printing out the JSON response in the console as we did earlier, we will parse and convert it to model objects and display them on the screen.

Getting ready

The API that we will use is from the randomuser website. Its supports pagination, and you can check it from the following URL:

https://randomuser.me/documentation#pagination

In the API, you will see that we can pass the page parameter to indicate the page index and the results parameter for page size; these two parameters will be used while building our demo to support pagination.

How to do it...

1. Open our previous demo, and get ready to build a UI screen to display a list of contacts that we will fetch from a server.

2. Open `Main.storyboard` and remove the connect button from the screen. While selecting the first view controller, go to **Edit | Embed In | Navigation Controller**.

3. Change the title of the navigation bar on the first screen to **Contacts**.

4. From **Object Library** in the left-hand side panel, drag a `UITableView` and place it on screen, with full width and height. Add constraints to the table view, as follows:

```
TableView.Trailing = Superview.Trailing
TableView.Leading = Superview.Leading
TableView.Top = Superview.Top
TableView.Bottom = Superview.Bottom
```

5. Drag a `UITableViewCell` and place it on the table view. Change its style to **Basic** and change its identifier to `contact`.

6. The final look of your UI will be something like this:

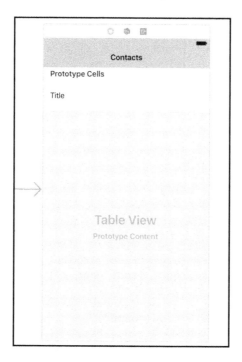

7. Link the `delegate` and `datasource` of the table view to the view controller.
   Link an `IBOutlet` to `ViewController.swift`, as follows:

```
@IBOutlet weak var contactsTableView: UITableView!
```

8. From `ViewController.swift`, remove the code of the `IBOutlet` of the connect
   button and the action function as well.

9. Create a new model `struct` called `Contact`. Open the `Contact.swift` file, and
   paste the following code:

```
import UIKit

enum Gender{
    case Male
    case Female
    case Other
}

extension Gender{
    init(gender: String) {
        switch gender.lowercased() {
        case "male":
            self = .Male
        case "female":
            self = .Female
        default:
            self = .Other
        }
    }
}

struct Contact{
    let gender: Gender
    let title: String
    let firstName: String
    let lastName: String
    let email: String
    let cellPhone: String
    let pictureURLString: String
    init(json: Dictionary<String, Any>) {
        let genderString = json["gender"]
          as? String ?? "other"
        self.gender = Gender(gender: genderString)
        if let name = json["name"]
          as? Dictionary<String, String>{
            self.title = name["title"] ?? ""
            self.firstName = name["first"] ?? ""
```

```
                    self.lastName = name["last"] ?? ""
               }
               else{
                    self.title = ""
                    self.firstName = ""
                    self.lastName = ""
               }
               self.email = json["email"] as? String ?? ""
               self.cellPhone = json["cell"] as? String ?? ""
               if let picture = json["picture"]
                 as? Dictionary<String, String>{
                    self.pictureURLString = picture["large"] ?? ""
               }
               else{
                    self.pictureURLString = ""
               }
          }
     }
```

10. Open the `ContactsManager` class; we need to change the `fetchContacts`
    function to support pagination. We need to pass the page index and the page size
    to the function to be fetched. The function will perform parsing to convert the
    JSON to a list of `Contact` model objects. Now, update the code of
    `ContactsManager.swift` to the following:

```
     typealias CompletionHandler = (_ success: Bool, _ contacts:
[Contact]) -> ()

     class ContactsManager: NSObject {
          func fetchContacts(page:
            Int, pageSize: Int, handler:
              @escaping CompletionHandler){
              let session = URLSession.shared
              let url = URL(string:
              "https://randomuser.me/api/
                ?page=\(page)&results=\(pageSize)")
              let dataTask = session.dataTask(with: url!,
                completionHandler: { (data, response, error) in
                  if let error = error {
                       print(error.localizedDescription)
                       handler(false, [])
                  } else if let httpResponse =
                    response as? HTTPURLResponse {
                       var success = false
                       var allContacts = [Contact]()
                       if httpResponse.statusCode == 200 {
                            if let responseData = data{
```

```
                          do{
                          let json = try
                          JSONSerialization.jsonObject
                          (with: responseData, options:
                          .allowFragments)
                           as! Dictionary<String, Any>
                          let contacts =
                          self.parseContactsJSON(json: json)
                          allContacts.append(contentsOf:
                          contacts)
                                  success = true

                          }
                          catch{
                              print(error)
                          }
                      }
                  }
                  handler(success, allContacts)
              }
          })
          dataTask.resume()
      }
      func parseContactsJSON(json: Dictionary<String, Any>) ->
[Contact]{
          var contacts = [Contact]()
          if let contactsJson = json["results"] as?
            [Dictionary<String, Any>]{
              for contactObj in contactsJson {
                  let contact = Contact(json: contactObj)
                  contacts.append(contact)
              }
          }
          return contacts
      }
  }
```

11. Now, the model classes are ready. Let's go back to the view controller. Add the following properties to the `ViewController` class:

```
var contacts = [Contact]()
var currentPageIndex = 0
let pageSize = 10
var noMorePages = false
var loadingPage = false
```

12. Update the `viewDidLoad` function to request the first page of contacts directly at the beginning:

```
override func viewDidLoad() {
    super.viewDidLoad()
    loadNextPage()
}
```

13. Add the following `loadNextPage` function to be called when you want to load a page of contacts:

```
func loadNextPage(){
    if noMorePages || loadingPage{
        return
    }
    loadingPage = true
    UIApplication.shared.isNetworkActivityIndicatorVisible =
      true
    let contactsManager = ContactsManager()
    contactsManager.fetchContacts(page: currentPageIndex,
      pageSize: pageSize) { (success, newContacts) in
        DispatchQueue.main.async {
          UIApplication.shared
            .isNetworkActivityIndicatorVisible = false
          self.loadingPage = false
          if success{
              if newContacts.isEmpty{
                  self.noMorePages = true
              }
              else{
                  self.contacts
                    .append(contentsOf: newContacts)
                  self.contactsTableView.reloadData()
                  self.currentPageIndex += 1
              }
          }
        }
    }
}
```

14. Finally, add the following extensions to implement the `UITableViewDelegate` and `UITableViewDataSource`:

```
extension ViewController: UITableViewDataSource{
    func tableView(_ tableView: UITableView,
      numberOfRowsInSection section: Int) -> Int {
        return self.contacts.count
```

```
    }
    func tableView(_ tableView: UITableView,
      cellForRowAt indexPath: IndexPath) -> UITableViewCell {
        let cell = tableView.dequeueReusableCell
        (withIdentifier: "contact")
        let contact = self.contacts[indexPath.row]
        cell?.textLabel?.text = "\(contact.title) \
          (contact.firstName) \(contact.lastName)"
        return cell!
    }
}

extension ViewController: UITableViewDelegate{
    func tableView(_ tableView: UITableView, willDisplay
      cell: UITableViewCell, forRowAt indexPath: IndexPath) {
        if indexPath.row == self.contacts.count - 1{
            loadNextPage()
        }
    }
}
```

15. Now, build and run; you will see something like this:

16. Try to scroll down; once you reach the end of the list, a new page will be requested and new contacts will be added.

How it works...

In the previous demo, we requested data from a server in the form of a JSON response, and we parsed this response to model objects. The model objects were displayed on the screen.

We started by updating the UI so that we can have a suitable component to display the list of contacts. UITableView is the perfect component to manage the list of items due to its simplicity and efficiency in managing memory. Since we are going to parse the contacts response to model objects, we started by creating a new model struct called Contact. The JSON representation of the contact object is as follows:

```
{
  "gender": "female",
  "name": {
    "title": "ms",
    "first": "anni",
    "last": "nikula"
  },
  "location": {
    "street": "8026 suvantokatu",
    "city": "pello",
    "state": "north karelia",
    "postcode": 48774
  },
  "email": "anni.nikula@example.com",
  "login": {
    "username": "greenkoala301",
    "password": "band",
    "salt": "u4PVgsmP",
    "md5": "d8ae579ffce37950527e6807ead32ebf",
    "sha1": "ef537ade37a9a8636568ba0f83e173622539637f",
    "sha256":
"2dedbd9f0f5e57685d3854ab3b3cae9a37647449290161a055987649f3fae7fe"
  },
  "dob": "1950-08-23 04:42:36",
  "registered": "2005-04-22 14:29:41",
  "phone": "02-346-115",
  "cell": "045-984-67-74",
  "id": {
    "name": "HETU",
    "value": "1050-680W"
  },
```

```
      "picture": {
        "large": "https://randomuser.me/api/portraits/women/80.jpg",
        "medium": "https://randomuser.me/api/portraits/med/women/80.jpg",
        "thumbnail":
"https://randomuser.me/api/portraits/thumb/women/80.jpg"
      },
      "nat": "FI"
  }
```

For the sake of simplicity, in our demo we care only about simple information (title, first name, last name, e-mail, gender, cell phone, and picture image URL). That's why, in the `Contact` struct, we added only these properties, which we will parse. `Gender` has been represented by `Enum`, as its values are fixed as `Male`, `Female`, and `other`. Other is used for those who do not consider themselves as a male or female or who don't want to expose their gender. Thanks to Swift, we can add an extension to `enum` and define a new initializer based on a string representation of the gender. We can do that because we receive the gender as text from a JSON response. In `Contact struct`, we add an initializer function to `init`, a new contact with a JSON dictionary. The implementation of the `init` function is straightforward, but I want to highlight something. We used the `??` operator heavily, which will set the value of the property to the value that comes after the `??` operator, in case the required value of JSON does not exist or the casting has failed. This will ensure that we always have a valid data-like empty string for string values, or zeros for numeric values.

In the `ContactManager` class, we changed the completion handler definition by adding a new parameter called `contacts`, which is the list that contains the Contact instances after getting a response from backend. The `fetchContacts` function now accepts two additional parameters: the page index and page size. We agreed to load contacts by pagination and not all at once. The function will use new parameters and append them on the URL request so that the server will know which list to return. iOS supports natively the JSON parsing using the `JSONSerialization` class. It has a class function called `jsonObject(with: , options: )`, which returns a dictionary representation for the JSON data. Once we get the dictionary representation of the response, we call a `parseContactsJSON()` function. This function gets the array of dictionaries (each dictionary represents a contact), and for each item, we initialize a new `Contact` model object using the dictionary.

Let's get back to the view controller now. We added some new properties to help us in managing the logic. The `contacts` array holds the current displayed contacts, and each time we get a new page of contacts, we append them to the current list. The `currentPageIndex` integer knows which page we should request when the user reaches the end of the current displayed list. The `pageSize` is a constant (defined by `let`), which tells us how many contacts we should get from a server per page. The `noMorePages` flag is `false`, which means we still have more pages in the server to be requested. However, the question is, how can we know whether there are more pages in the server or not? In our logic, if we receive an empty list from the server when we ask for a page, this means there are no more contacts to be loaded, and the flag will be set to `true`, so we will not load any pages anymore. The `loadingPage` flag indicates that there is a request running to load a page, so we disable requesting any pages until the current one finishes.

In the `loadNextPage()` function, we check first whether we can load more pages and that there is no active pagination. Once we pass this condition, we set the `loadingPage` flag to `true` till we finish the request, then we display the network activity indicator to the user. Once we get the response, we check the page size to see whether we can request more pages or not. Then, we append the incoming contacts list to the current list we have, and refresh the table view.

To trigger loading the next page, we override the `willDisplayCell` function in the `UITableViewDelegate` protocol. If the cell that is going to be displayed is the last cell, we call the `loadNextPage()` function.

Social sharing

Sharing content in social media is a common thing in our lives nowadays. We share our moods, ideas, thoughts, photos, videos, and so on every day in social networks. Social networks now are another world where people live and that drives us away from our real life and real communication. Anyway, as an iOS developer and regardless of whether you agree or disagree with the social networks life, you have to know how to share content from your app to social network or to other apps you have in your device. In this section, we will see how to share content from an iOS app by continuing the demo project we built before. During this time, we will share a contact information when a user clicks on the contact from the list.

Getting ready

The class that is responsible for the sharing of content for all available services is the
UIActivityViewController class. This class does all the magic behind the scenes, and
the user will just select the service they want to share using a dialog screen:

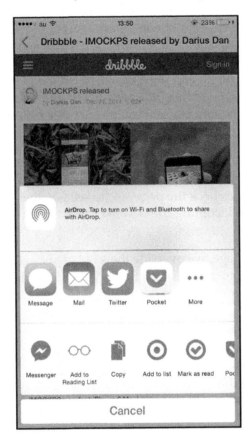

The UIActivityViewController will take content from your device. By default, it will
display all services that can share this content type. However,
UIActivityViewController gives you the option to exclude some services if you want.

The services (activities) the activity view controller displays can be categorized into two main categories: share activities and action activities. The share activities are as follows:

- postToFacebook
- postToTwitter
- postToWeibo
- message
- mail
- postToFlickr
- postToVimeo
- postToTencentWeibo
- airDrop

The action activities are as follows:

- print
- copyToPasteboard
- assignToContact
- saveToCameraRoll
- addToReadingList
- openInIBooks

Let's get started now and take a look at how to present `UIActivityViewController` to share contact information.

How to do it...

1. Let's continue using our previous demo to add a way to share the contact information when a user clicks on it.

2. Let's start by handling the selection of cells in a table view. Override the following function in `UITableViewDelegate`:

```
func tableView(_ tableView: UITableView, didSelectRowAt
  indexPath: IndexPath) {
    let contact = self.contacts[indexPath.row]
    self.shareContact(contact: contact)
}
```

3. Add the following function to share the content:

```
func shareContact(contact: Contact){
    let contactInfo = "Name: \(contact.firstName) \
      (contact.lastName) \nEmail: \(contact.email)\n
        Cell phone: \(contact.cellPhone)"
    let photoImageURL = URL(string: contact.pictureURLString)
    let activityViewController =
    UIActivityViewController(activityItems:
      [contactInfo, photoImageURL],
      applicationActivities: nil)
    self.present(activityViewController,
    animated: true, completion: {
        print("Sharing has been done")
    })
}
```

4. Now, build and run the app on a simulator; try to click on a contact. A dialog like the following will be presented:

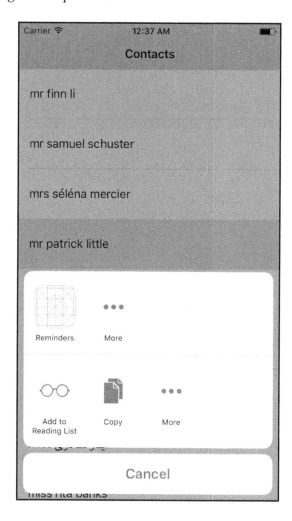

5. As the simulator has no apps installed or services enabled, let's try to test it on a device. Check the following screenshot from a device:

In the preceding screenshot, we can see a list of apps where we can share content, such as *Twitter*, *Facebook*, *Slack*, and so on.

Swiping through the list of apps allows you to see all apps installed to your device that accept sharing.

6. After I select *WhatsApp* to share with one of my contacts, the shared message looks like this:

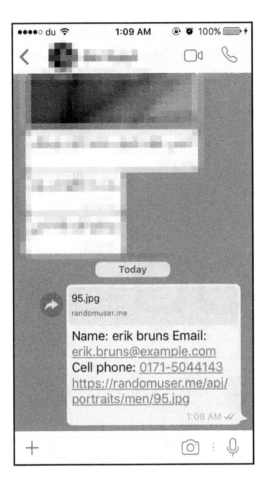

How it works...

Working with UIActivityViewController is straightforward, and we saw how with a couple of lines of code, we integrated sharing options to our app. The first thing to prepare is the items to share. You can share text (strings), URLs, images, data, or assets. Based on what services can handle these types, the activity view controller will display these services. We initialized the UIActivityViewController with the items that we wanted to share, such as the text and image URL. Then, we called present function to display the view controller.

You can exclude activities from the controller by simply doing something like the following:

```
activityViewController.excludedActivityTypes =
    [.addToReadingList, .print];
```

It will exclude the actions you don't want (addToReadingList and print).

12

Persisting Data with Core Data

In this chapter, we will cover the following topics:

- Designing data models
- Reading and insertions in Core Data
- Updating and deleting records from Core Data

Introduction

In mobile apps, you may need to save data locally in device disk-like files or database files. In a database, you can save a set of records (objects) and create relations between them. You can perform many types of operations with high performance, such as insertions, deletions, updates, fetching, filtering, and so on. Initially, we used to use SQLite to manage persistence in an iOS app, until Apple launched the **Core Data** framework.

Core Data is a great framework that manages the data layer of your application and model objects, persistence in device disk. Core Data is built over SQL, but it provides more features and a higher level of abstraction. In this chapter, we will build a simple Todo app. This app will teach you how to design data models with Xcode editor, add new records to Core Data, fetch and display the inserted records from Core Data, delete records from Core Data, and so on.

Designing data models

Before getting started with Core Data, you should take a look at how we will organize or design the data models and determine the relations between these models. The data model in Core Data is called Entity.

Xcode provides an editor to add entities and to specify the relations between them. The design of your data models should be simple and organized, so anyone looking at it should understand what is going on between your data models and what the relations are between them. Check the following example of a design of data models:

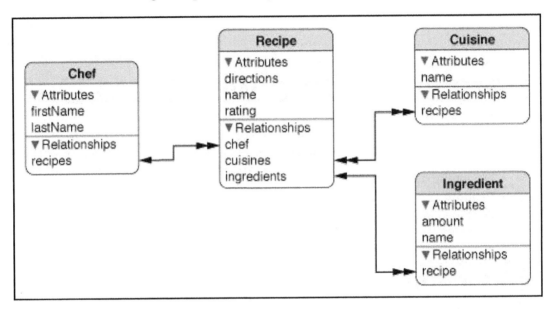

The example shows four entities and the relations between them. The first entity is a Chef entity, which has a list of attributes, such as firstName and lastName. It has a one-to-many relation to the Recipe entity, as each Chef can have many recipes but each recipe has only one chef. The same idea applies to other entities and, through attributes and relations, you will understand the relations between entities.

How to do it...

1. Create a new Xcode project with the **Single View Application** template and with the name TodoApp.
2. Ensure that the checkbox **Use Core Data** is checked so that Xcode can help you by generating boilerplate code in AppDelegate.swift:

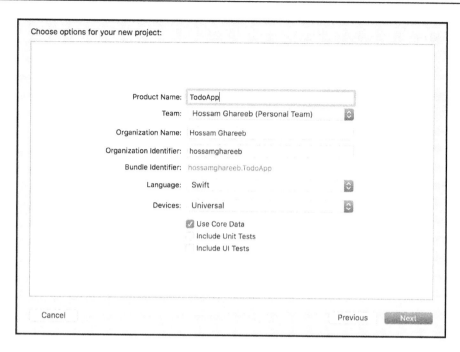

Choose options for your new project:

Product Name:	TodoApp
Team:	Hossam Ghareeb (Personal Team)
Organization Name:	Hossam Ghareeb
Organization Identifier:	hossamghareeb
Bundle Identifier:	hossamghareeb.TodoApp
Language:	Swift
Devices:	Universal

☑ Use Core Data
☐ Include Unit Tests
☐ Include UI Tests

Cancel   Previous   Next

3. Once you create the project, check the left-hand side panel and click on **TodoApp.xcdatamodeld,** which will open an awesome data models editor, as follows:

4. Let's add our first entity. Click on the **Add Entity** button at the bottom-left corner of the editor screen. Then, double-click on the entity to rename it as `TaskList`:

5. Add some attributes to the `TaskList` entity. Add the `name` attribute with type `String` and the `createdAt` attribute with type `Date`:

6. Now, let's add another entity. Repeat the previous steps, but rename the entity as `Task`. Add attributes to the entity, such as `name` with the `String`, `createdAt` with type `Date`, `isCompleted` with type `Boolean`, and `notes` with type `String`:

7. Let's add a relation between the `TaskList` and `Task` models. Select the `TaskList` entity, and under the **Relationships** section, click on the **+** button. Rename the **Relationship** as `tasks` and the **Destination** as `Task` model:

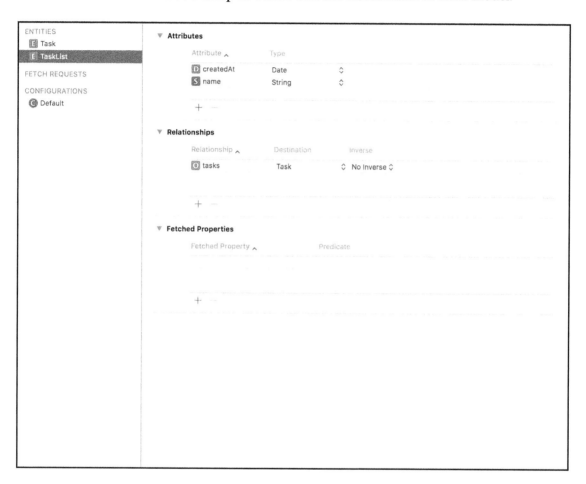

8. Now, select the `Task` entity and add a new relation. Rename the **Relationship** as list, and select `TaskList` under **Destination**. Under **Inverse**, select the `tasks` relation:

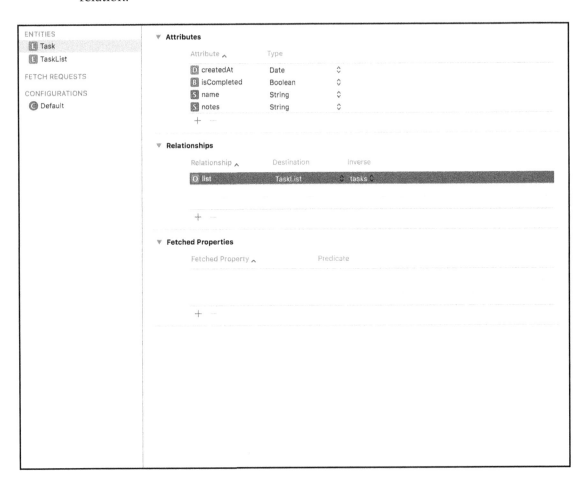

9. Now, go back to the `TaskList` entity. Select the `tasks` relationship and, from the right-hand side panel, select the **Inspector** tab. From the **Inspector** tab, change the relation type to **To Many**:

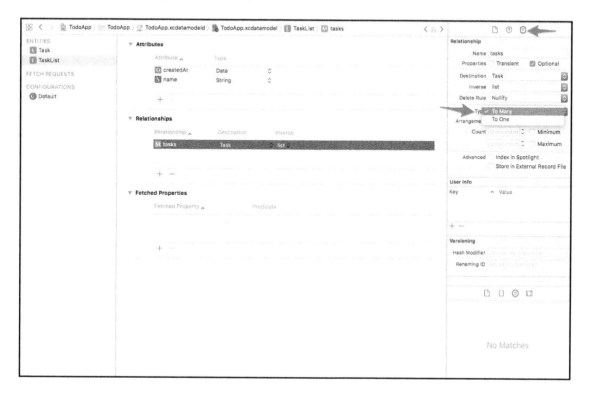

10. Change the editor style from the bottom-right corner of the editor screen; you should see something like this:

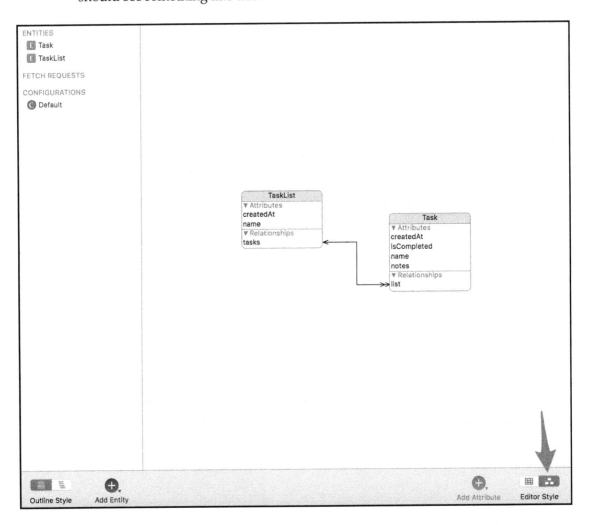

 Xcode 8.0 autogenerates the class files of `Task` and `TaskList` so that you can use them directly in code.

How it works...

In this section, we started our journey with Core Data by creating our data models. Xcode offers a great editor to manage your entities and the relationships between them. Since we will build a Todo app, we created two entities: the TaskList entity, which will be a container of specific kinds of tasks, and the Task entity, which encapsulates everything you need about a specific task. If we want to define a relationship between these two entities, we will see that each task list will have many tasks inside of it, but each task will be linked only to one task list. That's why we defined a one-to-many relation between these two entities. TaskList has a toMany relation to the Task entity, and Task has a toOne relation to the TaskList entity.

Reading and inserting records to Core Data

We have set up our data models, and now we are ready to do some operations in Core Data. In this section, we will see how to insert new records and fetch them back so that we can display them to our user. In our demo, we will design a screen so that the user can add new task lists and see the already added lists. The user will then be able to select a task list to open another screen, which has a list of tasks inside this list. We will add a functionality to add new tasks to this list.

How to do it...

1. Let's continue working in our demo to build our Todo app.
2. Create a new Group in Xcode called Model to add the model classes inside.
3. Create a new class called AbstractManager to work as a parent manager for the TasksListsManager and the TasksManager classes that we will create.
4. Add the following code in the AbstractManager class:

```
import UIKit
import CoreData

class AbstractManager: NSObject {

    /// The managedObjectContext for core data.
    lazy var managedObjectContext: NSManagedObjectContext = {
        let app =
            UIApplication.shared.delegate as! AppDelegate
        return app.persistentContainer.viewContext
```

```
            } ()
        }
```

5. Add a new class called `TasksListManager` with a subclass of `AbstractManager`. Add the following code in `TasksListManager.swift`:

```
import UIKit
import CoreData

extension TaskList{
    public class func newEntityWithName
        (name: String, context: NSManagedObjectContext) ->
            TaskList{
                let list = NSEntityDescription.insertNewObject
                (forEntityName: "TaskList",
                    into: context) as! TaskList
            list.name = name
            return list
        }
}

class TasksListManager: AbstractManager {

    func addNewList(name s: String){
        let list = TaskList.newEntityWithName
        (name: s, context: self.managedObjectContext)
        list.createdAt = NSDate()
        do{
            try self.managedObjectContext.save()
        }
        catch{
            print(error)
        }
    }
    func fetchAllLists() -> [TaskList]{
        return self.fetchLists(predicate: nil)
    }
    private func fetchLists
        (predicate: NSPredicate? = nil) -> [TaskList]{
        let fetchRequest =
            TaskList.fetchRequest() as NSFetchRequest
        fetchRequest.predicate = predicate
        do{
            let lists = try
                self.managedObjectContext.fetch(fetchRequest)
            return lists
        }catch{
            print(error)
```

```
        }
        return []
    }
}
```

In the preceding code, we added an extension to the `TaskList` entity; this adds a new function that creates an instance of `NSEntityDescription` that Core Data will use to insert a new record. The `TasksListManager` class will take care of inserting a new record of `TaskList` to Core Data and will fetch it again.

6. Now, the `TasksListManager` is ready to add new records to the database and to fetch all lists.
7. In `ViewController.swift`, rename it as `TasksListsViewController` so that it will map the controller of the screen that will manage task lists.
8. Open `Main.storyboard`, and select the initial view controller to embed it in **Navigation Controller**:

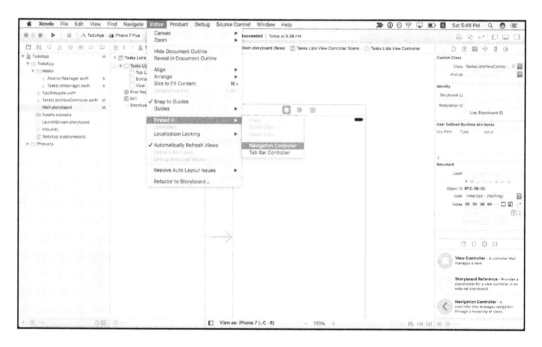

9. Drag a `UITableView` and place it as a subview to fill the screen.

10. Then, we need to make the `TasksListsViewController` the table view's `dataSource` and `delegate`. *Ctrl* + drag the table view to the view controller, and select `dataSource` and `delegate`:

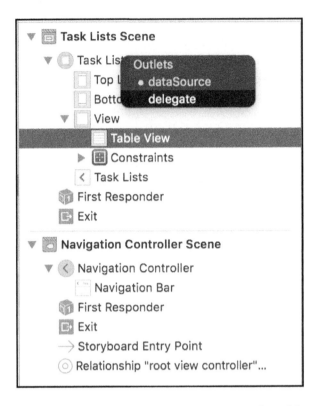

11. From **Object Library**, drag a `UITableViewCell` to the table view. Select the cell, and from **Attribute Inspector**, change the **Style** to **Right Detail**. In the **Identifier**, type `cell` in the text field.

12. From **Object Library**, drag a **Bar Button Item** and place it to the right of the navigation bar. From **Attribute Inspector**, change the **System Item** to **Add**.

13. The final look of the storyboard so far should be something like this:

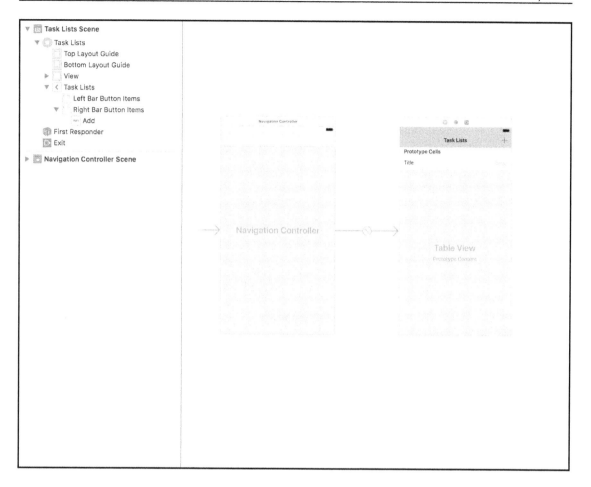

14. Now, link an **IBOutlet** to the table view the with name `tasksListsTableView`, and link an **IBAction** to the **Add** button with the name `didClickOnAddButton`:

```
@IBOutlet weak var tasksListsTableView: UITableView!
@IBAction func didClickOnAddButton(_ sender: Any) {
}
Add the following functions that will display an
UIAlertController with a text field to type
the task list name:
func displayAlertToAddTaskList(){
    let title = "New Tasks List"
    let doneTitle = "Create"

    let alertController = UIAlertController(title: title,
      message: "Write the name of your tasks list.",
```

```
        preferredStyle: .alert)
    let createAction =
      UIAlertAction(title: doneTitle,
        style: .default) { (action) -> Void in
      let listName =
        alertController.textFields?.first?.text ?? ""
        let tasksListsManager = TasksListManager()
        tasksListsManager.addNewList(name: listName)
        print(listName)
    }
    alertController.addAction(createAction)
    createAction.isEnabled = false
    self.currentCreateAction = createAction
    alertController.addAction(UIAlertAction
    (title: "Cancel", style: .cancel, handler: nil))
    alertController.addTextField { (textField) in
        textField.placeholder = "Task List Name"
        textField.addTarget(self, action: #selector
          (TasksListsViewController.listNameFieldDidChange
            (textField:)),
              for: .editingChanged)
    }

  self.present(alertController,
    animated: true, completion: nil)
}
//Enable the create action of the alert
  only if textfield text is not empty
func listNameFieldDidChange(textField:UITextField){
    self.currentCreateAction.isEnabled = (textField.text ??
      "").characters.count > 0
}
```

The previous code is straightforward; we first created an instance of the
UIAlertController class to display an alert to their user. The alert will
have an action button to save the task list and another action button to
dismiss the alert. We added a text field to the alert where the user can type
the name of the task list.

15. Now, define the following property to have a reference to the submit action button of the alert:

```
var currentCreateAction:UIAlertAction!
```

16. Now, update the `didClickOnAddButton` function to call the function that we've just created:

```
@IBAction func didClickOnAddButton(_ sender: Any) {
    displayAlertToAddTaskList()
}
```

17. Add the following extension to implement the `UITableViewDataSource` protocol:

```
extension TasksListsViewController: UITableViewDataSource{
    func tableView(_ tableView: UITableView,
      numberOfRowsInSection section: Int)
        -> Int {
        return 0
    }
    func tableView(_ tableView: UITableView, cellForRowAt
      indexPath: IndexPath) -> UITableViewCell {
        let cell = tableView.dequeueReusableCell
          (withIdentifier: "cell")
        return cell!
    }
}
```

18. Now, build and run; you will see an empty list, as follows:

19. When you click on the add button an alert controller will be displayed, as shown in the following screenshot and, as you can see, the **Create** button is disabled:

20. Once you type a name, the **Create** button of the alert will be enabled:

21. After clicking on the **Create** button, the list will be saved in Core Data, but unfortunately right now, we don't see anything yet on screen. Let's take a look at how to read the inserted lists and display them on screen.

22. Add the following property to hold the current displayed lists:

```
var tasksLists: [TaskList] = [TaskList]()
```

23. Add the following function to read tasks from Core Data and refresh the table view:

```
func loadTasks(){
        let tasksListsManager = TasksListManager()
        self.tasksLists = tasksListsManager.fetchAllLists()
        self.tasksListsTableView.reloadData()
}
```

24. Update the `viewDidLoad` function to call `loadTasks` to display the current list once the screen is displayed:

```
override func viewDidLoad() {
    super.viewDidLoad()
    // Do any additional setup
      after loading the view, typically from a nib.
    self.loadTasks()
}
```

25. Update the `displayAlertToAddTaskList` function to call `loadTasks` after inserting any new list:

```
let listName = alertController.textFields?.first?.text ?? ""
let tasksListsManager = TasksListManager()
tasksListsManager.addNewList(name: listName)
self.loadTasks()
```

26. Lastly, update the data source functions to display the data we read from a database:

```
extension TasksListsViewController: UITableViewDataSource{
func tableView(_ tableView: UITableView,
numberOfRowsInSection section: Int) -> Int {
    return self.tasksLists.count
}
func tableView(_ tableView:
  UITableView, cellForRowAt indexPath: IndexPath) ->
    UITableViewCell {
    let cell = tableView.dequeueReusableCell
      (withIdentifier: "cell")
    let list = self.tasksLists[indexPath.row]
    cell?.textLabel?.text = list.name
    cell?.detailTextLabel?.text =
      "\(list.tasks?.count ?? 0) Tasks"
    return cell!
    }
}
```

27. Now, build and run; our data will be loaded like this:

How it works...

In this section, we implemented the reading and insertions of objects in Core Data. First, we created the model classes that will be responsible for dealing with Core Data and executing requests. The AbstractManager is an abstract class that will have all common functionalities and properties that will be needed in any concrete manager. In the AbstractManager, we added a lazy property called managedObjectContext, which is a reference to the NSManagedObjectContext. The context is a place where all data objects live. The context will take care of persisting the changes made in model objects.

The first concrete manager that extends AbstractManager is TasksListManager. This manager will take care of all CRUD operations in the TaskList object. The first thing we did was to add an extension for our TaskList class to add the newEntityWithName function, which will create a new instance of TaskList by a given context. The NSEntityDescription has a class function called insertNewObject, which takes the entity name which is TaskList and the context which will have the new added object.

In the TasksListManager class, we added a function called addNewList; the function takes the list name as a parameter and creates a new instance using the class function we created in the extension. After we create the instance, we called self.managedObjectContext.save() to write our changes to disk. The second function is fetchAllLists(), which returns a list of objects of the TaskList class. The function internally calls a private function, which performs a fetch request with an option to provide a predicate. The NSPredicate gives you the option to filter, sort, or limit the fetched results. To fetch all results, we pass it as a nil for now. The TaskList.fetchRequest() returns an instance of NSFetchRequest to be executed by calling self.managedObjectContext.fetch(fetchRequest), which informs the context to start fetching the given fetch request.

Going back to TasksListsViewController, we added the displayAlertToAddTaskList() function that will display an alert dialog with a text field so that the user can type the list name. The alert controller is an instance of UIAlertController. We added the first action which, just like the create action, will be disabled at the beginning till the user types a valid list name. That's why we have a reference to the create action to enable it later. We added a text field to the alert controller so that the user can type the list in it. The function passed a closure to add your configuration for the text field in it. We added a target-action to the event of editingChanged, so it will call the listNameFieldDidChange(textField:) function, where we validate the list name to enable or disable the create action.

Inserting new objects to Core Data is nothing without knowing how to read them back to display them to the user. In the loadTasks() function, we created an instance of TasksListManager() and called the fetchAllLists function. Then, we reloaded the table view. In the cellForRow function of dataSource, we changed the cell label text to the list name and the cell details label text to the number of tasks inside this list.

Updating and deleting records from Core Data

While dealing with objects in databases, you will need to know how to update or delete objects. In Core Data, these kinds of operations are made easy and, with just simple APIs, you can perform these operations. In this section, we will see how a user can edit the name of task list or delete it.

How to do it...

1. Let's start with deleting lists. Open the `TasksListManager.swift` file, and add the following function:

```
func deleteList(list: TaskList){

    self.managedObjectContext.delete(list)
    do{
        try self.managedObjectContext.save()
    }
    catch{
        print(error)
    }
}
```

2. Add the following extension to implement the `UITableViewDelegate` protocol and override the `editActionsForRow` function:

```
extension TasksListsViewController: UITableViewDelegate{
    func tableView(_ tableView: UITableView,
       editActionsForRowAt indexPath: IndexPath) ->
         [UITableViewRowAction]? {
       let deleteAction = UITableViewRowAction(style:
           .destructive, title: "Delete", handler:
             { (deleteAction, indexPath) in
                 let tasksListsManager = TasksListManager()
                 let listToBeDeleted =
                   self.tasksLists[indexPath.row]
                 tasksListsManager.deleteList(list:
                   listToBeDeleted)
                 self.tasksLists.remove(at: indexPath.row)
                 self.tasksListsTableView.deleteRows(at:
                   [indexPath], with: .fade)
```

```
        })
        return [deleteAction]
    }
}
```

3. Now, build and run the app. Once the list of movies appears, swipe left from any list, and you will see the option to delete:

4. Once you click on **Delete**, the list will be deleted with fade animation:

5. Double-check that everything is working fine, kill the app, and reopen it. You should see that the list is completely deleted when you fetch all lists.

6. Let's add another option now to edit a task list name. Update the `editActionsForRow` function to add another action for edit:

```
func tableView(_ tableView: UITableView,
    editActionsForRowAt indexPath: IndexPath) ->
    [UITableViewRowAction]? {
```

```
let deleteAction = UITableViewRowAction(style:
  .destructive, title: "Delete", handler:
    { (deleteAction, indexPath) in
        let tasksListsManager = TasksListManager()
        let listToBeDeleted =
          self.tasksLists[indexPath.row]
        tasksListsManager.deleteList(list:
          listToBeDeleted)
        self.tasksLists.remove(at: indexPath.row)
        self.tasksListsTableView.deleteRows(at:
          [indexPath], with: .fade)
  })
let editAction = UITableViewRowAction(style:'
  .normal, title: "Edit", handler:
    { (editAction, indexPath) in
        let listToBeUpdated =
          self.tasksLists[indexPath.row]
          self.displayAlertToAddOrUpdateTaskList
            (toUpdateList: listToBeUpdated)
  })
return [deleteAction, editAction]
}
```

7. Note that there is a call for a `displayAlertToAddOrUpdateTaskList()`
   function, which is the updated version of `displayAlertToAddTaskList()`.
   Consider the following updated function:

```
func displayAlertToAddOrUpdateTaskList
  (toUpdateList: TaskList?){
    var title = "New Tasks List"
    var doneTitle = "Create"
    if toUpdateList != nil {
        title = "Update Tasks List"
        doneTitle = "Update"
    }

  let alertController = UIAlertController(title: title,
    message: "Write the name of your tasks list.",
    preferredStyle: .alert)
  let createAction = UIAlertAction
    (title: doneTitle, style: .default)
      { (action) -> Void in
      let listName =
        alertController.textFields?.first?.text ?? ""
      let tasksListsManager = TasksListManager()
      if let updatedList = toUpdateList{
          updatedList.name = listName
          tasksListsManager.saveContextForUpdates()
```

```
            }
            else{
                tasksListsManager.addNewList(name: listName)
            }
            self.loadTasks()
            print(listName)
        }
        alertController.addAction(createAction)
        createAction.isEnabled = false
        self.currentCreateAction = createAction
        alertController.addAction(UIAlertAction(title:
          "Cancel", style: .cancel, handler: nil))
        alertController.addTextField { (textField) in
            textField.placeholder = "Task List Name"
            textField.addTarget(self, action:
              #selector(TasksListsViewController
                .listNameFieldDidChange(textField:)),
                   for: .editingChanged)
            if let updatedList = toUpdateList{
                textField.text = updatedList.name
            }
        }

        self.present(alertController,
          animated: true, completion: nil)
    }
```

8. Now, update the `TasksListManager` class to add the following function:

```
func saveContextForUpdates(){
    do{
        try self.managedObjectContext.save()
    }
    catch{
        print(error)
    }
}
```

9. Now, build and run. Assume that the current list we have is like the following:

10. When you swipe left to the first item in the task list, you will see two options: **Edit** or **Delete**:

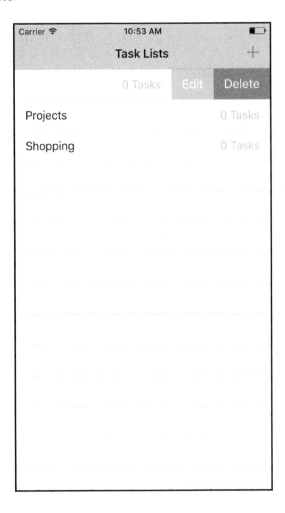

11. When you click on **Edit**, a pop-up dialog will appear, as follows:

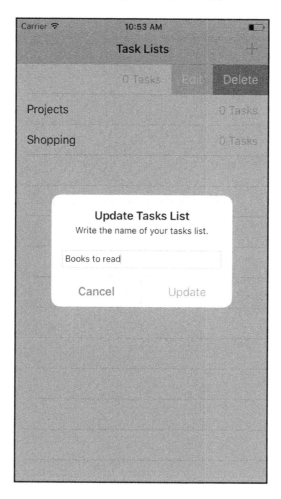

12. Once you click on **Update**, the table view will be reloaded and the lists will be updated:

How it works...

In this section, we have implemented two important functionalities, which are updating and deleting objects. Although these functionalities are very important, they are easy to perform, thanks to Core Data, which provides easy and simple APIs to get these jobs done. We started implementing deletion and created the `deleteList()` function in the `TasksListManager`. As we said before, all data model objects live in a `managedObjectContext`. That's why we asked the context to delete the object by calling `self.managedObjectContext.delete(list)`; then, we saved the context.

In `TasksListsViewController`, we overode the `editActionsForRow()` function, which is one of the delegate functions of `UITableViewDelegate`. The function returns a list of actions that needs to appear when the user swipes any cell in the table. We added two actions, one for the delete action and one for the edit action. In the delete action, when the user clicks on the delete button, we create a new instance of `TasksListManager` to call the `deleteList` function. Once the list is deleted from Core Data, we directly remove it from our array and reload the table view.

In editing mode, we reused the `displayAlertToAddTaskList()` function to support displaying the alert dialog while inserting or updating a task list. We renamed the function as `displayAlertToAddOrUpdateTaskList`, and we added an optional parameter called `toUpdateList`. This parameter will be nil in the case of inserting a new task list and will be a reference to the updated list in the case of updating an existing task list. When the user clicks on the submit button, we update the name directly to the updated list and ask the context to save the change directly.

13
Notifications

In this chapter, we will cover the following topics:

- Setting up Push Notifications
- Setting up a local server to send Push Notification
- Working with Interactive Push Notifications
- Working with local notifications

Introduction

Most of our apps nowadays highly depend on notifications when they implement most of its features. Notifying users with specific actions is the best practice rather than letting them keep checking the app for any updates. All of us now are aware of Push Notifications while receiving messages or notifications from your friends in social networks, new e-mails, reminders from apps to do specific actions, and so on. Push Notifications now are being enhanced in each new version of iOS to deliver the user the best benefit of push notifications and support newer features.

In this chapter, we will give you a great coverage of the most important topics in notifications. We will start by working with push notification, which are the most important part of notifications in iOS. This type of notifications is sent via server side to mobile phones, which requires Internet connection on the iOS device. Then, we will see how to create interactive notifications and present images. Presenting images is one of the great features in iOS 10. Notifications may not only be Push Notifications; however, you can keep sending notifications to your user locally, which requires no Internet connection at all.

Setting up Push Notifications

The first step in working with Push Notifications is to know how to set up Push Notification in your app. This step causes a headache for most iOS developers, as it requires a lot of setup instructions, which may lead to a Push Notification that doesn't work in the end, unfortunately. In this section, based on my experience, I will try to list the steps that you should follow to set up Push Notifications. After setting it up, we will build a simple demo app that asks the user permission to send push notifications. Then, we will try to build a simple local server to send notifications from.

Getting ready

When you think of Push Notifications, you have to know that there are a lot of things involved in this setup:

- **Apple developer account**: You must have a paid developer account to work with Push Notifications. In this account, you can create the app identifiers, provisions, and certificates to be used in the setup. In this account, we need the following:
    - **Provision profile**: This is a provision profile that has Push Notification service enabled. The development provision profile needs a list of devices, UDID's that are involved in testing. This provision will be added in the Xcode project.
    - **Push Notification certificate**: This certificate is a special type of certificate which is specific only for Push Notifications. This certificate will be used only by the server that will send the Push Notifications.
- **Xcode project**: In Xcode project settings, we will need only to add the provision profile, which has Push Notification service enabled.
- **Source code**: This is the code that will be required to set up Push Notifications. This code will do the following:
    - Register for push notifications by asking the user permission to send these notifications
    - Receive the device token after the user accepts to receive Push Notifications and it connects to the server that will send the notifications

- **Server**: This is the server that will fire the notifications to the Apple servers, and they will be sent directly again to your device. To do this, the server will need to talk to Apple servers and it will need the following:
  - The device token so that Apple servers can know which device to talk to
  - The push notification certificate which has been created from Apple developer account

This is the summary of what is required to set up push notifications. When you finish the setup, make sure that you come back to this list to review what you did.

How to do it...

1. Create a new Xcode project with a **Single View Application** template and with the name `PushApp`.
2. Change the app identifier of the project to `ae.example.pushapp`.
3. Log in to your Apple developer account and click on the **Account** tab at the top:

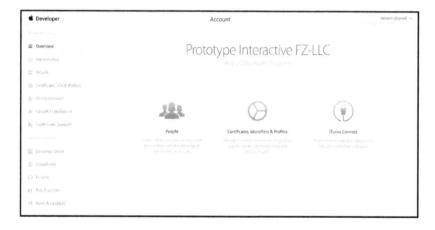

4. On the left-hand side, you will find a menu. Click on **Certificates, IDs & Profiles**.

5. The Apple developer account will be opened with details, as follows:

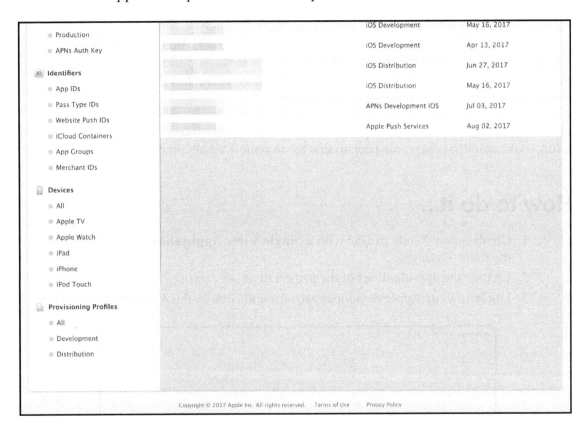

6. In the menu on the left-hand side, click on **App IDs** and then click on the **+** button at the top-right corner.

7. Under **App ID Description**, enter `PushApp` in the **Name** section, and under **App ID Suffix**, choose **Explicit App ID** and type `ae.example.pushapp` in **Bundle ID**:

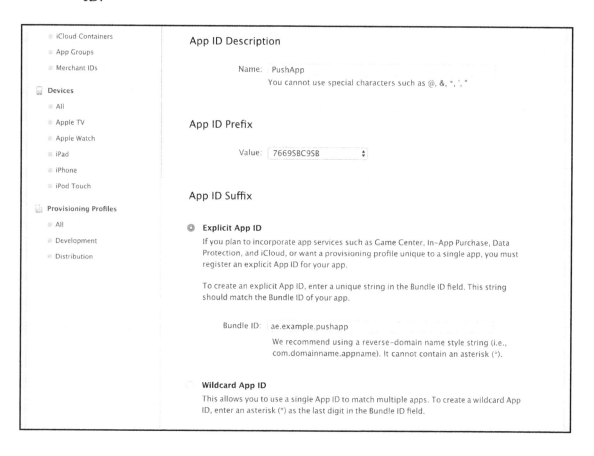

8. In the same page and under**App Service**, make sure that **Push Notification** is selected and then click on **Continue**:

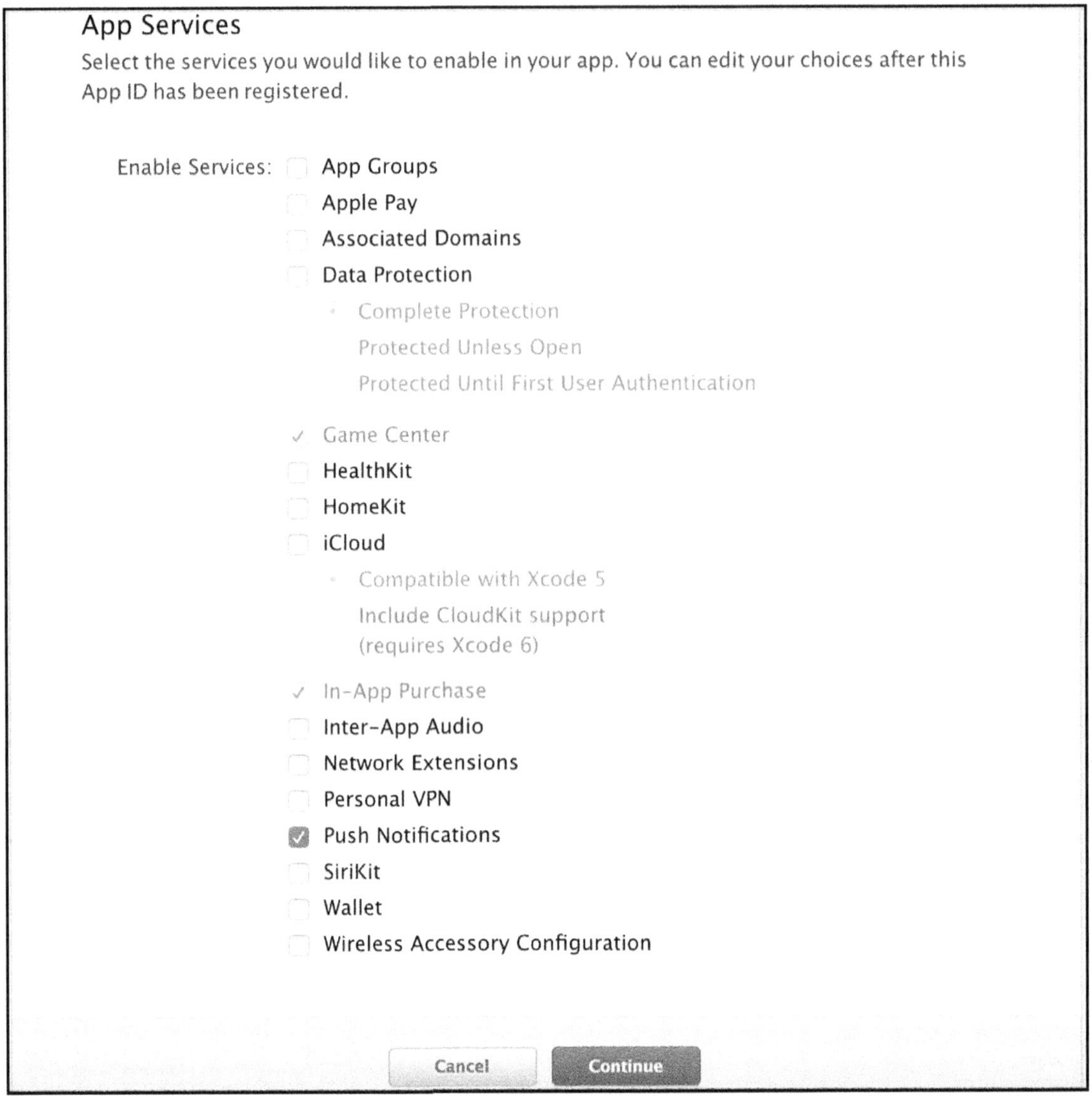

App Services

Select the services you would like to enable in your app. You can edit your choices after this App ID has been registered.

Enable Services: ☐ App Groups

☐ Apple Pay

☐ Associated Domains

☐ Data Protection

· Complete Protection

Protected Unless Open

Protected Until First User Authentication

✓ Game Center

☐ HealthKit

☐ HomeKit

☐ iCloud

· Compatible with Xcode 5

Include CloudKit support
(requires Xcode 6)

✓ In-App Purchase

☐ Inter-App Audio

☐ Network Extensions

☐ Personal VPN

☑ Push Notifications

☐ SiriKit

☐ Wallet

☐ Wireless Accessory Configuration

Cancel   Continue

---

9. A confirmation page will be displayed; ensure that **Push Notifications** is set as **Configurable** and then click on **Register**:

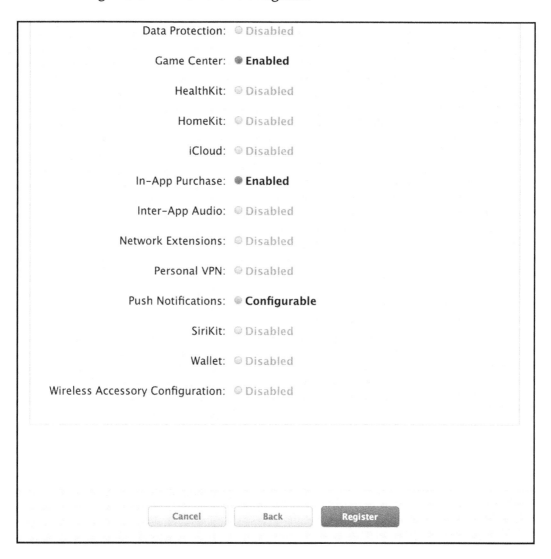

Now, let's create the Push Notification certificate.

10. In the left menu, click on **Development** under **Certificates**. Then, click on the top plus button and select **Apple Push Notification service SSL (Sandbox)**:

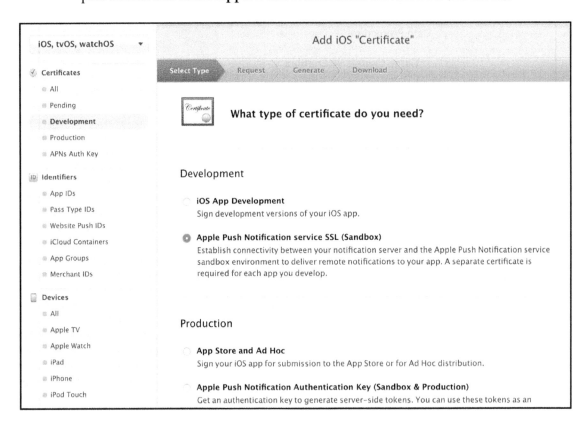

11. Then, select the app identifier **ae.example.pushapp** from the list:

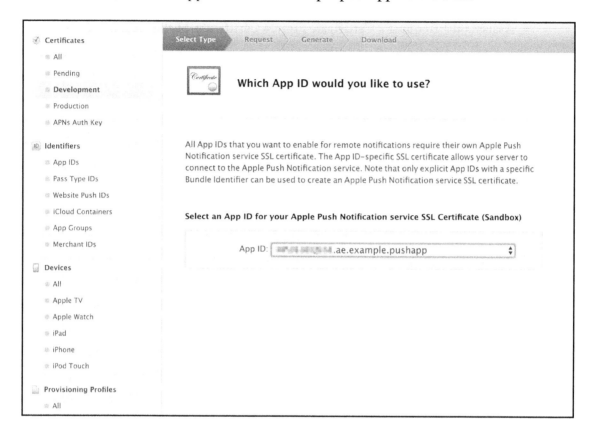

12. Then the page will ask you to create a **certificate signing request** (CSR). Open the **Keychain Access** app in your Mac, and select **Keychain Access | Certificate | Assisstant | Request a Certificate From a Certificate Authority...**:

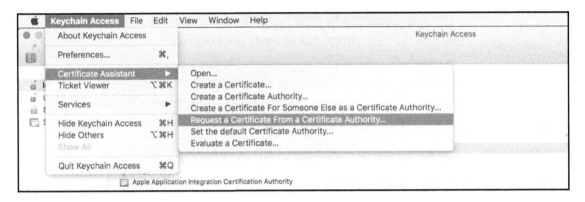

13. A window will open asking you to enter some information. Just enter your e-mail address, name, and select **Saved to disk** to save in your desktop, for example:

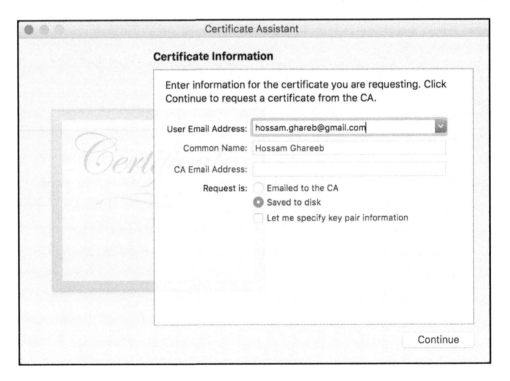

14. Now, return to the website, and click on **Continue** to upload the signing request that you have saved in Desktop:

15. Then the certificate will be ready; click on **Download**:

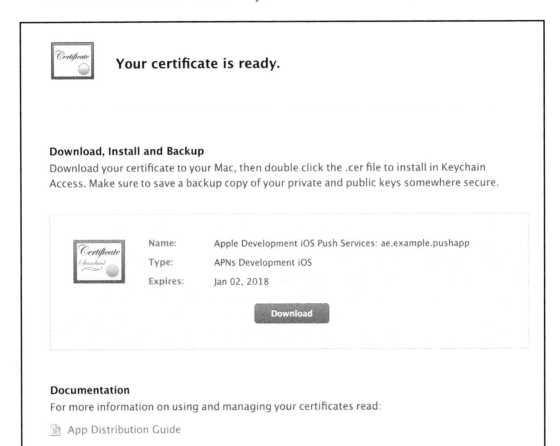

16. Now, the last thing is the app provision profile. Select **Development** from under **Provisioning Profiles**, and select **iOS App Development** and click on **Continue**:

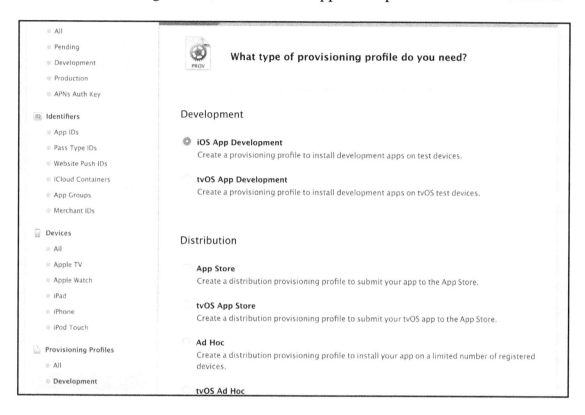

17. Then, select the **App ID** from the list:

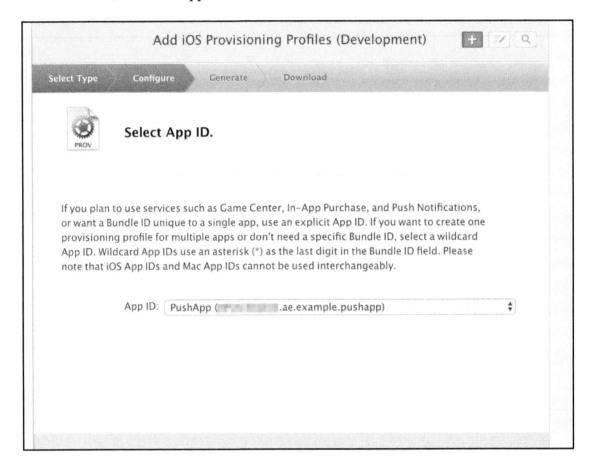

18. Write a name to the provision, and select the device that you want to test it on. Then the provision will be ready to be downloaded:

Your provisioning profile is ready.

Download and Install

Download and double click the following file to install your Provisioning Profile.

Name:	PushAppProvisionDev
Type:	iOS Development
App ID:	▓▓▓▓▓▓.ae.example.pushapp
Expires:	Jan 2, 2018

Download

19. Now, return to Xcode and update the project development certificate and provision:

20. Lastly, open the **Capabilities** tab and enable **Push Notifications**:

21. Open the `AppDelegate.swift` file to add the code that will register for push notifications. At the top of file, add the following `import` statement:

```
import UserNotifications
```

22. Then, add the following function:

```
func registerForPushNotifications(){
    let application = UIApplication.shared
    let center = UNUserNotificationCenter.current()
    center.requestAuthorization(options:
        [.alert, .sound]) { (granted, error) in
        // actions based on whether
           notifications were authorized or not
        print(granted)
        print(error ?? "No error")
```

```
        }
      application.registerForRemoteNotifications()
    }
```

23. Then, update the `didFinishLaunchWithOptions` function to call the previously added function:

```
func application(_ application: UIApplication,
  didFinishLaunchingWithOptions launchOptions:
    [UIApplicationLaunchOptionsKey: Any]?) -> Bool {
  // Override point for customization
    after application launch.
  registerForPushNotifications()
  return true
}
```

24. Now, let's implement the following two functions from among which one will be called based on success or failure:

```
func application(_ application: UIApplication,
    didRegisterForRemoteNotificationsWithDeviceToken
      deviceToken: Data) {
    let deviceTokenString = deviceToken.reduce("", {$0 +
      String(format: "%02X", $1)})
    print(deviceTokenString)
}
func application(_ application: UIApplication,
  didFailToRegisterForRemoteNotificationsWithError
    error: Error) {
    print(error)
}
```

25. Now, let's build and run the app. Once you open the app on the device, you will see the following alert:

26. Now, check your debug area; you should see the device token printed:

27. Now, the push notifications service has been set up correctly once you receive the device token from the system.

How it works...

In this section, we have gone through the setup process of the push notification service. Doing anything wrong or missing one of the steps that we have introduced will lead to unexpected behavior while working with push notifications. The most important steps have been done through the Apple developer account to create the app certificate, APNS certificate, and the app provision profile. After you create all these files, you can easily embed them in the Xcode project.

Starting from iOS 10, push notification APIs have been moved to a grand new framework called `UserNotifications`. This framework has everything needed to set up push notifications in your app. The registration for push notifications has been done in the `registerForPushNotifications()` function. In this function, we get a reference to the user notification center by calling `UNUserNotificationCenter.current()`, and then we called the `requestAuthorization` function, which takes a block to be called once the authorization finishes. This block has two parameters: granted--which has two values: true, if the user grants access to send notifications, and false, otherwise--and the error if the authorization fails.

In `AppDelegate`, there are two callback functions related to push notifications, the `didRegisterForRemoteNotificationsWithDeviceToken` and `didFailToRegisterForRemoteNotificationsWithError`. The first function will be called in successful registration and the device token will be passed. The second one will be called if the app fails the registration and the error will be passed.

Setting up a local server to send Push Notifications

In the previous section, we saw how to set up push notifications from the Apple developer account and in the Xcode project. Then, we wrote the code in **AppDelegate** to register for push notifications. Everything is good, but it will be nothing if we don't know how to send push notifications to the device. In this section, we will set up a local server that will send push notifications to the device using the APNS certificate and the device token.

Getting ready

To send push notification easily, we will introduce a good and easy tool that you can set up in your local machine. Check the following tool in GitHub, which is called **Houston**: `https://github.com/nomad/houston`

Houston is a ruby gem that can be installed in your Mac, and here you go; you can send push notifications with very few steps.

How to do it...

1. Run the previous app on a device and keep a record of the device token, as we will use it to send notifications.
2. Open the Houston project in GitHub and follow the instructions there to install Houston.
3. The Push Notification certificate that you have downloaded should be with the `.cer` extension. Double-click on certificate, and it will open **Keychain Access**:

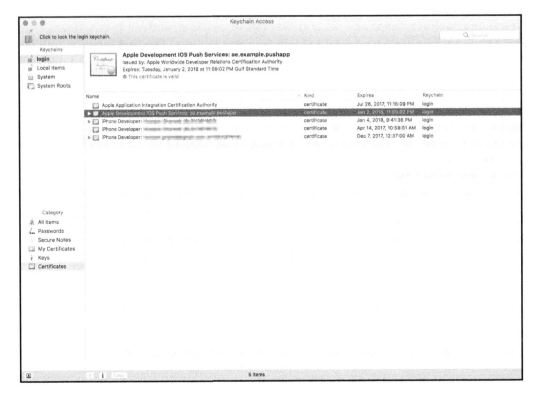

4. Right-click on the certificate and click on **Export** " ":

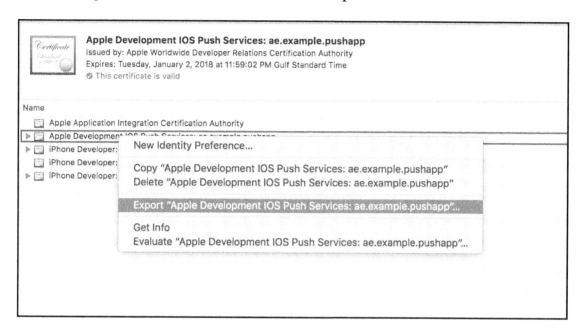

5. Ensure that the `.p12` extension is selected:

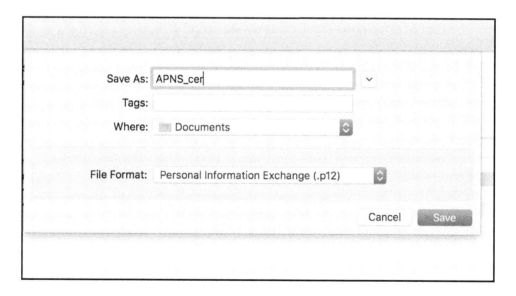

6. Click on the **Save** button to save the file in your disk. After saving it, we need to convert the certificate file from `.p12` to `.pem`. The `.pem` will be used by Houston to send notifications.

7. Open the terminal and navigate to the folder that has the certificate.

8. Now, run the following command to generate a new `.pem` certificate:

```
$ openssl pkcs12 -in cert.p12 -out
  apple_push_notification.pem -nodes -clcerts
```

9. Create a new text file, and write the following code:

```
require 'houston'

# Environment variables are automatically read, or can be
  overridden by any specified options. You can also
# conveniently use `Houston::Client.development` or `
  Houston::Client.production`.
APN = Houston::Client.development
APN.certificate =
  File.read("/Users/hossamghareeb/Documents/
    apple_push_notification.pem")

# An example of the token sent back when a device registers
  for notifications
token =
  "699C8C3E87A7412E356365F80
    CEE08C737D541EB135EC5470334C85A5F4E2FCC"

# Create a notification that alerts a
message to the user, plays a
sound, and sets the badge on the app
notification = Houston::Notification.new(device: token)
notification.alert = "Hello, World!"

# Notifications can also change the badge count, have a
custom sound, have a category identifier, indicate available
Newsstand content, or pass along arbitrary data.
notification.badge = 57
notification.sound = "sosumi.aiff"
notification.category = "INVITE_CATEGORY"
notification.content_available = true
notification.mutable_content = true
notification.custom_data = { foo: "bar" }

# And... sent! That's all it takes.
APN.push(notification)
```

10. Replace the device token in the file with a device token of the device that you're using. You can get it from the **Debug** area when you run the app. Then, save the file as a `push.rb` file.

11. In the terminal now, run the following command:

```
ruby push.rb
```

12. Check the device; you will see the Push Notification, as follows:

How it works...

In this section, we saw how simple it is to send Push Notifications when you have a server. For simplicity, we've used the local machine as a server to send push notifications thanks to Houston. It manages to wrap the message and the certificate and send them to the Apple Push Notification server with the device token. The Apple server understands which device it should communicate with and which app should take care of the notification. The certificate that you export from Keychain is in the `.p12` format, but the server needs the `.pem` format, and that's why we converted our certificate to that extension. In Houston ruby code, the `alert` property takes the push notification message that you want the user to read when they receive the notification. The `custom_data` property takes a custom JSON object that can contain useful information that you may need in your app when you handle the Push Notification when the user clicks on it.

Working with interactive Push Notifications

Users need to interact with Push Notifications by performing actions, such as tapping on it to see what are you telling them or swiping the notification to see multiple actions customized only for your app. If the app is in the foreground and the app received the Push Notification, the push notification will not be shown. However, in iOS 10, the `UserNotifications` framework has provided a way to make it presentable. If the app is in the background and the user received the push notification for your app, the push notification message will be presented. Clicking on the Push Notification will automatically open your app. Swiping on the notification will show two actions, by default. The **View** action is to open the app and the **Clear** action is to clear the notification from the notification center.

In this section, we will see how to handle tapping on the notification and how to customize the default actions of the notification.

How to do it...

1. Open the same demo project and click on the `AppDelegate.swift` file.
2. The first thing that we will do is enable the presentable of Push Notification if the app is in foreground and handle the tapping of the Push Notifications.
3. Update the function of `registerForPushNotifications` to be like the following:

```
func registerForPushNotifications(){
    let application = UIApplication.shared
    let center = UNUserNotificationCenter.current()
    center.delegate = self
    center.requestAuthorization(options:
      [.alert, .sound]) { (granted, error) in
        // actions based on whether
          notifications were authorized or not
        print(granted)
        print(error ?? "No error")
    }
    application.registerForRemoteNotifications()
}
```

4. At the end of the file, add the following extension to conform to the `UNUserNotificationCenterDelegate` protocol:

```
extension AppDelegate: UNUserNotificationCenterDelegate{
    public func userNotificationCenter(_ center:
      UNUserNotificationCenter, willPresent notification:
        UNNotification,
          withCompletionHandler completionHandler:
            @escaping (UNNotificationPresentationOptions) ->
              Swift.Void){
          completionHandler(.alert)
    }
// The method will be called on the delegate when the user
  responded to the notification by opening the application,
  dismissing the notification or choosing a
  UNNotificationAction. The
  delegate must be set before the application returns from
  applicationDidFinishLaunching:.
public func userNotificationCenter(_ center:
  UNUserNotificationCenter, didReceive response:
  UNNotificationResponse, withCompletionHandler
  completionHandler: @escaping () -> Swift.Void){
    let userInfo =
      response.notification.request.content.userInfo
    if let aps = userInfo["aps"]{
        print(aps)
    }
    if let customData = userInfo["foo"]{
        print(customData)
    }
    completionHandler()
  }
}
```

5. Now, run the app, and while the app is in the foreground, send a notification from the terminal. You will see as the following screenshot; the notification is presentable:

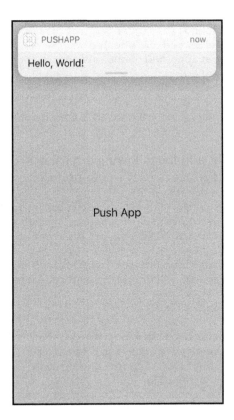

6. Now, try to send a notification while the app is in the background. Then, try to tap on the notification and then check the Debug area; you will see a log, as follows:

```
true
699C8C3E87A7412E356365F80CEE08C737D541EB135EC5470334C85A5F4E2FCC
No error
{
    alert = "Hello, World!";
    badge = 57;
    category = "INVITE_CATEGORY";
    "content-available" = 1;
    sound = "sosumi.aiff";
}
bar
```

All Output ◇   ⊜ Filter   🗑 | ▢▢

7. You will note that the same information you set in the Houston push notification file is received in the app.

Let's see now how we can create custom functions for the push notification:

1. At the top of the `AppDelegate.swift` file, add the following constants:

```
let ChatMessageCategory = "ChatMessageCategory"
let ReplyActionIdentifier = "ReplyActionIdentifier"
let CoolActionIdentifier = "CoolActionIdentifier"
```

2. Update the `registerForPushNotification` function to register the actions if permission granted:

```
func registerForPushNotifications(){
    let application = UIApplication.shared
    let center = UNUserNotificationCenter.current()
    center.delegate = self
    center.requestAuthorization(options:
        [.alert, .sound]) { (granted, error) in
        // actions based on whether
            notifications were authorized or not
        if granted{
            self.customizePushNotificationActions()
```

```
            }
        }
        application.registerForRemoteNotifications()
    }
```

3. Now, add the following function to register the actions for the Push Notification of a specific category:

```
func customizePushNotificationActions(){
    let center = UNUserNotificationCenter.current()
    let replyAction = UNNotificationAction(identifier:
      ReplyActionIdentifier, title:
        "Reply", options: .foreground)
    let coolAction =
      UNNotificationAction(identifier:

        CoolActionIdentifier, title: "👍",
        options: .destructive)
    let notificationCategory =
      UNNotificationCategory(identifier:
        ChatMessageCategory, actions:
          [replyAction, coolAction],
          intentIdentifiers:
          [], options:
          .customDismissAction)
      var categories = Set<UNNotificationCategory>()
      categories.insert(notificationCategory)
      center.setNotificationCategories(categories)
    }
```

4. Finally, update the delegate method to add a condition to check the actions:

```
public func userNotificationCenter(_ center:
  UNUserNotificationCenter, didReceive response:
  UNNotificationResponse, withCompletionHandler
  completionHandler: @escaping () -> Swift.Void){
    let userInfo =
      response.notification.request.content.userInfo
    if let aps = userInfo["aps"]{
        print(aps)
    }
    if let customData = userInfo["foo"]{
        print(customData)
    }
    switch response.actionIdentifier {
    case ReplyActionIdentifier:
        print("User did click on reply. Display the chat log
```

```
            and text box to reply.")
    case CoolActionIdentifier:

        print("Send cool emojo 👍 to the user")
    default:
        print(response.actionIdentifier)
    }
    completionHandler()
}
```

5. Now, run the app and put it in the background.

6. Update the push.rb file to add the new action identifier, as follows:

```
require 'houston'

# Environment variables are automatically read, or can be
overridden by any specified options. You can also
# conveniently use `Houston::Client.development` or `
Houston::Client.production`.
APN = Houston::Client.development
APN.certificate =
File.read("/Users/hossamghareeb/
Documents/apple_push_notification.pem")

# An example of the token sent back 1
when a device registers for notifications
token = "699C8C3E87A7412E356365F80CEE08C73
   7D541EB135EC5470334C85A5F4E2FCC"

# Create a notification that alerts
   a message to the user, plays a sound, and sets the badge on
      the app
   notification = Houston::Notification.new(device: token)
   notification.alert = "Hey man, we are
      going to cinema tomorrow. Are you in?"

   # Notifications can also change the badge count, have a
   custom sound, have a category identifier, indicate
   available Newsstand content, or pass along arbitrary data.
   notification.badge = 57
   notification.sound = "sosumi.aiff"
   notification.category = "ChatMessageCategory"
   notification.content_available = true
   notification.custom_data = { foo: "bar" }

   APN.push(notification)
```

7. Now, send the message as we did before. Once you get the message, drag down to see the custom action, as shown in the following screenshot:

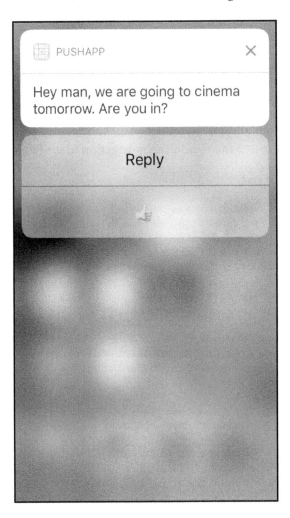

How it works...

We saw how easy it is to handle the interactions of push notifications and add your own custom actions. To get notified when the user taps or does any specific action to the push notification, you have to set the delegate for `UNUserNotificationCenter` and implement the function of the `UNUserNotificationCenterDelegate` protocol. In the `userNotificationCenter(_ center: UNUserNotificationCenter, willPresent notification)` function, it will be called when the user receives a push notification while the app is in the foreground state. By default, the notification will not be shown, but if you override this function, you have the chance to add your own logic to decide whether to present the notification or not. Calling `completionHandler(.alert)` inside the function will present the notification.

The `userNotificationCenter(_ center: UNUserNotificationCenter, didReceive response)` function will be called when the user interacts with the push notification while the app is in the background state. The function passes an instance of `UNNotificationResponse`, which gives you a way to access the user information dictionary.

In the `customizePushNotificationActions()` function, we define the custom actions that the user will see in the push notification. Each push notification can have a unique category, and each category will have its own actions. Facebook, for example, can have a category for a friend request notification, and the actions can be *accept* and *reject*. A new comment for your post can have another category with *Reply* and *Like* actions. In the example demo, we created the first two actions. Each action should be initialized with a unique identity, title, and options that identifies whether the notification will open the app in the foreground state or not. The foreground option will cause the app to open when you click on it. The destructive option will just destroy the notifications. Once you have a list of actions, you can create the categories. Each category should have a unique key and the list of actions that will appear in this category. Once you are ready with your categories, call `center.setNotificationCategories(categories)` to subscribe them. In the delegate method, you can later detect the custom action that has been clicked by getting its identifier by calling `response.actionIdentifier`.

Working with local notifications

We talked a lot in the previous sections about **Push Notification**, which is a notification that can be sent from a server side to the app and requires the Internet connection. There is another type of notification, which is the local notification. **Local notification** is a notification that you can build and register within the app itself with no need for a server to send the notifications. This type of notification can be used for reminders, alarms, and so on. In this section, we will build a screen where a user can create a reminder and the app will notify the user locally.

How to do it...

1. Open the storyboard file in the demo project. Select the initial view controller and click on **Editor** | **Embed In** | **Navigation Controller**.
2. Change the title of the navigation bar to **Add Reminder**.
3. Add a text field at the top of the screen to act as a title for the reminder.
4. Then, add a text view below the text field so that the user can enter a body for the reminder.
5. Below the text view, add a date picker so that the user can choose the date and time of the reminder.
6. Add a navigation bar button at the right to add the reminder when the user clicks on it.
7. Add `IBOutlets` and `IBActions` to the UI components, as follows:

```
@IBOutlet weak var titleTextField: UITextField!
@IBOutlet weak var reminderDatePicker: UIDatePicker!
@IBOutlet weak var bodyTextView: UITextView!
@IBAction func didClickOnAddButton(_ sender: Any) {
}
```

8. The final look of the screen UI should be something like this:

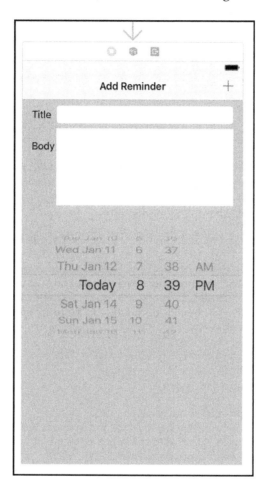

9. Update the `viewDidLoad` function to be like the following:

```
override func viewDidLoad() {
    super.viewDidLoad()
    // Do any additional setup after
      loading the view, typically from a nib.
    self.reminderDatePicker.minimumDate = Date()
    self.titleTextField.delegate = self
}
```

10. Now, update the `didClickOnAddButton` to fetch the information from the UI and schedule the notification:

```swift
@IBAction func didClickOnAddButton(_ sender: Any) {
    guard let title = titleTextField.text, let body =
      bodyTextView.text else {
        print("Please enter all information")
        return
    }
    let content = UNMutableNotificationContent()
    content.title = title
    content.body = body
    content.sound = UNNotificationSound.default()
    let triggerDate = Calendar.current.dateComponents
      ([.year, .month, .day, .hour, .minute, .second],
      from: self.reminderDatePicker.date)

    let trigger = UNCalendarNotificationTrigger
      (dateMatching: triggerDate, repeats: false)
    let center = UNUserNotificationCenter.current()
    let identifier = "ReminderNotification"
    let request = UNNotificationRequest(identifier:
      identifier, content: content, trigger: trigger)
    center.add(request, withCompletionHandler: { error in
        if let error = error {
            print("Error in scheduling the
                notification \(error)")
        }
        else{
            DispatchQueue.main.async {
                print("Scheduling done successfully")
                self.titleTextField.text = ""
                self.bodyTextView.text = ""
            }
        }
    })
}
```

11. Finally, add the following extension to allow `ViewController` to be the delegate of the text field:

```
extension ViewController: UITextFieldDelegate{
    func textFieldShouldReturn(_ textField: UITextField) ->
    Bool {
        textField.resignFirstResponder()
        return true
    }
}
```

12. Now, run the app on device, and enter some information like the following:

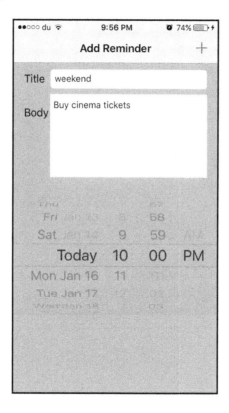

13. If you lock the phone and wait till the time you have set, you will see a local notification, as follows:

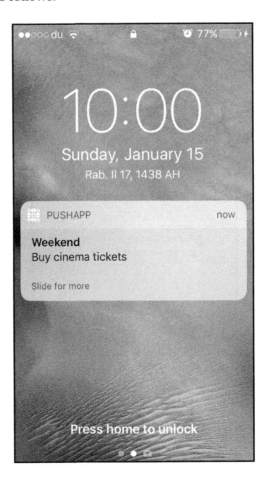

How it works...

Working with a local notification is straightforward, and as we saw, the code is very simple. We added a UIDatePicker in the screen to let the user pick the date and time for the reminder. Date picker has a useful property called minimumDate, which prevents the user from selecting a date before the current date. Before we process for scheduling the notification, we first check that the user has entered all information in the fields. Once the data is ready, we create an instance of UNMutableNotificationContent to set the title, body, and the sound of the notification. Once the notification content is ready, we need something to tell the notification center the time that we should fire the notification. The UNCalendarNotificationTrigger gets information about the date of the notification, and you can set up the trigger to repeat the notification if you want. After preparing the content and the trigger, you can create a new instance of UNNotificationRequest that will be added later to the notification center. The completion block is called once the request is added to the center, and a reference of the error (if occurred) will be passed to the block. After the successful scheduling of the notification, we reset the fields again, and because these updates are UI updates, we executed that in the main thread.

14
App Search

In this chapter, we will cover the following topics:

- App indexing using NSUserActivity
- App indexing using Core Spotlight APIs

Introduction

With the marvelous amount of information we have today in web and mobile apps, searching becomes the best way to get to what you need accurately and in no time. Think of Google search you get all the information you need by typing simple words into the search field. Now, in iOS, users can get information about your app in search results, even if the app is not installed. When you make your app content searchable, users can access this content through Spotlight and Safari search results and Siri suggestions. Implementing app search for your app is very easy and straightforward; iOS provides different techniques and index types to do this. In this chapter, we will try to give you a good introduction about app search adoption.

App indexing using NSUserActivity

The first technology of indexing for app indexing is working with NSUserActivity. This class helps you to index items when users perform activities in your app, such as opening specific screens or interacting with app content. Using this activity class will help a user to find the information that they need in search results and will improve your app's ranking. NSUserActivity is not intended to index an app's arbitrary data; it only indexes the user's activities. If you want to index app-specific data, you will need to use Core Spotlight APIs and that's what we will do in the next section:

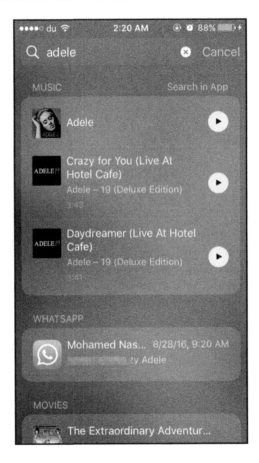

In the following demo, we will build a simple wallet app where a user can track their expenses by entering the item name and price. Once the user enters a new item in the wallet, we will create a user activity so that the system can index it in the private index.

Getting ready

There are two types of indexing in iOS and they're related to user privacy. Both indexes store searchable items related to app content. The following are the differences between the two indexes:

- **Private On-Device Index**: Each iOS device has a private index and its content is never shared publicly or synced with other devices. Once the search item is marked as an on-device index, only the device's user can see that item in search results.
- **Apple's Server-side Index**: The data will be stored on server side and will be publicly available.

By default, search items represented by NSUserActivity will be private, which means that they will be added to the on-device index. However, you can still mark them as eligible for public indexing if they contain activities that all users can view.

How to do it...

1. Create a new Xcode project with the **Single View Application** template with the name AppSearch.
2. Click on the initial view controller and embed it in **Navigation Controller** by clicking on **Editor | Embed In | Navigation Controller**.
3. Change the title of the navigation bar to My Wallet.

4. Drag a UITableView, and add it as a subview, and make it cover the screen. The constraints of the table view will look like this:

```
tableview.trailing = superview.trailing
tableview.leading = superview.leading
tableview.top = superview.top
tableview.trailing = superview.trailing
```

5. Then, drag a UITableViewCell to the table view. Open the **Attributes Inspector** tab and change the **Style** to **Right Detail** and the **Identifier** to cell.
6. Right-click on the table view and connect the delegate and datasource to the ViewController.
7. Drag a **Bar Button Item** and place it to the right of the navigation bar. From the **Attributes Inspector** tab, change the **System Item** to **Add**.

8. Connect an `IBAction` method to the bar button item, as follows:

```
@IBAction func didClickOnAdd(_ sender: Any) {
}
```

9. Open `ViewController.swift` and add the following `import` statement:

```
import CoreSpotlight
```

10. Add the following `struct` to define the wallet item:

```
struct Item{
   let name: String
   let price: Float
}
```

11. Add the following attributes to the `ViewController` class:

```
@IBOutlet weak var itemsTableView: UITableView!
var createAction: UIAlertAction?
var alertController: UIAlertController?
var currentActivity: NSUserActivity?
var items = [Item]()
```

12. Update the `didClickOnAdd` function to display a pop-up alert with text fields to add a new item:

```
@IBAction func didClickOnAdd(_ sender: Any) {
   let alertController = UIAlertController(title: "New Item",
      message: "Enter the name and price of the new item.",
         preferredStyle: .alert)
   self.alertController = alertController
   alertController.addTextField { (textField) in
         textField.placeholder = "Item Name"
         textField.addTarget(self, action:
         #selector(ViewController.textFieldDidChange
         (textField:)), for: .editingChanged)
   }
   alertController.addTextField { (textField) in
         textField.placeholder = "Item Price"
         textField.keyboardType = .numberPad
         textField.addTarget(self, action:
         #selector(ViewController.textFieldDidChange
         (textField:)), for: .editingChanged)
   }
   let createAction = UIAlertAction
      (title: "Submit", style: .default) { (action) in
```

```
    print("Submit")
    if let fields = alertController.textFields{
        let item = Item(name: fields[0].text!, price:
          (fields[1].text! as NSString).floatValue)
        self.items.append(item)
        self.itemsTableView.insertRows
          (at: [IndexPath(row: self.items.count - 1,
            section: 0)], with: .fade)
        self.createSearchableActivityForItem(item)
    }
}
createAction.isEnabled = false
self.createAction = createAction
let cancelAction = UIAlertAction
  (title: "Cancel", style: .cancel, handler: nil)
alertController.addAction(createAction)
alertController.addAction(cancelAction)
self.present(alertController,
  animated: true, completion: nil)
}
```

13. Then, add the following function to track the editing of text fields:

```
func textFieldDidChange(textField: UITextField){
    if let _ = self.alertController, let action =
      self.createAction, let fields =
      self.alertController?.textFields{
        var isValid = true
        for textField in fields{
            if let text = textField.text{
                isValid = isValid &&
                  text.characters.count > 0
            }
        }
        action.isEnabled = isValid
    }
}
```

14. Add the following function to create a searchable activity when the user inserts a new item:

```
func createSearchableActivityForItem(_ item: Item){
    let activity: NSUserActivity =
      NSUserActivity(activityType:
        "com.hossamghareeb.ItemType")
    // Set properties that describe
      the activity and that can be used in search.
    activity.title = "\(item.name)"
```

```
      activity.userInfo = ["name":
        "\(item.name)", "price": "\(item.price)"]
      let attributeSet = CSSearchableItemAttributeSet()
      attributeSet.contentDescription =
        "Price: $\(item.price) \n Adde on: \(NSDate())"
      attributeSet.title = "\(item.name)"
      activity.contentAttributeSet = attributeSet
      // Add the item to the private on-device index.
      activity.isEligibleForSearch = true
      self.currentActivity = activity
      activity.becomeCurrent()
  }
```

15. Finally, add the following extension to conform to the `UITableViewDataSource` protocol:

```
extension ViewController: UITableViewDataSource{
    func tableView(_ tableView:
      UITableView, numberOfRowsInSection section:
        Int) -> Int {
        return self.items.count
    }
    func tableView(_ tableView: UITableView, cellForRowAt
    indexPath: IndexPath) -> UITableViewCell {
        let cell =
        tableView.dequeueReusableCell
        (withIdentifier: "cell")
        let item = self.items[indexPath.row]
        cell?.textLabel?.text = item.name
        cell?.detailTextLabel?.text = "$\(item.price)"
        return cell!
    }
}
```

16. Now build and run the app; you will see an empty list with a plus button. Click on the add button; you should see a pop-up alert like the following:

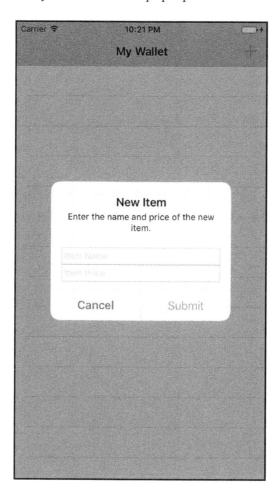

17. The **Submit** button will be disabled if one of the fields is empty. Try to fill the fields with data, as follows, and the state will be changed:

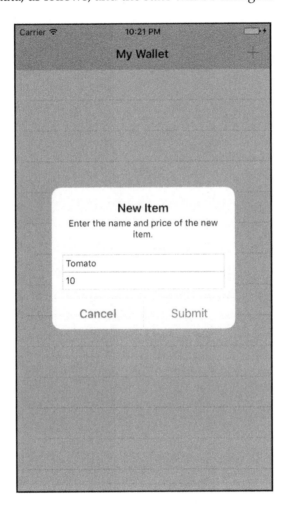

18. Add more items; the list should be similar to the following screenshot:

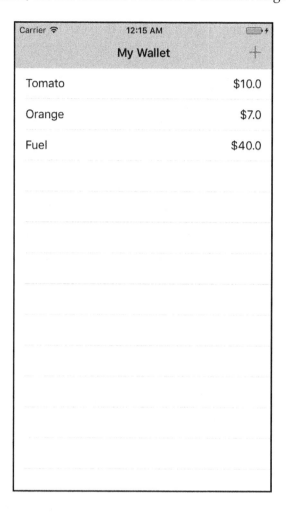

19. After each new insertion, an activity is indexed to the on-device private index. To ensure that the indexing is done correctly, press the home button and go to the Spotlight search screen. Type `Tomato` in the search bar; our app should appear at the top:

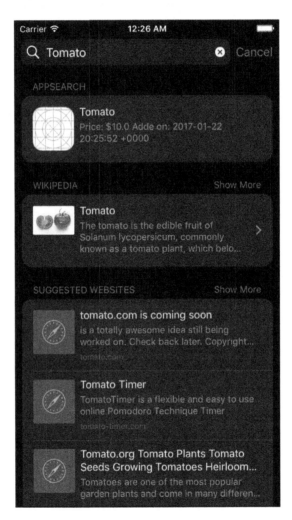

How it works...

In the previous demo, we gave you a good introduction to Search APIs and how to index users' activities and navigation points in an on-device private index. We started with the easy part, which is building the UI of the screen in the storyboard, and then we added our logic in the `ViewController.swift` file. We added the import statement for the `CoreSpotlight` framework, as the `contentAttributeSet` property takes a `CSSearchableItemAttributeSet` object, which is part of the `CoreSpotlight` framework. After the import statement, we added the `Itemstruct`, which is a simple structure for item properties, such as name and price. The items displayed on the screen will be saved in the `items` property array. Let's jump to the `didClickOnAdd` function. We created an instance of `UIAlertController` to display two text fields to the user for the item name and price. The `addTextField` function adds a new text field to the alert controller and you can pass a configuration block to configure the text field, such as changing the placeholder or the keyboard type. For both text fields that we add, we add a target to track the `editingChanged` event, which will call the `textFieldDidChange` function once any change happens in a text field. Tracking the editing of text fields will help us check the text entered by a user and then we can enable or disable the submit action button of the alert; you will note that the submit action is disabled by default at the beginning. We kept a reference to the submit action of the alert so that we can enable or disable it at any time. It will be enabled as long as the two text fields are not empty. We kept a reference to the alert controller so that we can retrieve the text fields' information.

Once a user clicks on the submit button, we create a new instance of the `Item` structure and add it to the items array. Then, we insert this item as a new row to the table view and call the `createSearchableActivityForItem` function. This function creates a new instance of `NSUserActivity` with a unique key of the activity type. This key is important and should be unique to your app organization, as we can use it later, when a user clicks on the activity from search results. Activity has properties such as `title`, which is the title of the activity, and `userInfo`, which will be passed when the user clicks on it later. The `contentAttributeSet` property lets you define many attributes to describe the activity item. This description will be displayed below the title in the search results. The `isEligibleForSearch` property allows the system to place it in the private on-device index. The call of `activity.becomeCurrent()` will make the current activity current and the user continue this activity from the search index.

There's more...

What will happen when the user clicks on an activity from the search results list? When the user clicks on an activity, the app will open and you should restore the app state based on the selected activity. To handle this, the app delegate should implement the following function in `AppDeleage.swift`:

```
func application(_ application: UIApplication, continue
  userActivity: NSUserActivity, restorationHandler: @escaping
  ([Any]?) -> Void) -> Bool {
    if userActivity.activityType ==
      "com.hossamghareeb.ItemType" {
        /// Restoring app state should be done here.
    }
    return true
}
```

App indexing using Core Spotlight APIs

In the previous recipe, we saw how you can index a user's activities so that the user can find them in Spotlight search and, when the user clicks on it, he will be able to continue his activity by restoring the app state. In this recipe, we will see how to index app content using the Core Spotlight framework. This framework is meant to work best with user or app-specific data. This kind of indexing will help users to find their content in Spotlight searching and they can click on it to find more information about this content. The Core Spotlight framework supports indexing items anytime, even when the app loads directly. In the following demo, we will build a simple demo on how to present some data in an app and index that data in Spotlight.

How to do it...

1. Create a new Xcode project with the **Single View Application** template with the name `FoodIndex`.
2. Click on the initial view controller and embed it in **Navigation Controller** by clicking on **Editor** | **Embed In** | **Navigation Controller**.
3. Change the title of the navigation bar to **Nutritions**.

4. Drag a `UITableView`, and add it as a `subview`, and make it cover the screen. The constraints of the table view will look like this:

```
tableview.trailing = superview.trailing
tableview.leading = superview.leading
tableview.top = superview.top
tableview.trailing = superview.trailing
```

5. Then, drag a `UITableViewCell` to the table view. Open the **Attributes Inspector** tab and change the **Style** to **Subtitle** and the **Identifier** to `cell`.

6. Right-click on the table view and connect the `delegate` and `datasource` to the `ViewController`.

7. The final look of the view controller in the storyboard should be like this:

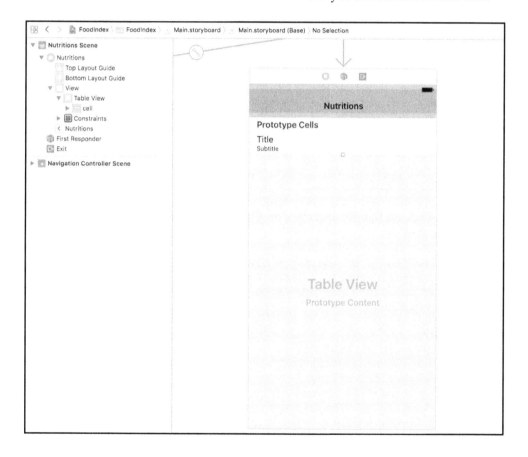

8. Create a new property list file from **Resource** with the name **Food**:

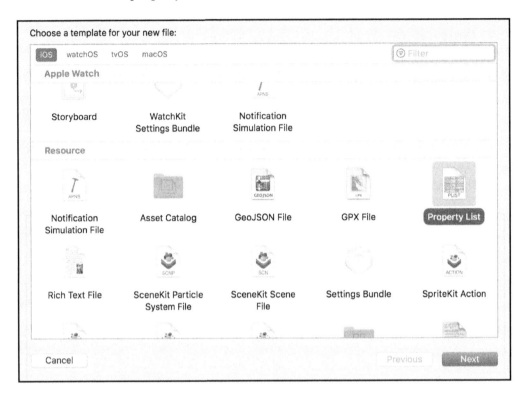

9. Double-click on the file and click on **Open As Source Code**. Update the text to be as illustrated:

```
<?xml version="1.0" encoding="UTF-8"?>
<!DOCTYPE plist PUBLIC "-//Apple//DTD PLIST 1.0//EN"
 "http://www.apple.com/DTDs/PropertyList-1.0.dtd">
<plist version="1.0">
<array>
    <dict>
      <key>title</key>
      <string>Almond</string>
      <key>calories</key>
      <integer>165</integer>
      <key>protein</key>
      <integer>6</integer>
      <key>fat</key>
      <integer>15</integer>
      <key>carbs</key>
      <integer>6</integer>
```

```
      </dict>
      <dict>
        <key>title</key>
        <string>DATES</string>
        <key>calories</key>
        <integer>230</integer>
        <key>protein</key>
        <integer>2</integer>
        <key>fat</key>
        <integer>0</integer>
        <key>carbs</key>
        <integer>61</integer>
      </dict>
      <dict>
        <key>title</key>
        <string>CHEESECAKE</string>
        <key>calories</key>
        <integer>3350</integer>
        <key>protein</key>
        <integer>60</integer>
        <key>fat</key>
        <integer>213</integer>
        <key>carbs</key>
        <integer>317</integer>
      </dict>
      <dict>
        <key>title</key>
        <string>BROCCOLI</string>
        <key>calories</key>
        <integer>40</integer>
        <key>protein</key>
        <integer>4</integer>
        <key>fat</key>
        <integer>1</integer>
        <key>carbs</key>
        <integer>8</integer>
      </dict>
  </array>
  </plist>
```

10. Now open `ViewController.swift` and add the following `import` statement:

```
import CoreSpotlight
```

11. Add the following structure at the top of the file:

```
struct Item{
    let title: String
    let calories: Int
    let protein: Int
    let fat: Int
    let carbs: Int
    func description() -> String {
        return "Calories \(self.calories) kcal, Protein: \
        (self.protein) g, Fat: \(self.fat) g, Carbs: \
        (self.carbs) g"
    }
}
```

12. Add the following attribute to keep a reference to the list of items:

```
var items = [Item]()
```

13. Update the `viewDidLoad` method, as follows:

```
override func viewDidLoad() {
    super.viewDidLoad()
    // Do any additional setup after loading the view,
      typically from a nib.
    if let path = Bundle.main.path(forResource: "Food",
      ofType: "plist") {
        if let array = NSArray(contentsOfFile: path) as?
          [[String: Any]] {
            for itemDic in array{
                let itemTitle = itemDic["title"] as! String
                let calories = (itemDic["calories"] as!
                  NSNumber).intValue
                let protein = (itemDic["protein"] as!
                  NSNumber).intValue
                let fat = (itemDic["fat"] as!
                  NSNumber).intValue
                let carbs = (itemDic["carbs"] as!
                  NSNumber).intValue
                let item = Item(title: itemTitle,
                              calories: calories,
                              protein: protein,
                              fat: fat,
                              carbs: carbs)
```

```
                        self.items.append(item)
                        createSearchableItemFrom(item)
                    }
                }
            }
        }
```

14. Add the following function to create a searchable record in Spotlight:

```
func createSearchableItemFrom(_ item: Item){
    // Create an attribute set to describe an item.
    let attributeSet =
      CSSearchableItemAttributeSet(itemContentType:
      "com.hossamghareeb.foodItem")
    // Add metadata that supplies details about the item.
    attributeSet.title = item.title
    attributeSet.contentDescription = item.description()
    // Create an item with a unique identifier, a domain i
       identifier, and the attribute set you created earlier.
    let item = CSSearchableItem(uniqueIdentifier: item.title,
       domainIdentifier: "com.hossamghareeb.foodItem",
       attributeSet: attributeSet)
    // Add the item to the on-device index.
    CSSearchableIndex.default().indexSearchableItems([item])
       { error in
         if error != nil {
            print(error?.localizedDescription ?? "")
         }
         else {
             print("Item indexed.")
         }
    }
}
```

15. Add the following extension to conform to the `UITableViewDataSource` protocol:

```
extension ViewController: UITableViewDataSource{
    func tableView(_ tableView: UITableView,
      numberOfRowsInSection section: Int) -> Int {
        return self.items.count
    }
    func tableView(_ tableView: UITableView, cellForRowAt
      indexPath: IndexPath) -> UITableViewCell {
        let cell =
          tableView.dequeueReusableCell(withIdentifier:
            "cell")
        let item = self.items[indexPath.row]
```

```
            cell?.textLabel?.text = item.title
            cell?.detailTextLabel?.text = item.description()
            return cell!
        }
    }
```

16. Now run the app; you should see a list of food items like the following:

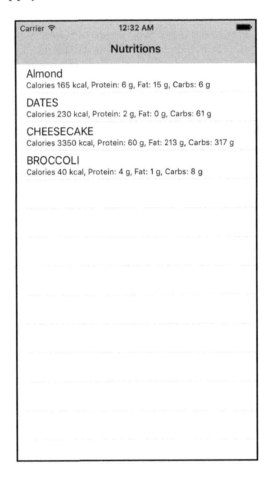

17. After all the items have been indexed, open the Spotlight search and search for `cheesecake`. The search results should look like this:

How it works...

In the demo, we saw how to use the Core Spotlight search framework to index app-specific data. The UI part was pretty easy and it's very similar to the one we built in the previous recipe. In the `ViewController.swift` file, we added the import statement for the `CoreSpotlight` framework, as the APIs that we will use are part of this framework. We created a new structure for the food item to work as encapsulation for the food item details. In the `viewDidLoad` function, we got a path for the `plist` file using `Bundle.main.path(forResource: "Food", ofType: "plist")`. The path can be used to get an array of dictionary objects. Each dictionary has all the information about the food item that will be used to create an instance of the `Item` structure. After we create an instance of the item, we call the `createSearchableItemFrom()` function. This function will take care of all the logic required to list the item in the index. It first creates an instance of `CSSearchableItemAttributeSet` with the title and item description. The attribute set will be used to create a new instance of `CSSearchableItem`, along with a unique identifier and domain identifier. This searchable item can be passed directly to `SSearchableIndex.default().indexSearchableItems([item])` so that the index will add the item and be ready to appear in search results.

15

Optimizing Performance

In this chapter, we will cover the following topics:

- Memory management with ARC
- Measuring performance
- Measuring energy impact
- On-demand resources

Introduction

Taking care of the app performance is one of the most important topics in iOS. All of us have faced apps that run smoothly without lagging or heating up your device. On the other hand, we have faced apps that lag a lot and cause memory pressure and overhead on the system. To build a successful app, you should take care of its performance and memory usage. Ensure that there isn't any memory pressure or memory leaks. The iOS system is smart enough to monitor the memory of all apps and kill any app that tries to cause memory pressure on the device. The system sends warning notifications to the app, before killing it to free some memory. In this chapter, we will cover some concepts of memory management and how to measure and optimize the performance of the app.

Memory management with ARC

In this recipe, we will talk about memory management in iOS using **ARC** (**Automatic Reference Counting**). ARC was first introduced in iOS 5 to help developers to manage the app memory. However, while ARC takes care of releasing objects, you still have to set up your reference types correctly to avoid any leaks and retain cycles. In the following recipe, we will try to build a simple app that has a lot of memory issues, and we will see how to catch these issues and what the correct ways to solve them are.

Getting ready

There are some definitions and concepts about memory management that you need to know before starting our demo. In iOS, each object has a reference count in memory, and once this count reaches *ZERO*, the object will be deallocated from memory. The reference count of any object refers to how many objects have a strong reference to that object. This reference sends a retain message to that object to increase its reference count by *ONE*. Once any object is done from any object, a release message should be sent to that object to decrement its reference count by *ONE* till it reaches *ZERO*, and then it will be deallocated.

Before ARC, we had **MRC** (**Manual Reference Counting**), in which it was the developer's responsibility to release or retain objects. In ARC, all releases and retains are done automatically by an Xcode compiler. The compiler inserts all calls for releases or retains in the appropriate places at runtime.

We have two types of references; strong and weak. Let's see the difference between them:

- **Strong**: The strong reference increments the reference count by *ONE*, and the referenced object will remain in memory as long as the referencing object is still in memory and doesn't refer to another object.
- **Weak**: It doesn't increment the reference count, but it just keeps a reference to the object. If the referenced object has been deallocated from memory, the reference will be set to `nil` and not to a garbage memory.
- **Unowned**: It's the same as a weak reference; but the only difference is that it will not nullify the reference and it will keep pointing to a garbage memory if the referenced object has been deallocated, which would cause your app to crash if you tried to access it.

In ARC, all that you need to do is to decide when to use strong, weak, or unowned references. In Swift, the default is strong for the references you create; if you want to use a weak or unowned reference, you have to mark it like this:

```
weak var scrollView: UIScrollView!
unowned var parent: AnyObject
```

Retain cycles

Retain cycles are one of the most common problems in memory management, which cause leaks in memory. The following figure will illustrate how a retain cycle occurs:

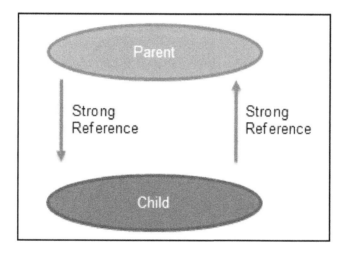

We have two objects: parent and child. The parent object has a strong reference to the child object, as the child needs to exist as long as the parent object exists. The child object also needs to speak to the parent object, and that's why, we have a strong reference to the parent. In that case, we have created a retain cycle. The retain cycle is the case when you have two objects having a strong reference to each other. The problem of the retain cycle is that each one will wait for the other to break the strong reference so that they can be deallocated. This leads to a leakage in memory, as these two objects will never get deallocated from memory.

The solution of the problem is to break the cycle by using a weak or unowned reference instead of a strong reference in one of the references, as follows:

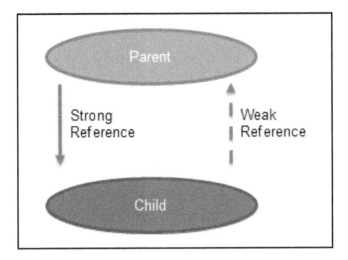

As we see, the child-to-parent reference is changed to a weak reference. When you think of it, you will note that it makes sense to choose the child-to-parent relation to be weak because the child object would never exist if the parent object didn't exist.

Working with closures

Closures are heavily used in Swift and that's why we need to understand how they work. Closures capture all references used inside to make sure that these objects will not be deallocated till the closures finish their job. Owing to this, there is a case that a retain cycle can occur while using closures. This case happens when you assign a closure to a property of a class instance, and then, inside the body of that closure, the instance is captured. In that case, the instance has a strong reference to the closure, and the closure has a strong reference to the instance. To break this, we use something called `weakself` to use a weak reference of `self` inside the closure.

How to do it...

1. Create a new Xcode project with the **Master-Detail Application** template and with name `MemoryManagement`. Check out the following screenshot:

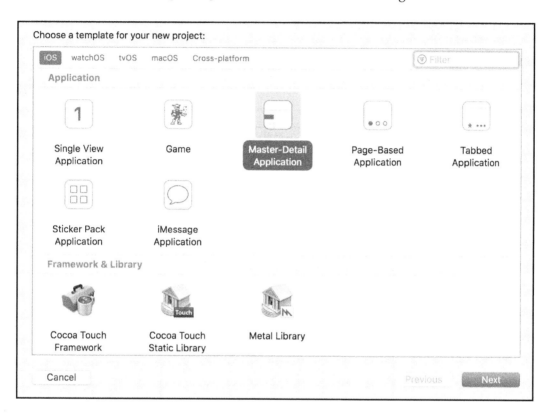

2. The new project will be created with sample code for a master-detail template app. Open the source file `DetailViewController.swift`.

3. Add the following class at the top of the file:

```
class Child{
   var parent: UIViewController?
}
```

4. Then, in the `DetailViewController` class, add the following property:

```
let child = Child()
```

5. Update the `viewDidLoad` function like this:

```
override func viewDidLoad() {
    super.viewDidLoad()
    // Do any additional setup after loading the view, typically from a
nib.
    self.configureView()
    self.child.parent = self
}
```

6. Now, run the app and keep clicking on the right navigation bar button to add more timestamps:

7. Keep clicking on the timestamp to open details and then go back. In this case, we're creating retain cycles and leaks in memory. To detect if we have any leakage in memory or not, we have to use the **Leaks Instrument** too.

8. Let's detect this cycle. Long press on the **Run** button in Xcode to open a small menu:

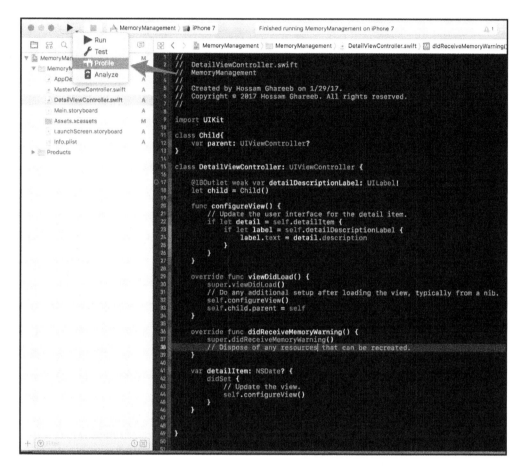

9. Choose **Profile** from the pop-up menu and then the **Instruments** app will open.
10. A list of instruments will be opened, so you can select from one of them; choose the **Leaks** instrument:

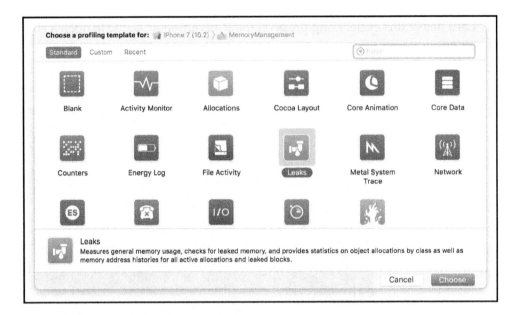

11. Click on the **Choose** button; then, a window will be opened to record:

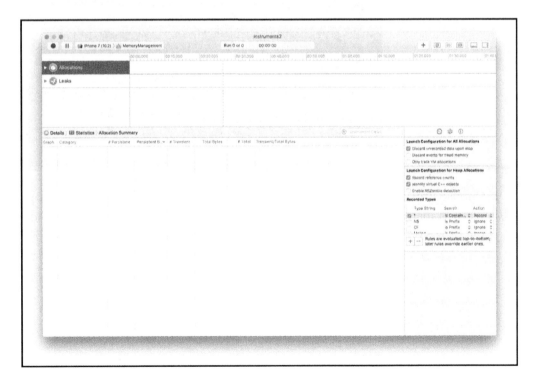

12. At the top-left corner, click on the red record button to start recording. Use the app and add some timestamps. The recording will look like this:

13. You will note that everything seems perfect in the **Leak Checks** row.

14. Now, try to open the details screen multiple times. Leaks will show in the **Leaks Checks** section:

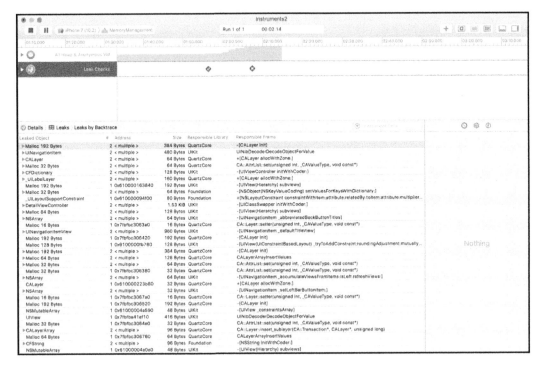

15. As you can see, there are marks indicating the leaks in memory that we have in the app.

16. Now try to update the Child class to be like the following:

```
class Child{
    weak var parent: UIViewController?
}
```

17. Close the current recorder, and start a new one. Add some timestamps and open details screens multiple times. The memory will be fine and no leaks will be found:

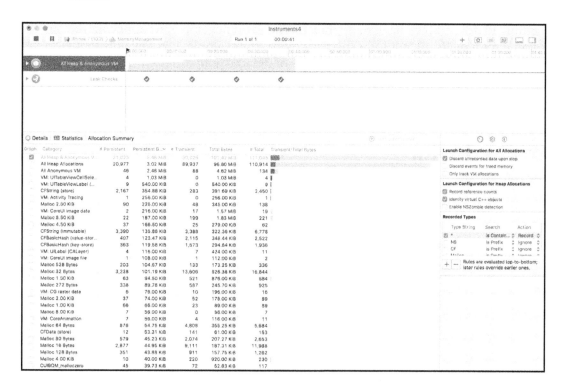

How it works...

In our previous demo, we saw how to accidentally create a retain cycle in between objects, which can later lead to a memory leak. We created a new class called `Child`, which had a strong reference to a parent object. The parent object, `DetailViewController`, had a strong reference to its child. Doing this will lead to a memory leak, and that's the same as what we detected in the `Instruments` application. To break this cycle, we had to change one of the references to be a weak reference. In the `Child` class, we changed the `var parent: UIViewController?` to `weak var parent: UIViewController?`. Marking it as weak helped us to break the retain cycle and fix the memory leak issue.

Measuring performance

Performance is one of the most important things that you should take care of in your app. Your users need to use your app smoothly with no interruption or hanging. They have something to do, and they have to do it fast. When you develop your application, you develop it for a platform, not for a specific device. For example, you develop an iOS application, which will run on different types of devices with different CPU capabilities. That's why, measuring your app performance is very important, so you can find the areas that need optimization.

How to do it...

1. In these measurements, we will not write any code. So, you can pick any Xcode project you have to run these experiments on.
2. First, we will try to measure the CPU usage of an app to see how our app uses the multiple cores/threads that we have.
3. Open the Xcode project, and click on **Profile** as we did in the preceding recipe.
4. Choose **Time Profiler** from the list of instruments:

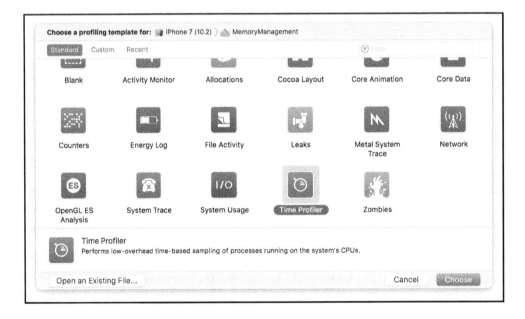

5. Choose the device/simulator and the app from the target device and process list.
6. Click on the **Record** button at the top-left corner.
7. Use the app that you want to record normally, and then click on the **Stop** button.
8. After clicking on the stop button, the analysis of CPU usage will be like this:

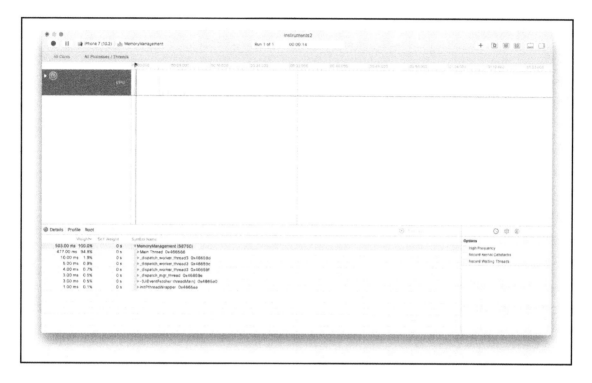

9. When you zoom in, you can see the details of the CPU usage, like this:

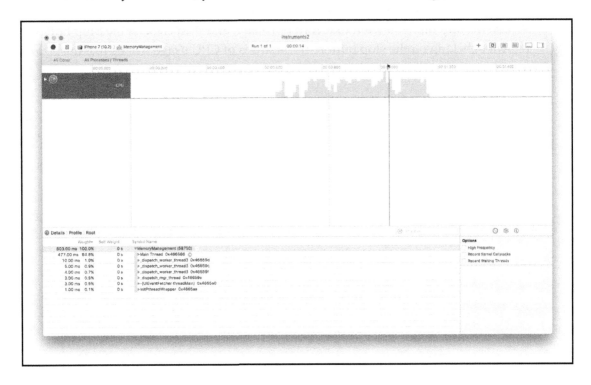

10. Open the threads data view to see the app's use of threads to perform work:

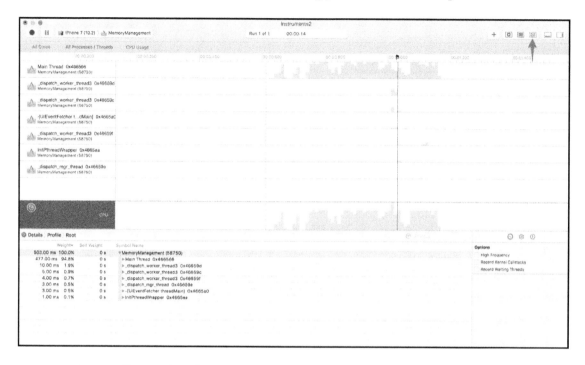

11. You will note that the main thread is taking care of all the work in the app.
12. Let's check another tool together to check the CPU usage. Run the app on your device or simulator.

13. In Xcode, open the **Debug Navigator** area and click on CPU:

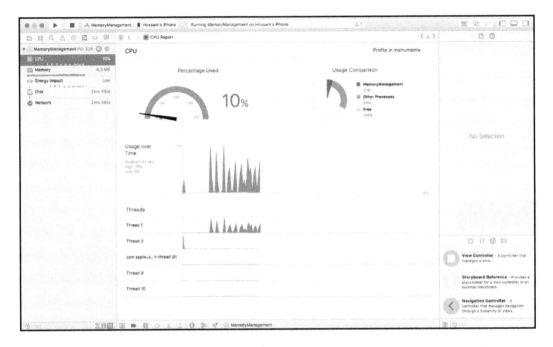

14. The view gauges the CPU usage for the app and also compares it to other apps.

15. In the same screen--and from the left panel--if you tried to click on **Memory**, you will get as well the same comparison and usage, but only for memory:

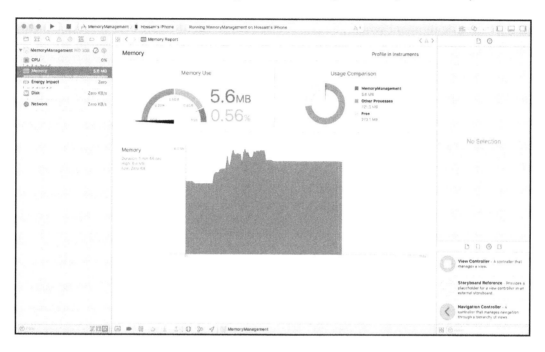

16. You can use this view to do an experiment to see the memory usage before and after fixing the retain cycle issue.

How it works...

Instruments help a lot in measuring the app performance and the CPU usage. The steps we explained previously in the preceding section are self-explanatory and very easy to use. When you find any issue in the CPU usage or higher usage at a specific level while using the app. You have to check this part of code at that point and revise it, so you can find any optimization to do. Also, we saw how to get information about threads usage and how the app distributes the work among threads and utilizes the multicore in the system to perform tasks quickly and without interrupting the main thread.

Measuring energy impact

All users suffer from the draining of the life of their mobile phone's battery during usage. What a frustrating moment when you see your phone is about to die and you don't have access to any power supply. Developers, your device, and the operating system are all involved in taking care of the battery life. Any inefficient way of performing a task in the app may cause an impact on the battery life and needs your intervention to do it in a better way. In this recipe, we will see how to measure the app energy usage from **Instruments**.

How to do it...

1. Pick any Xcode project you have, and click on **Profile**.
2. Choose **Energy Log** from the following list of instruments:

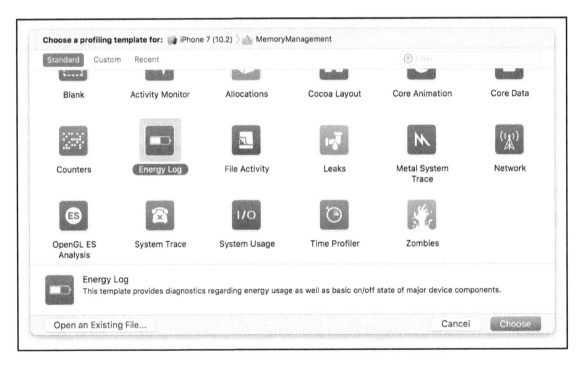

3. Choose the device/simulator and the app from the target device and process list.
4. Click on the **Record** button at the top-left corner.
5. Use the app that you want to record normally, and then click on the **Stop** button.
6. You should see a detailed analysis of the energy used:

7. There is another way to log the energy usage while you're away from **Instruments**.

8. Go to your iOS device and then go to **Settings** | **Developer** | **Logging**:

9. When you click on the **Developer** option, another screen will open; select **Logging**:

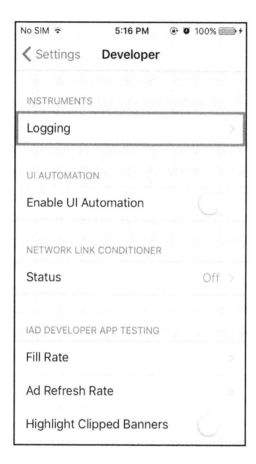

10. Enable **Energy** logging, and then click on **Start Recording**:

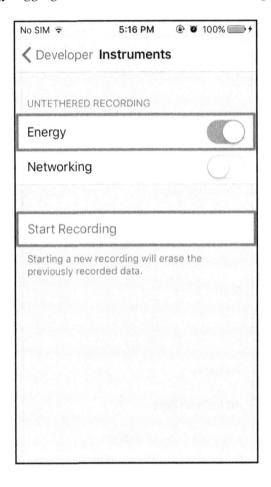

11. Use the device normally.
12. After using the device, go to **Settings** | **Developer** | **Logging** and click on **Stop Recording**:

13. Open the **Instruments** app and choose **Energy Log**. Then, go to **File** | **Import Logged Data from Device**:

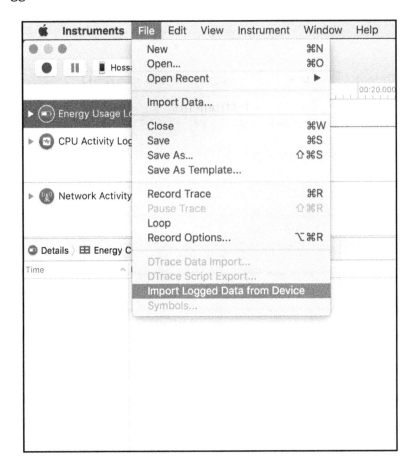

14. The collected data will be displayed as live logging.

How it works...

When you go through the collected data in the **Energy Log** instrument, you should search for any spikes or areas that have unexpected activity. These areas should be reviewed in your source code to optimize them.

The way of logging energy usage when the device is not connected to the Instruments app helps a lot to take your time to measure the app anytime while normal usage. In that case, you will get realistic measurements. The way we explained how to enable or disable logging in the iOS device is efficient enough to log the usage for the whole day if you want and even when the device goes into sleep mode. The only disadvantage of this method is that if the battery dies or you switch off the phone, all log data is lost.

On-demand resources

The on-demand resources are contents that are hosted in Apple Store servers and not in the app bundle of the app. When you download the app from App Store, the content will not be available until the app requests them. The app later will request the on-demand resources, and the operating system will take care of downloading and storing the content. The resources types can be of any type, except for executable source code. In this recipe, we will see how to manage the on-demand resources and download them.

Getting ready

Before getting started with on-demand resources, let's get more information about it to help you get a better understanding. Let's take a look at the benefits of using on-demand resources in your app:

- **Small App Size**: The small app size helps the user to download the app fast and gives the limited storage devices the opportunity to download more apps.
- **Lazy download contents**: Some of your app's content is only needed in certain states. Keeping these resources in an app bundle is useless if the user hasn't reach this state. With on-demand resources, we can download this content only when the user is about to reach the state.
- **Rarely used resources**: Some resources are rarely used and can be used only once, such as app tutorials. These resources are likely to be requested only once, or when the user asks for them.
- **In-App Purchase:** You can add more content to in-app purchases, and your user can purchase and download the content.

In the on-demand resource, we use tags to identify the resource. Each resource can have multiple tags. The tag is just a string that describes the content. For example, you're working on a game and have weapons resources related to the final level of each milestone. You can give each weapon resource tags like these: final-level and weapon.

Now you know we have two types of resources: the on-demand and app bundle resources. As we said, each resource has one or more tags. Once the tags are ready in Xcode, you can assign each tag one of three categories. Let's check them out:

- **Initial Install Tags**: The resources are downloaded at the same time as the app, and the size of the app in the App Store includes the size of these resources.
- **Prefetch Tag Order**: The resources will be downloaded after the app is installed. These resources will be downloaded in the same order they are added in the prefetch tag order group in Xcode.
- **Download Only On Demand**: The resources will be downloaded only when they are requested by the app. This category is the default category for all resources.

How to do it...

1. Create a new Xcode project with a **Single View Application** template and with name OnDemandDemo.
2. Open **Main.storyboard**, and add two buttons on the initial view controller.
3. Change the title of the first button to **Dubai** and the second button to **Abu Dhabi**. When a user clicks on either of these, a screen with images for that city should be displayed.
4. Click on the initial view controller, and go to **Edit | Embed In | Navigation Controller** to embed it in your navigation controller.
5. Drag a **UIViewController** from **Object Library** and place it beside the initial view controller. The name of this controller will be ImagesViewController.

6. Create a segue from the initial view controller to `ImagesViewController` with the identifier `showImages`:

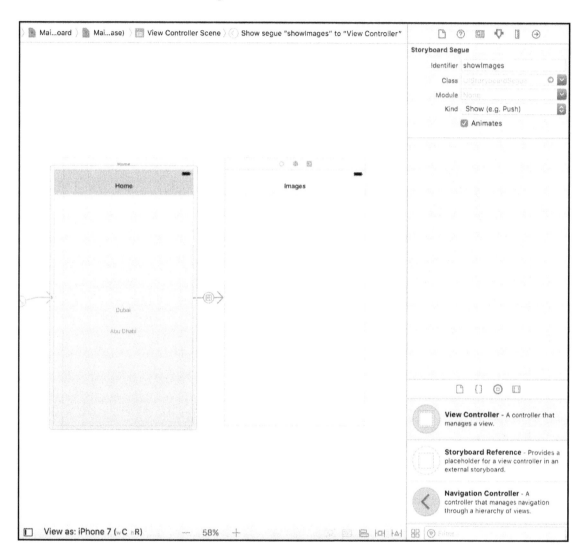

7. Create a new `ImagesViewController` swift class and change the class type of the second view controller in the storyboard.

8. Open `ImagesViewController` in the storyboard file and place four image views, as follows:

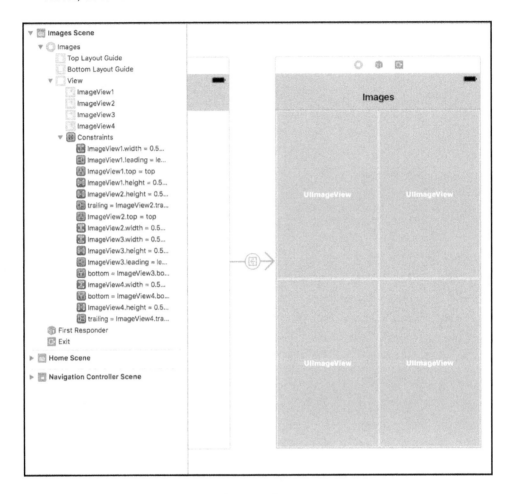

9. Link the four image views with **IBOutlets** to `ImagesViewController.swift` like this:

```
@IBOutlet weak var imageView1: UIImageView!
@IBOutlet weak var imageView2: UIImageView!
@IBOutlet weak var imageView3: UIImageView!
@IBOutlet weak var imageView4: UIImageView!
```

10. In initial view controller `ViewController.swift`, link **IBActions** to the two buttons, like this:

```
@IBAction func didClickOnDubaiButton(_ sender: Any) {
}
@IBAction func didClickonADButton(_ sender: Any) {
}
```

11. Open `ViewController.swift` and add the following property:

```
var currentCity = ""
```

12. Update the action functions of the cities buttons:

```
@IBAction func didClickOnDubaiButton(_ sender: Any) {
  currentCity = "dubai"
  self.performSegue(withIdentifier: "showImages", sender: nil)
}
@IBAction func didClickonADButton(_ sender: Any) {
  currentCity = "abu-dhabi"
  self.performSegue(withIdentifier: "showImages", sender: nil)
}
```

13. Override the `prepareForSegue` function to pass the city name to `ImageViewController`:

```
override func prepare(for segue: UIStoryboardSegue, sender: Any?)
{
  if segue.identifier == "showImages" {
    if let destinationViewController = segue.destination as?
      ImagesViewController{
        destinationViewController.selectedCity = currentCity
      }
    }
  }
```

14. Open `ImagesViewController` and add the following property:

```
var selectedCity: String?
```

15. In Xcode, click on the project and then select the target. Under the **Build Settings** tab, search for **Assets**. Double-check that the **On Demand Resource** is enabled:

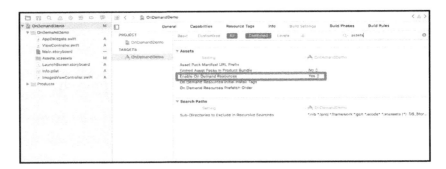

16. Open the `Assets.xcassets` file and you will find four images for **Abu Dhabi** and **Dubai**. Select the first four images for **Abu Dhabi**, and from the **Attribute Inspector**, under **On Demand Resource Tags**, type **abu-dhabi**.

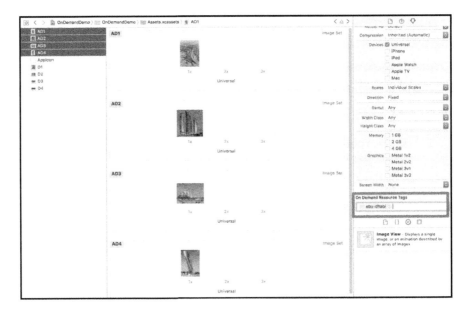

17. Do the same for **Dubai** images, change their tags to `dubai`:

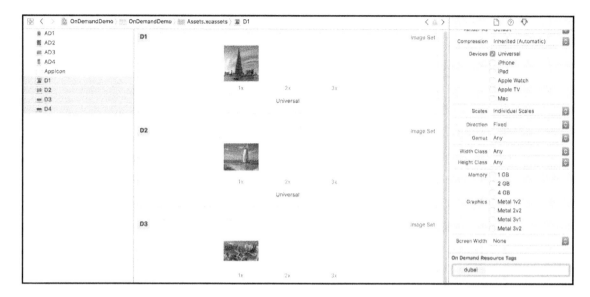

18. Click on the target again and then go to the **Resource Tags** tab; you will see all the tags that we have created listed there:

19. Click on the **Prefetched** filter instead of **All**; it will show you the four categories of assets tags. Users can drag and drop assets to the appropriate category:

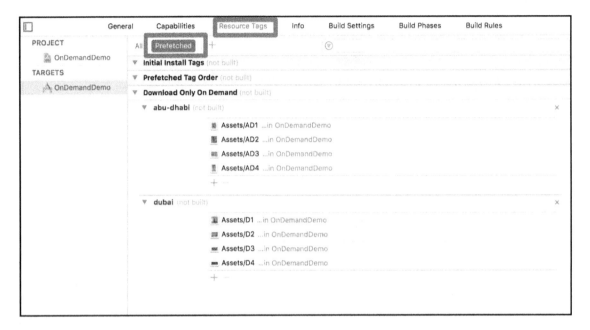

20. Open the `ImagesViewController.swift` file to start requesting the resources based on the city name.

21. Add the following property in the `ImagesViewController` class:

```
var resourceRequest: NSBundleResourceRequest?
```

22. Update the `viewDidLoad` function to be like the following:

```
override func viewDidLoad() {
  super.viewDidLoad()

  // Do any additional setup after loading the view.
  if let city = self.selectedCity{
    let tags = NSSet(object: city)
    resourceRequest = NSBundleResourceRequest(tags: tags as!
    Set<String>)
      // Request access to tags that may already be on the device
      resourceRequest?.conditionallyBeginAccessingResources
        (completionHandler: { (resourcesAvailable) in
          if resourcesAvailable{
            // the associated resources are loaded, start using
```

```
      them
    OperationQueue.main.addOperation {
      self.displayImages()
    }
  }
  else{
    // The resources are not on the device and need to be
     loaded
    self.resourceRequest?.beginAccessingResources
     (completionHandler: { (error) in
      if (error != nil){
        return
      }
      OperationQueue.main.addOperation {
        self.displayImages()
      }
    })
  }
 })
 }
}
```

23. Then, add the following function:

```
func  displayImages(){
  if let city = self.selectedCity{
    let imgName = city == "dubai" ? "D" : "AD"
    self.imageView1.image = UIImage(named: "\(imgName)1")
    self.imageView2.image = UIImage(named: "\(imgName)2")
    self.imageView3.image = UIImage(named: "\(imgName)3")
    self.imageView4.image = UIImage(named: "\(imgName)4")
  }
}
```

24. Now, build and run the app. Click on **Dubai** to download the resources for **Dubai** city:

25. The images will appear once the downloading finishes.
26. Go to Xcode, and in the left panel click on the **Debug Navigator** tab.

27. Select the **Disk**, and check the **On Demand Resources** section:

How it works...

We started first by building the UI of the demo app, and as we saw, it was very simple. We created an initial screen with two buttons. Each button maps to a city, and when you click on it, it opens a resources screen to display images for that city. In the `ViewController` class, we added the `currentCity` property to change it according to the button selected, and this value later will be passed to the `ImagesViewController` property `selecteCity` in the `prepareForSegue` function. To add tags to resources, you go to **Assets.xcassets** and select the assets that will have the same tag and add it in the **On Demand Resource Tags** section in the **Attribute Inspector** tab. Each asset can have multiple tags if you want. When you go to the app target, and open the **Resource Tags** tab, you can categorize the tags based on the categories that we have illustrated in the *Getting ready* section.

To download the on-demand resources, you need an instance of `NSBundleResourceRequest`, which can be initialized with `Set` of tags of the resources. Before downloading any resource, it's a good practice to first check whether they're available on the device, so there is no need to request them. The `conditionallyBeginAccessingResources` function tells you whether the requests tags are available or not, but it doesn't download the content. However, calling the `beginAccessingResources` function downloads the content. In both functions, the completion handler callbacks are not called on the main thread. That's why, before calling the function `displayImages()`, we execute this call in the main thread by calling `OperationQueue.main.addOperation`.

Index

Lightning Source UK Ltd.
Milton Keynes UK
UKOW07f2257120617
303198UK00003B/273/P